T0305040

The Neoliberal Revolution in Eastern Europe

NEW THINKING IN POLITICAL ECONOMY

Series Editor: Peter J. Boettke, *George Mason University, USA*

New Thinking in Political Economy aims to encourage scholarship in the intersection of the disciplines of politics, philosophy and economics. It has the ambitious purpose of reinvigorating political economy as a progressive force for understanding social and economic change.

The series is an important forum for the publication of new work analyzing the social world from a multidisciplinary perspective. With increased specialization (and professionalization) within universities, interdisciplinary work has become increasingly uncommon. Indeed, during the 20th century, the process of disciplinary specialization reduced the intersection between economics, philosophy and politics and impoverished our understanding of society. Modern economics in particular has become increasingly mathematical and largely ignores the role of institutions and the contribution of moral philosophy and politics.

New Thinking in Political Economy will stimulate new work that combines technical knowledge provided by the 'dismal science' and the wisdom gleaned from the serious study of the 'worldly philosophy'. The series will reinvigorate our understanding of the social world by encouraging a multidisciplinary approach to the challenges confronting society in the new century.

Recent titles in the series include:

The Neoliberal Revolution in Eastern Europe

Economic Ideas in the Transition from Communism

Paul Dragos Aligica

Mercatus Center, George Mason University, USA

Anthony J. Evans

ESCP-EAP European School of Management, UK

NEW THINKING IN POLITICAL ECONOMY

Edward Elgar
Cheltenham, UK • Northampton, MA, USA

Published by
Edward Elgar Publishing Limited
The Lypiatts
15 Lansdown Road
Cheltenham
Glos GL50 2JA
UK

Edward Elgar Publishing, Inc.
William Pratt House
9 Dewey Court
Northampton
Massachusetts 01060
USA

A catalogue record for this book
is available from the British Library

Library of Congress Control Number: 2008017415

Mixed Sources
Product group from well-managed
forests and other controlled sources
www.fsc.org Cert no. SA-COC-1565
© 1996 Forest Stewardship Council

FSC

ISBN 978 1 84720 637 4

Printed and bound in Great Britain by MPG Books Ltd, Bodmin, Cornwall

Contents

v

Acknowledgements

This book would not have been possible without three major research projects involving extensive data collection and sustained field work: *The Social Change – GPI Field Work Program* (2004–2006) run by Mercatus Center at George Mason University and coordinated by Brian Hooks and Claire Morgan; *Three Social Science Disciplines in Central and Eastern Europe* (2000–2002) run by Social Science Information Centre, Berlin and Collegium Budapest and coordinated by Max Kaase, Vera Sparschuh and Agniezka Wenninger; and *The Dioscuri-Access Projects* (2002–2007) run by by Institut für die Wissenschaften vom Menschen, Vienna and Central European University Budapest and coordinated by Janos Matyas Kovacs and Viola Zentai. The book is rooted in the tremendous opportunities offered by these projects in which we were directly involved and we gratefully acknowledge our debt to all those that made that possible. The value of our contributions is given in large measure the numerous interviews and conversations we had with the Western and Eastern European economists. We want to express our gratitude to them.

We would like to extend additional thanks to Max Kaase, Vera Sparschuh and Agniezka Wenninger, and to the Social Science Information Centre Berlin and Collegium Budapest for allowing us to generously quote from Kaase, Sparschuh and Wenninger (2002) and also to use in Chapters 2 and 3 of our book several paragraphs published in *Three Social Science Disciplines* as part of a chapter written by Paul Dragos Aligica.

Chapter 8 is based on an article initially published in *East European Economics*, vol 46, May/June 2008, 'The Spread of the Flat Tax in Eastern Europe. A Comparative Study'. We thank M.E. Sharpe Inc. for authorizing us to use a large part of it in our book. A version of Chapter 9 was published as 'Learning in time: new institutionalism and the Central and Eastern European economic reform experience', *Global Business and Economics Review (GBER)(2006)*, **8** (1/2). We would like to thank Inderscience Publishers and GBER.

We are indebted to the critical dialogue that we have shared with a number of scholars, and in particular we wish to thank Peter Boettke, Richard Wagner, Elinor Ostrom, Vladimir Tismaneanu, Vincent Ostrom, Jeffrey Hart, Michael McGinnis, Karol Boudreaux, John Clark, Henry Hale, Janos Matyas Kovacs, Adrian Miroiu and Matei Calinescu. As friends, colleagues and teachers their feedback has been crucial to improve the content and structure of this book. Needless to say, any remaining errors of omission or commission are entirely our own.

Anthony has enduring gratitude for his wife, Faith, who has both physically and emotionally supported his research in this area. Social scientists require passports as much as blackboards and he couldn't have conducted such a study without her continued backing. He apologizes for the late nights and doggedness, but knows she understands. Anthony would also like to thank Davide Sola and Jerome Couturier at ESCP-EAP European School of Management for allowing him to devote research leave in summer 2007 to this work. Parts of this book were written at the library of the University College London's School of Slavonic and East European Studies (SSEES) and he also appreciates the use of the British Library of Political and Economic Science at the London School of Economics.

Finally, we owe a great debt to those whose ideas and passion for ideas have inspired and guided us and who managed to create the institutional infrastructure for assisting research projects like ours. It is remarkable that so many of these people are associated with the Mercatus Center at George Mason University and the Institute for Humane Studies, and we are privileged that they have given our work their personal support over the years. We have benefited immensely from the opportunity of being associated with these two great institutions and we would like to express our deep gratitude to them.

Introduction

The fast political and economic transition from communism to democracy and market economy in Eastern Europe in the 1990s has been preceded and paralleled by a lengthy and yet unfinished transition in the realm of economic and political ideas. This change in the realm of beliefs was the precondition and one of the major forces that set into motion the changes leading to the collapse of the Communist regime and the emergence on its ruins of a liberal order. As economics Nobel Prize winner Douglass North put it: 'The demise of Communism in Eastern Europe in 1989 reflected a collapse of the existing belief system and a consequent weakening of the supporting organizations' (North, 1997, p. 18). North's assessment is echoed by other scholars deeply familiar with the region. The transition from the Marxist-socialist way of conceptualizing the political economy system to a new and different perspective shaped the attitudes, motivation and political behavior of the Eastern European administrative and political elites (Tismaneanu, 1992). In this process, the economics 'epistemic community' – researchers, professors, publicists and specialists in economics – played a pivotal role. In fact, rarely in history has any other social science discipline been elevated to the high status that economics managed to achieve in post-communist Eastern Europe. Yet, despite this salience, very few studies have ventured to explore this shift in economic ideas that seems to be such a critical factor in shaping and understanding the transition process (Kovács, 1994; Risse-Kappen, 1994; Wagener, 1998; Kaase, Sparschuh and Wenninger, 2002). Even fewer studies have seized upon the potential that the crucial East European case has to illuminate the larger phenomenon of diffusion and adoption of economic ideas, a phenomenon that undoubtedly has in the so-called Eastern European 'neoliberal revolution' an exemplary instantiation (Campbell and Pedersen, 2001; Robison, 2006; Roy et al., 2007). This book is an attempt to respond to the challenge posed by these overdue research agendas.

The first test confronting such a project is the clash with the tacit consensus according to which the relationship between economic ideas and the poor economic performance of the Soviet block is self-explanatory. Because the system inspired by the Marxist political economy did not 'deliver the goods', Marxist economics ideas were rejected: an example of 'marketplace of ideas' at work and a straightforward explanation of the process of ideas diffusion and change in Eastern Europe. This book, while accepting this simple but robust interpretation, goes beyond it and focuses at a deeper level by taking a closer look at a number of the complex institutional and ideational processes involved. Thus the study directly questions those that seem to think that an inquiry on the spread and adoption of economic ideas is pointless as the answers are obvious and conclusive. As such, it is addressing frontally one of those prejudices shared, as Coats and Collander (1989, pp. 4–10) put it, 'both by the dominant academic methodology and the common sense views'. That common prejudice invites a superficial and hasty answer: the ideas that win or survive are so because they are 'the best'. From that perspective, the rest is just accidental and of marginal interest. This book is based on an alternative assumption, i.e. that the answers to the question 'how and why do economic ideas spread or die?' are not only more complex but also, precisely because of that, extremely relevant for our understanding of social and institutional change.

Consequently, the study explicitly builds on the current resurgence of interest in ideas as determinants of social action and institutional structure and change. A significant number of authors have seen their views converging around the older notion that ideas of production, dissemination and change are crucial for the direction and rhythm of social change (Barry, 1989; Boudon, 1989; Haas, 1990; Hall, 1993; Jacobsen, 1995; Yee, 1996; Stone, 1996; Goldstein and Keohane, 1993a; Blyth, 1997, 2002a; North, 2005; McCloskey, 2006). Therefore, in order to understand institutional change it is crucial to explore why and how actors change their explicit or implicit views about what they see as a problem and its solutions. In this literature, special attention is given to social scientific and general theoretical ideas, as factors having considerable impact upon economic and political processes (Haas, 1990, p. 11). Social science and philosophical ideas, broadly defined, inform and shape the way politics is done. They become a component of politics because their way of grasping reality is used to define the interests that political actors articulate and the strategy they use to defend these interests. This is even truer when, in the broad category of scientific ideas, one is dealing with economics and political science. Changing social scientific beliefs should thus be seen in this light as a transforming force and therefore attention towards prevalent ideas is not only justified, but mandatory for the effective study of social change. But the current interest in the role and diffusion of ideas goes beyond the agenda of social theory. In fact, this very agenda is shaped by important contemporary ideological developments. The reality is that despite what optimists proclaim recurrently (Fukuyama, 1992; Bell, 1960), the competition of ideologies, grand political paradigms and worldviews seems to be far from over. Therefore, a better understanding of how and why such complex belief about the nature and goals of social order diffuse, evolve or disintegrate, of the institutional and social processes associated with them, as well as of the most effective conceptual frameworks to be employed in their analysis, continues to represent more than a mere academic challenge. Thus, a study exploring the lessons of the East European shift of political and economic ideas could also be considered a contribution to the understanding of the dynamics of such large belief systems and their associated conditions and consequences.

The starting point of the study is the association that has been made in the literature and public discourse between the Eastern Europe transformations and the so called 'neoliberal revolution' in political and economic ideas. Starting with the 1980s the global spread of pro-market ideas has become a phenomenon of remarkable salience having a significant impact on public policy and mesmerizing the attention of the academic literature and of the mass media. This set of ideas has been labeled in various ways: Economic Rationalism, Monetarism, Thatcherism, Reaganomics, Neoconservatism, Managerialism, Contractualism, Washington Consensus and Market Fundamentalism (England and Ward, 2007). The labels have varied in function of ideological biases and analytical purposes, yet all have pointed out to the same social fact: the expansion of a specific family of theories and beliefs about the relationship between markets and the state accompanied by corresponding policy and institutional changes. In time, all these labels have been condensed under the banner of 'neoliberalism', described as 'a remarkable transformation of the last decades of the twentieth century' that has occurred 'in the way national policy makers attempt to manage economic activity': a series of policy experiments 'undermining both the legitimacy and potential efficacy of 'big government', a time of market deregulation, state decentralization and reduced state intervention into economic affairs in general (Albert, 1993; Munck, 2003; Arestis and Sawyer, 2004; Gamble, 2006).

'Neoliberalism' is thus defined in the literature as both a doctrine and a social practice (Prakash and Hart, 1999; Arestis and Sawyer, 2004; Blyth, 2002b; Harvey, 2005). The core of the doctrine has been identified by many in the notion that 'all, or virtually all, economic and social problems have a market solution, with the corollary that state failure is typically worse than market failure'. The practice means the application of this doctrine 'to an ever-expanding area of life in the real world, via the privatization of state industries and public services, the elimination of "dependency cultures" and the introduction of market-mimicking arrangements to those areas of government activity that remain unprivatized' (Arestis and Sawyer, 2004, p. 40). These policy innovations 'premised on the extension of market relationships' (Larner, 2000) and associated with a 'decline of the State' (Ohmae, 1995; Strange, 1996) are considered to have led to the consolidation of a 'new and distinctive mode of governance' (Beeson and Firth, 1998). Indeed, the trend consisted of more than just a change of rhetoric. The very substance of neoliberal ideas was relatively radical in its implications, at least from the perspective of the political and economic status quo. Neoliberalism, writes Larner (2000), 'has been a political project concerned with institutional changes on a scale not seen since the immediate aftermath of the Second World War'. Its objective was to 'fundamentally transform some of the most basic political and economic settlements of the postwar era, including labor relations, redistributive tax structures, social welfare programs, nationalized industries and public provision of health and education'. And, as it has been repeatedly pointed out, 'while there has been much debate over about the causes, and the scope of these changes, few doubt that neoliberalism has become an important part of our world' (Dore and Berger, 1996; Boyer and Drache, 1996; Crouch and Streeck, 1997; Hirst and Thompson, 1996; Kitschelt et al., 1999; Hay, 2001). Given all of the above, the explosion of interest in the phenomenon is understandable: the shadow of the ideas and practices associated with it looms large on some of the most salient political and intellectual debates of the moment. To sum up, the term 'neoliberalism' is a convenient shorthand for a range of ideas, practices and approaches to the conduct of government that are associated with 'a preference for small goverments and a reliance on market mechanisms to determine economic outcomes' (Beeson and Firth, 1998). The association of these ideas and practices with the globalization phenomenon as well as with the profound transformation produced by the collapse of the Soviet block gave them a uniquely global dimension and relevance.

One of the most interesting aspects of the discussions about 'neoliberalism' and the 'neoliberal revolution' is that they ultimately gravitate towards the ideational factor – that is to say, towards an ideas-centered conception of social order and change. When people conceptualize 'global restructuring' as an 'imperialist political project' emanating from the 'ideological heartlands of the United States and the United Kingdom' (Steger, 2002; Larner, 2003) the assumptions and implications are unambiguous. The very notion that we are dealing not with structural, impersonal forces but with plans and projects as well as a 'center' instigating the spread of a specific ideology, imposes a shift of attention to ideas and the role of ideas in history. For some authors, the growth and spread of markets is the result of a learning process: people come to understand that markets are a better way of organizing economic activity. In people's minds the idea of market comes to be associated with choice and economic efficiency (Boettke, 1994; Cowen, 1998). For other authors, the spread of neoliberal ideas and the neoliberal phenomenon itself are the consequence of a relentless propaganda campaign. In other words of 'a quite successful ideological operation' to spread beliefs inciting to radical change aimed at 'disabling social and political organization for transformation by preaching the all-knowing and omnipotent mechanisms of the free market' (Munck, 2003). One way or another, the theme of the social role of ideas emerges as pivotal. This conclusion is reinforced if things are seen in a larger historical perspective. As Eric Helleiner (2003) explains, 'for those familiar with international economic history, the dramatic political success of the neoliberal movement in the 1980s and 1990s was reminiscent of the 1850s and 1860s when classical economic liberal ideas also swept across much of the world'. That is to say, the two periods are moments when public opinion goes through a transformation and 'the terms of discourse reflect a significantly changed acceptance of market mechanisms and a shift in public–private relations in the direction of greater support for (and increased reliance on) the private sector' (Biersteker, 1995, p. 178; Munck, 2003). Again, ideas mark history.

To conclude, the diversity and complexity of the neoliberal phenomenon escapes a unique and rigid definition. Yet, irrespective of theoretical or ideological biases, in analyzing its meaning and nature, the attention comes to be sooner or later focalized on ideas. And thus, many critics of neoliberalism had to accept the role of ideas despite the constraints of their own theoretical paradigms. Caught between the notion that abstract 'structural' forces were evolving and pushing as a winner the neoliberal formula and the notion that certain social actors and their beliefs may have a role in that development, people tend to side with the second alternative. Thus the debates about neoliberalism sooner or later came down to the problem of the role of belief systems and human agency. Marxism and structuralism notwithstanding, ideas seem to matter. As Heilbroner and Milberg (1995) note, ideas lead to changes and to understand the changes one needs to understand the ideas behind them. Or as authors such as Munck (2003) or Larner (2003) argue, policy and institutional transformation 'entailed a confrontation of ideas and rhetoric on a normative level'.

Thus, seen in the larger context of the current developments and the literature reflecting them, this book focuses on what one could consider to be a core dimension of the recent East European and global transformations: the ideas inspiring and legitimizing the process of economic and institutional change in the crisis of socialism and the collapse of communism. As one of the main contributors to the resurgence of the ideas-focused research agenda in political sciences put it,

> (. . .) attending to economic ideas in moments of crisis is key. Such ideas make institutional reconstruction possible by providing the authoritative diagnosis as

to what a crisis actually is and when a given situation actually constitutes a crisis. They diagnose 'what has gone wrong' and thus 'what is to be done'. In short, the nature of a crisis is not simply given by its effects, dislocations, or casualties, nor are the actions of agents simply determined by their 'given' interests. Instead, the diagnosis of a situation as a 'crisis' by a particular set of ideas is a deliberate construction that makes the uncertainty agents perceive explicable, manageable, and indeed, actionable. (Blyth, 2002b, p. 77)

The parameters of the book could be further focalized if one sees the expansion of neoliberalism as a development on three major fronts. First it was an attack on the Keynesian and welfarist consensus of the 'embedded liberalism' that acted as the foundation for the 1944 Bretton Woods arrangements and that 'dominated the thinking of Western policymakers for the first few decades after the war' (Ruggie, 1982; Kirshner, 1998a). The second was an offensive against socialism – especially in Latin America, where the ideological left had reinvented itself through the intricate 'structuralist' theory put forward by Raul Prebisch and his ECLA school and the 'dependency' theorists criticizing capitalist imperialism (and neo-imperialism) on 'peripheral' regions (Helleiner, 2003, p. 687). Most of the current literature on neoliberalism as an ideas-driven process is focused on these first two fronts. Yet there was a third front. The most spectacular confrontation in the battle of ideas took place in the communist Eastern Europe, where Marxism had enjoyed an unprecedented hegemony after 1945. And it is precisely on that front that neoliberalism managed to get its most decisive victory. Seen in retrospect, the erosion of the Marxist belief system and its gradual replacement with Western beliefs on how the economy and society should be organized seems to be one of the most spectacular developments in the political and intellectual history of the twentieth century.

This is exactly where the present book intends to make its contribution. Our study is a tentative effort to develop two related research agendas: the study of the spread of 'neoliberalism' – as seen from the perspective of Eastern European evolutions; and the study of Eastern European transition – as seen from an ideas-centered perspective. From an operational standpoint, the book tries to isolate one specific aspect of the process of interest (the diffusion and adoption of a particular set of ideas about the political-economic order by a specific population – the economics epistemic community of the region) and to document and analyze it from different angles. A book thus construed has to deal from the very beginning with the problem that both the 'neoliberalism' phenomenon and the process of 'transition' have a large number of complex facets and dimensions. The ambiguity generated by the overlap of these dimensions and facets makes the discussion vulnerable to misunderstandings and confusions. Out of the intricate mix of ideas, policies, institutions and social groups that define the 'neoliberal phenomenon' in Eastern Europe as elsewhere, the book is focusing only on one limited but crucial component: the political economy theories. The population studied is the group of professional scholars dealing with economic theory and policy issues. The focus is on the dynamics of ideas between the Western and Eastern European economics epistemic communities and implicitly within and between the epistemic communities of the region. It is important to note that the investigation is not directly concerned with the entire sequence 'ideas–policies–consequences– economic performance' but with one specific moment of this sequence: the moment of ideas diffusion and the ensuing process of paradigm shift. The problem of the policy application of ideas and the resulting consequences is dealt with only in a derivative manner. The focus is on the 'spread of ideas' phase.

To sum up, this is an exploratory study looking at the economics epistemic communities in Eastern Europe and the ways it embraced the pro-market neoliberal ideas thus leading the way of the massive structural transition in institutions and policies in that part of the world. While engaging in this task, the study will systematize the existing literature, bring to fore fresh facts and perspectives, challenge some old assumptions surrounding the theme and suggest new interpretations. As such, the book is built around a set of twin objectives that reinforce each other: On the one side, it is an attempt to better understand the Eastern European case by approaching it through the lenses of different theories and conceptual frameworks emerging in or related to previous studies of the diffusion and adoption of economic ideas. On the other side, it is an attempt to explore the Eastern European case with the goal of getting through it a better grasp of the processes associated to the transmission of economic ideas. In other words, the study uses the case of the Eastern Europe transition as a vehicle to understand the process of spread of (neoliberal) political economy, and uses the conceptualization, theories and frameworks associated to the study of the spread and change of ideas as means to better understand the Eastern European case.

With these objectives in view, the study is structured as follows: The first section concentrates on the factual and empirical dimension of the Eastern Europe case. It starts by identifying and describing the relevant paradigms or families of political economy. Then it continues with a overview of the 'facts' of economic ideas diffusion and paradigm shift by looking with the help of the most up-to-date and comprehensive studies available at nine countries of the region: Central-East European (Poland, Czech Republic, Slovak Republic and Hungary), South Eastern European (Romania and Bulgaria) and Baltic (Latvia, Estonia and Lithuania). The second section further explores the theme of the embrace of pro-market ideas behind the Iron Curtain by applying a series of concepts and theories aimed at generating alternative interpretations and explanations. The implicit assumption of many commentators and students of the phenomenon is that one single, relatively simple way of framing and theorizing the growth of pro-market ideas could explain the Eastern European case (and by implication all cases from elsewhere in the world). Instead, this section suggests that a pluralistic approach involving complementary perspectives and theories originating in various fields and disciplines is more useful in illuminating and interpreting the phenomenon in question. An exercise of reading the case through successive theoretical lenses is going to illustrate this point. The third section takes a step further by focusing on a series of cases that illuminate in a more detailed way the relevant facets and dimensions of the phenomenon of change of economic ideas in Eastern Europe. The broad macro-level perspective is replaced by one focused at the micro-level. This refocusing is sufficient to expose a series of myths or misunderstandings that are plaguing the general perception of the Eastern European transformation of economic ideas: the belief in the complete standardization and regimentation of economic thinking as a result of the spread of Western ways of doing economics, the notion that the Eastern Europeans have been passively embracing this uniformity and homogenization, and the myth that extreme forms of pro-market views (so called 'market fundamentalism') have been dominating the region.

Consistent with the exploratory nature of the study, the three sections of the book open three possible avenues for further investigations. The hope is that, when taken together, these three separated but related investigative tracks will build complementing interpretations, offer a reliable basis for more elaborated and more focused explorations and, in the end, create the conditions for a more nuanced and realistic understanding of the nature and significance of the neoliberal revolution in economic ideas in Eastern Europe.

PART I

The spread of Western economic ideas in Eastern Europe: an overview

The objective of this section is to provide an overview of the 'basic facts' of the spread and change of economic ideas in Eastern Europe as a precondition of an informed analysis and interpretation of the phenomenon. However, before engaging this task, the section starts with a clarification of the conceptual contours of three major protagonists of the study: 'neoliberalism', 'neoclassical economics' and indeed, 'Marxism'. A significant part of the literature dealing with the 'neoliberal revolution' in Eastern Europe has been pervaded by discussions that fail to mention what kind of ideas were embraced before 'neoliberalism' and with what results. That overlook creates the impression that 'neoliberalism' was either an intruder or something of a usurper and that better alternatives were somehow sidestepped by the march of 'market fundamentalism'. And thus, the dialectics between the dominant paradigm before the 1989 transformations and what came after is entirely overlooked although it may explain better the success of pro-market ideas in Eastern Europe than the speculative arguments that make tabula rasa of 50 years of experimentation with socialist ideas in that part of the world. To avoid this error, one has to look at both the winners and the losers. Once that is done, the rest of the section focuses on the specifics of the phenomenon of spread and change of ideas itself.

A research on these lines should, from an operational standpoint, necessarily incorporate several levels of case studies. First is the micro-level – instances of activities and developments taking place in universities, publications, research institutions, etc. – countless instances of ideas-related episodes scattered all over the region. Then are the country cases – more specifically the countries from Eastern Europe out of which nine are the object of special attention in this study: Bulgaria, Czech Republic, Hungary, Estonia, Latvia, Lithuania, Poland, Romania and Slovakia. (The USSR/Russia situation is not discussed directly but only in the measure in which it is relevant for the Baltic countries' evolution and as a background influence for the rest of the ex-Soviet space.) Finally, the third level consists of the large, consolidated regional case, 'the case of Eastern Europe' – the sum of all micro-level and national cases aggregated in an overarching regional unit of observation.

As one may expect, the efforts of studying and collecting data regarding economic ideas diffusion and change in Eastern Europe are at their very beginning. Therefore, for obvious reasons, any synthesis study today is by its nature explanatory and tentative. Furthermore, the varieties of situations, countries, conditions, languages and cultures involved require a daunting effort. Getting familiar with the specific developments at the level of each country, while being familiar with each nation's publications and language, is a titanic task for any individual researcher. Such undertaking is only feasible as a team project and even then it raises its own problems and challenges. For instance, one needs researchers who are not only familiar with the developments in each country but also, at the same time, able to work within a common conceptual and methodological framework shared by the entire team. Fortunately, this book has been able to make use of the results of the first such large-scale comparative international teamwork.

More precisely, in addition to the standard bibliographical sources, Chapters 2 and 3 of this section of the book reflect the most comprehensive and up-to-date empirical investigation of the evolution of political economy ideas in Eastern Europe, based on the most recent data collection efforts. The overview is building on the results of a large European Union funded expert survey operationalized through Collegium Budapest and the Social Science Information Centre – GESIS Berlin, as part of the project 'The State of Three Social Science Disciplines in Central and Eastern Europe' with the participation of institutions such as Institut für die Wissenschaften von Menschen, Vienna, Centre Marc Bloch, Berlin, Maison des Sciences de l'Homme, Paris. The survey, based on a questionnaire and the reports written as a response to it, was applied to the core East European 'accession' countries: Bulgaria, Czech Republic, Hungary, Estonia, Latvia, Lithuania, Poland, Romania and Slovakia. An important part of the findings were published in Kaase, Sparschuh and Wenninger (2002) making out of this book the most inclusive synopsis of the state of social sciences in Eastern Europe to date. The methodology of the project implied a double internal review. Top scholars of each country were nominated as investigators and commentators. The investigators used the

questionnaires and the data gathered by them to bolster their own expertise and to write country reports or 'country cases'. In parallel, information
collected through another questionnaire run by the Informations-zentrum
Sozialwissenschaften Berlin and circulated among the key research and
academic centers of each country was used to corroborate information,
complement and strengthen these initial country reports. Once produced,
each country report entered a new stage in which it was reviewed and com-
mented on by a different top scholar from the one who wrote the report.
The result of this multilayered and methodical effort was an ample survey
on the disciplinary developments in the region and a unique database
regarding the phenomenon of interest for our study.

The following discussion anchors the overview of the 'basic facts' of the
process of economic ideas diffusion and change in Eastern Europe in this
database using a framework with two dimensions. First, the countries are
grouped into three clusters: the Central-East European nations (Poland,
Czech Republic, Slovak Republic and Hungary), the Southeast European
nations (Romania and Bulgaria) and the Baltic nations (Latvia, Estonia
and Lithuania). Second, reflecting Kaase, Sparschuh and Wenninger
(2002), the discussion of each of the three groups will be approached following an outline framed by a set of well-defined themes relevant to the
understanding of dynamics of economic ideas before and after the 1989
transformations: The state of Marxism as a reigning paradigm; the
pace and outlets of Western influence (including the pre-war traditions
and the impact of Western theories pre-1989); the institutional, social
and ideational processes associated to the paradigm change tipping
point; the institutionalization process in academia, public policy and
research units; and the professional/disciplinary elites change. Finally,
an additional issue of major importance that could not be entirely captured by the above-mentioned framework is discussed separately: the role
of the international and European institutions as conduits for epistemic
change.

To sum up, the subsequent discussion is not meant to present a comprehensive survey of the multiplicity of facets, processes and circumstances
associated with the change of economic ideas in Eastern Europe. In this
respect it is important to emphasize that today there is no substitute for
reading the excellent Kaase, Sparschuh and Wenninger (2002) book in
which each country development is discussed at length and in depth. The
goal of the following pages is to offer an informed regional-level picture of
the phenomenon – a bird's eye view background for further discussions and
interpretations. One hopes that once juxtaposed, the overviews of all the
concurrent aspects of the Eastern European dynamics of ideas will not
only offer a richer image of the complex transformations that took place

there, but also a counterweight to the temptation to engage in swift generalizations or superficial conjectures that marks in a persistent way the
already hefty literature dealing with 'neoliberalism' and the 'neoliberal
revolution' of the 1980s and 1990s.

1. Economic ideas: demarcations and schools of thought

Many discussions of the profound transformation taking place in Western Europe, Latin America and Eastern Europe use implicitly or explicitly models, conjectures and theories in which 'neoliberalism' represents a key variable. Sometimes seen as an independent variable, sometimes as a dependent one, sometimes introduced as a 'key variable' and sometimes as part of an analysis of the facilitating conditions, the recourse to the 'neoliberal' factor is more often than not a significant theme. Yet, the visibility of the concept is misleading. In reality its use hinders rather than helps the analytical effort: despite its salience, it remains an under-conceptualized and under-operationalized notion. As Ray, Denzau and Willett (2007, p. 21) put it, neoliberalism 'is a term often used in political economy very broadly and vaguely to refer to market-oriented policy ideas and strategies in the second half of the twentieth century'. But besides that, ambiguity and confusion reign.

Indeed something called 'neoliberalism' is invoked in many studies, but especially when it comes to Eastern Europe, somehow manages in most cases to slip and escape a clear conceptualization. The unit of observation and the specification of the phenomenon in question vary from author to author. Authors sometimes employ it to refer to theories and schools of thought (such as 'neoclassical economics', 'Washington consensus') and sometimes they add an ideological overtone (as in 'market ideology', 'market fundamentalism'); in some cases they focus their approach on specific policies or public policies ('privatization', 'deregulation', 'stabilization'), while in other cases they use the notion to refer to institutions and institutionalization processes: market-creating institutions (for property rights and contract enforcement), market-regulating institutions (for externalities, and asymmetric information) or market-stabilizing institutions (for monetary and fiscal management). And then there are cases when the notion stands for various combinations of any of the above (Arestis and Sawyer, 2004; Steger, 2002; Robison, 2006; England and Ward, 2007).

Our study is based on the postulate that if there is a hard core in the fuzzy set of the 'neoliberalism' phenomena, that core could be identified primarily at the level of economic theory ideas. One could not imagine any meaningful definition of neoliberalism without making reference to the specific concepts and theories referring to the nature of political-economic order. More specifically, to the beliefs regarding the operation of the economy as a system and the ways that operation should be reformed or improved in function of a collection of implicit norms and principles. Any understanding of the 'neoliberal phenomenon' as a whole or of any of its facets, goes through the understanding of those ideas. Neoliberalism, write Roy, Denzau and Willett (2007, p. 21), 'can be understood as both a reference to the distinct but related experiments applying market-oriented ideas in various political, social, and economic contexts' or as a 'broader reference to certain core ideas that are shared among them'. One way or another, the position of ideas is pivotal. And irrespective of the label used, one thing remains the same: the substance of those ideas is given by specific cause-and-effect beliefs about the operation of the economy. In other words, they imply or are based on what is called 'economics' or 'political economy'.

The core of neoliberalism is thus intrinsically linked to economics as a social science. That doesn't mean at all that because of this reference to 'positive' science the discussion loses the normative or practical relevance. As Robert Solo points out, 'the pure science of economics is a part of political economy, understood as a system geared to the formation and implementation of economic policy'. But, at its turn, political economy is also part of a larger system: the encompassing political system. The generalizing theories of economics have a limited meaning if they are not seen in this larger context and are 'not coupled with the selection of goals and priorities, and the evaluation of costs and benefits'. That introduces new dimensions: both theories and norms should be 'wedded into yet another form of ideational system. Beyond policy formation and the exercise of collective choice, there is a need to fashion and develop technologies for the implementation of policy, for the control and evaluation of operations, and for the reevaluation of policy and choice' (Solo, 1991, pp. 75–8). In other words, following Solo's hint, the main elements of a political economy school of thought are (a) a general theory, (b) a normative perspective, (c) a corresponding strategy and policy technology. The general theory offers 'a framework that reduces the infinity of details of the phenomenon or issue studied to a set of significant regularities'. The task of general theory or economics in the broader political economy paradigm is 'to provide the most inclusive overview possible of some class of social phenomena, and in so doing, qua policy science, to provide the informational base for an overall posture in the formation of public policy'. On the other hand, information, regardless of its accurateness, 'will be insufficient by itself for public choice and policy decisions'. General theory serves well defining policy alternatives, but it is unable to offer a framework for evaluating the goals and values from which those alternatives originate. The normative element would delve into such questions. Economics is ultimately economic policy-oriented and economic policy depends on both normative standards and the theoretical and information base. The key statements of the general theory are empirical, 'possibly falsifiable by reference to shared experience'. At the core of a normative discourse are statements of another order. They are not empirical, nor can they be falsified by experimental trial.

Thus, to conclude, one may say that a political economy system (such as 'neoliberalism') consists of the theoretical and normative core plus the strategic and tactical policy-oriented extensions (Solo, 1991, pp. 76–7). That is to say that one could distinguish in the neoliberal cluster of ideas several concentric circles. At the center is an economics heart – causal (cause-and-effect) theories about the nature of social order. That is embedded within normative beliefs about freedom, social justice and efficiency. Built around them is another circle: strategies and policies. The conclusion is straightforward: for any study that takes as a pivot the process of economic ideas diffusion, the theoretical core of those ideas represents the focal point. Indeed without a clearly individualized conceptual core, one couldn't even speak of a study of 'ideas'. The first task of such an investigation is then to identify the theoretical component. In our case, more specifically: What were the specific economic theory ideas that grew or diffused in Eastern Europe thus marking the 'neoliberal revolution' in that part of the world? Identifying them with clarity allows to isolate the units of observation and analysis and to better focus the investigation. At the same time, by implication, a related question gets to be addressed: What were the ideas that got discarded and replaced?

SCHOOLS OF THOUGHT IN POLITICAL ECONOMY

A crucial observation for a study of neoliberal ideas is that such political-economic ideas, by their very nature, do not exist in isolation but are grouped in clusters of various configurations. In fact this is a typical working hypothesis for the studies of the spread of economic ideas (Coats and Collander, 1989, p. 10). These clusters could be well described as 'paradigms'. They are, following a definition given by Hall,

> an overarching set of ideas that specify how the problems are to be perceived, which goals might be attained through policy and what sorts of techniques can be used to reach those goals . . . Like a gestalt, they structure the very way in which policy-makers see the world and their role within. (Hall, 1992, pp. 91–2)

As we have seen they are belief systems that are not purely theoretical but they have normative and 'constitutive' dimensions, too. Defining the 'ideas' this study is interested in as 'paradigms' and using as an initial guide the insights given by the 'paradigm shift' literature, is probably the best step further in the effort to give clear conceptual contours to the discussion. Once the notion of paradigm is used, the problem of the dynamics or change of the political economy beliefs systems automatically evokes the classical philosophy of science discussion generated by Kuhn's influential book, *The Structure of Scientific Revolutions* (1962). The literature points out several facets of the notion of 'paradigm': a set of beliefs, a myth and a successful metaphysical speculation, a way of seeing an organizing principle governing perception, an entire theoretical worldview, a series of laws, a methodological recipe, and a set of fundamental values (Kuhn, 1962, pp. 4, 2, 17, 117–21, 120). The mere list of the various facets of the notion of paradigm reminds us that the economic ideas of interest to our study are complex clusters that could not be reduced to a mere abstract formula. The focus on the economics hard core of the 'neoliberal phenomenon' is a very constructive heuristic and analytic device. On the one hand, we think of it 'like the sun in a solar system' drawing around it the rest of the elements of the system. On the other hand, one should not try to reduce the system to just the central element. In other words, even if for analytic and heuristic reasons the attention should be indeed on the economic theory core, one should never forget the other layers of the circle and the difficulty of disentangling the normative elements and practical elements from the more theoretical component of the paradigm.

Regardless of the way the analysis units of this study are conceptualized, a research on these lines will raise some problems of operationalization. Because the unit (the paradigm, cluster of ideas, belief system, etc.) is less individualizable than a proposition or even a theory, and because paradigms have many layers or dimensions with different dynamics, the question of how to categorize theories into their respective paradigms, and how to study the change, can be a difficult one. Yet, a study dealing with the dynamics of ideas such as the present one needs to be based precisely on such a clear-cut taxonomy. The taxonomy of paradigms, the way theories are grouped together, is a difficult task even in natural sciences. The problem is evident and it should be no surprise that it is even thornier in social sciences. For instance, Copernicus's theory shared much of Aristotle's physics (among others Aristotle's commitment to aethereal spheres). Yet, in grouping Copernicus with Kepler and Newton, we consider that other aspects of his theory are more important than his beliefs about the way heaven moved. The choice to put his work in a category is not an automatic one (Solo, 1991, pp. 76–7). Things are no different in political economy. In function of the defining criterion chosen, several taxonomies of political economy paradigms may come into sight.

Fortunately for the present study, irrespective of the way paradigm is defined, in the case of the twentieth-century political economists, the habit of thinking in terms of schools and paradigms has been widespread. Although the first intuition is that the array of possible permutations of concepts, frameworks, theories, causal or normative beliefs and worldviews is infinite, in fact the standard textbooks present a limited number of such combinations. In *Theories of Political Economy*, a book dealing precisely with this topic, James Caporaso and David Levine (1992) take the very basic conceptualization of *economy* and *politics* as a defining criterion:

> It matters in thinking about the issues in political economy whether we treat, for example, authority or the state as central concepts in politics. At the same time it matters whether we think material reproduction, the market, or constrained choice is the central concept in economics. Different notions of economics and politics, lead to different political economies. (Caporaso and Levine, 1992, p. 3)

After making the point that different conceptualizations lead to different paradigms, they emphasize the importance of understanding the categorical distinction between politics and economics, as well as the significance of the separateness and relationship of the two spheres of the economic and the political. If we focus on the various ways of conceptualizing the two spheres and their relationship, we could develop various combinations. And thus, taking the relationship between economics and politics as a defining criterion, Caporaso and Levine outline what they identify as the 'major paradigms of political economy'.

The Classical approach argues for the capacity of markets to regulate themselves. In this paradigm, the economy is treated as a system separable in principle from politics and family life with the market as a reality *sui generis* connected to but not a subsidiary organ of the state. The economy is not or should not be political. The Marxist paradigm is an extension of the classical project. While continuing the idea of the economy as a distinctive arena of society it advances a distinct conception of the relationship between the political and the economic. Its emphasis is on the powerful forces originated in the dynamics of the capitalist economic process and the historical political implications of that dynamics. Also Marxism develops a critique of the classical claim for market self-regulation. To demonstrate that capitalism is not viable in the long run, it stresses the so-called 'contradictions of capitalism' (Caporaso and Levine, 1992, p. 3).

The Neoclassical theory is also an extension of the classical view of the economy as a separable system but instead of the classical analytical scheme it applies a utilitarian framework. In the neoclassical approach, the relation of politics to economics is defined on the basis of the idea of market failure. Market failure is defined with reference to individual preferences and the efficient use of resources and represents a condition in which a market does not efficiently allocate resources to achieve the greatest possible consumer satisfaction. The four main expressions of market failures are in the areas of public goods, market control, externalities and imperfect information. In each case, a market acting without any government-imposed direction does not direct an efficient amount of our resources into the production, distribution or consumption of the good. 'For the neoclassical thinker economics refers to private transactions in pursuit of utility maximization, politics to the use of public authority in the same cause' (Caporaso and Levine, 1992, p. 4).

Finally, the Keynesian paradigm is a critique of the claims for market self-regulation of the classical and neoclassical schools. Like the neoclassical, it emphasizes a type of market failure. But this type of market failure is deeper and possesses a more fundamental challenge to the institutions of a private market system: 'Its critique of the market calls into question the role assigned to the public authority by the classical theorists. Changes in that role carry implications for the classical innovation – the depoliticization of the economy' (Caporaso and Levine, 1992, p. 4). Adding to these basic categories, the authors also discuss the implications for political economy of different methods and approaching economy and politics: the economic approach to politics; state-centered alternatives of conceptualizing the relation between politics and economics and the justice-centered approach. Nevertheless, all gravitate around these major approaches or, to be more precise, to three of them – the Classical view being more or less only of historical significance (Caporaso and Levine, 1992, p. 3).

In *The Ideal Worlds of Economics: Liberal, Radical, and Conservative Economic World Views*, Benjamin Ward (1979) uses a different type of criteria but the emerging paradigms taxonomy is largely similar to the Caporaso and Levine one. Ward's goal is

> to persuade the reader that economics is thoroughly permeated by ideology in its structure, in the way it asks questions and answers them, and in the way policy implications are drawn from it. The discipline is striking and distinctive in that there are three ideologies that are widely held by professional practitioners and whose implications for these most fundamental aspects of the subject are very different from one another. (Ward, 1979, p. vii)

These three are the liberal, radical and conservative. All have variants and different forms and their spectrum is conceived as rather broad but all those forms might be reduced to the basic pure three forms or 'optimal views': 'there is in fact no fourth alternative in economics today. These are

the only world views we have . . . The variants tend clearly to fall within one
or another of the world views on each issue' (Ward, 1979, p. vii).

From Ward's standpoint each worldview does pass 'the test of being
assertable in ways that contradict no known facts'. Furthermore, in terms
of policy implications each is consistent with reasonable codes of morality
while each is coherent, the parts being mutually compatible and mutually
reinforcing. 'And yet when discussing the same problems, such as the economic activities of the government or economic development or socialism
the shift from one view to another is really like shifting from one world to
another' (Ward, 1979, p. viii). In his view, various ideas, values and concepts tend to cluster in three configurations but in his case, as distinct from
Caporaso and Levine, the defining criterion has a normative nature: 'communication across world views does not occur with great frequency in economics and almost every attempt to communicate across world views is
essentially an attempt to alter value systems' (Ward, 1979, p. viii).

The point is that even if the problem is approached using a normative criterion, three contemporary clusters, schools or paradigms seem to emerge.
This conclusion receives a systematic articulation from Ken Cole, John
Cameron and Chris Edwards (1991). For them, economics is not a unified
science. There are, in fact, three essentially opposed perspectives that
cannot be synthesized into a single school of thought. Each perspective has
to be understood and presented in its own terms, as a logical system. The
development of economics is seen as the outcome of battles between
schools of thought to provide explanations and criticism over current
issues. 'Such battles are strongly related to conflicts in the sphere of politics
and as such economic theory cannot be divorced from political practice'
(Cole, Cameron and Edwards, 1991, p. viii). Cole, Cameron and Edwards
make the problem of values the key defining criterion of an economic
paradigm.

From their standpoint, there are three, and only three, schools of economics: 'Three breeds of economics which form a basis for successful
inbreeding but have never given rise to healthy cross breeds. The only link
between these three pure breeds of economics is their concern with valuation' (Cole, Cameron and Edwards, 1991, p. 5). What is crucial in the taxonomy introduced by the three authors is the fact that that the theory of
values is explicitly singled out as pivotal for the way schools or paradigms
are grouped. The different schools of economic thought follow different
theories of value implying different models of social behavior and different
policies. The three are: the subjective preferences school, the cost of production school, and the abstract labor school. Cole, Cameron and Edwards
formulate a comprehensive set of adoption and change criteria. Each of
these paradigms faces the test of realism, rationalism and activism. If the

theory just describes parts of social experience without deriving policy pre-scriptions it will be rejected by activists (those taking the ability to change the reality as the key criterion). If the theory is not linked to the realities of the present, it will be rejected by realists. If the theory does not link the description to prescriptions through rigorous application of reason, the theory runs the risk of inconsistency loosening its appeal to rationalists. All three schools or paradigms meet these three criteria for survival. Each points to an area of experience as matching its description, displays a clear logic of arguments, and has specific policy conclusions (Cole, Cameron and Edwards, 1991, pp. 5–8). These conclusions are reinforced by other attempts like Glass and Johnson (1989) that develop a tripartite character-ization of economic theory, too.

In summary, a tripartite division of the contemporary political economy thought seems to be a salient feature of any paradigmatic taxonomy in the field. Nevertheless, it is important to keep in mind that these tripartite tax-onomies are at the broadest possible level of generalization. One could develop more elaborated taxonomies that introduce the Austrian, the Institutional and the post-Keynesian schools as autonomous paradigms. And, in fact, these more refined distinctions will be used later by this current study. But, for now the basic point is that if sufficient degrees of generality are allowed, one could organize the existing families of schools of thought into three major clusters. Yet, even if Benjamin Ward's point regarding the reduction to 'optimal views' is vindicated, it is neither necessary to go along with him and to accept his rhetorical overemphasis that communication across worldviews does not occur with great frequency, nor to agree with Cole, Cameron and Edwards' point that the only link between these three 'pure breeds of economics' is their concern with valuation. It is more real-istic to relax these strong theses and see the paradigms as part of a complex web of ideas that could be cut in different ways in function of different cri-teria but irrespective of the way you try to make the cut the separated parts would have roughly similar contours and parameters. That doesn't rule out indeed the possibility of intercommunication within the web or even some instances of interbreeding.

The present study takes as a starting point the broad consensus regard-ing the existent paradigms in current political economy as defined by the authors discussed before. In the next pages, the focus will be on two basic schools: Eastern Marxism and the Western Neoclassical Synthesis. The reason is simple; neoliberal ideas did not diffuse eastward in a void. To understand the process one needs to also understand what happened to the ideas that occupied the territory before them. Too many discussions of neoliberalism in the literature forget to mention what kind of ideas were embraced before 'neoliberalism' and with what results. If the dialectics between the dominant paradigm before the 1989 transformation and what came after is entirely overlooked, although it may explain far better the success of pro-market ideas in Eastern Europe, then any speculation about the 'geopolitics of neoliberal hegemony' will be missed. To avoid this analytical mistake one has to look at both the winners and the losers.

THE NEOCLASSICAL SYNTHESIS AND THE MARXIST PARADIGMS

The two sets of economic ideas whose competition is the focus of this discussion are the Eastern Marxism and the Western neoclassical synthesis. While the choice of Marxism is self-explanatory, the choice of the neoclassical synthesis requires an explanation. There is a consensus among the economists that the political economy ideas diffused in Eastern Europe and the paradigm shift brought by them were defined in terms of a specific postwar development of Western economics known as the neoclassical synthesis. In this respect an important point should be made: The neoliberal revolution in Eastern European ideas was not an extremist phenomenon of change promoted by 'market fundamentalism' as it is insistently implied by some authors. The synthesis, broadly defined, was de facto world standard among Western academic, professional and government economists. Also known as 'the mainstream', 'mainstream economics' or the 'orthodoxy', it was also overwhelmingly the main object of diffusion in Eastern Europe economics epistemic communities. Before any supply side, monetarist, public choice or any other 'market fundamentalism' principles could be understood and embraced in Eastern Europe the very basic idea of modern economics had to be absorbed and embraced. That meant that the 'neoliberal revolution' in Eastern Europe was not so much a process of uncritically embracing Hayek's social theory or Friedman's monetarism but one of familiarization with Samuelson's 'neoclassical synthesis'. The term 'neoclassical synthesis' was coined by Paul Samuelson to denote the consensus view of economics which emerged in the mid-1950s in the US – 'a compromise doctrine has emerged from the combination of classical, neoclassical, Keynesian and neo Keynesian analysis' (Samuelson, 1951, p. 336). In the third edition of his economics textbook he wrote:

> In recent years, 90 percent of American Economists have stopped being 'Keynesian economists' or 'anti-Keynesian economists'. Instead they have worked toward a synthesis of whatever is valuable in older economics and in modern theories of income determination. The result might be called neoclassical economics and is accepted in its broad outlines by all but about 5 per cent of extreme left wing and right wing writers. (Samuelson, 1955, p. 212)

The structure of the paradigm could be easily understood once focused on its historical origins. The challenge posed by the emergence of Keynesian economics to economics was twofold. On the one hand, ignoring it would have left out what, by that time, was considered to be a potent explanation of depressions and recessions. On the other hand, Keynesianism had a different scope and therefore it could not impose itself on neoclassical economics little by little similarly to how neoclassical economics had imposed earlier on classical economics. The solution was a coexistence, in which neoclassical economics was considered applicable under conditions of full employment and Keynesism as a theory explained recessions. The standard neoclassical economics theories were labeled microeconomics and the Keynesian ones macroeconomics. The neoclassical theories of value, price and income distribution would be called microeconomics and the study of fluctuations in total output would be called macroeconomics. The whole was called the neoclassical/Keynesian synthesis (Weintraub, 1993; Blackhouse, 1985; Blaug, 1997).

Due to its policy influence and prestige, the neoclassical synthesis is not a mere theory but an overarching conceptual framework, having all attributes of a meta-level paradigm, a set of implicit rules and approaches for constructing economic theories. Its fundamental principles pivot around the individual and individual decision-making process. The core of those fundamental ideas includes 'economic agents' having 'rational preferences among outcomes' (or 'agents optimizing subject to constraints' or 'maximize utility and profits') etc. Theories are constructed out of these elements, or guided by these heuristics. The influence and clout of this synthesis has been so vast during the past 50 years, that even when disagreeing with it or departing from it other, non-orthodox theories take it as their main reference point (Weintraub, 1993; Kirzner, 1960; Blaug, 1997).

The public success of the 'synthesis' was decisive in its pre-eminence in the epistemic community. That success was both conceptual and practical. Crucial in this respect was its application during the Kennedy and the Johnson administrations, during which it was at its peak. As inflation increased in the late 1960s, the empirical success and in turn its theoretical foundations were increasingly questioned. The most serious challenge was the stagflation of the mid-1970s when it became clear that the policy it inspired was not able to maintain steady growth and low inflation (Snowdon et al., 1994; Blackhouse, 1985). While initially the problem was the failure to explain the economic phenomenon, later the attention switched to deeper conceptual problems. The synthesis seemed to suffer from what was called 'schizophrenia', a structural mismatch between its micro and macro dimensions. The essential fault was identified in its asymmetric treatment of micro-level actors as being highly rational and of macro-level markets as being inefficient in optimally adjusting wages and prices. Although since 1975 the neoclassical synthesis both in its theoretical core and its applied dimension has been fighting for survival, the broader paradigmatic environment created remained unchallenged. In spite of all its problems, by that time it was deeply rooted in the epistemic community. A general paradigmatic vision in which the neoclassical element was the foundation on which the macro-structure could be erected.

By then, the neoclassical synthesis acquired broader features, and it was a vision about what economics was and how economic research should be done. Theories, which were not detailed, were the ones defining the synthesis, but a general paradigmatic vision in which the neoclassical element was the foundation on which the macro-structure could be erected. Especially after the new classical macroeconomics asserted itself as a possible exit solution to the synthesis's problems, the image consolidated: the notion of a system, with interacting components, 'maxima' and 'minima' and 'stable equilibria'. In this way, emulating the successful physical sciences, the neoclassical enterprise become intrinsically associated to the idea of successful science and became linked to science itself (Weintraub, 1993). Thus the neoclassical synthesis stands in the epistemic community not only for the study of the 'truths about incentives, prices and information, the interrelatedness of decisions and the unintended consequences of choices' but also for a scientific attitude, 'a self-consciousness about the use of evidence, a clarity in the rules of theory development, and assessment, and a general attitude of scientific rationalism' (Weintraub, 1993, pp. 135–9). And indeed at the same time it is the core of what was labeled as 'neoliberal doctrine' or 'neoliberalism', a position that it occupies with the entire clout (and drawbacks) of being associated in the minds of the economics epistemic community with the very idea of a scientific approach.

That is to say that, indeed, the 'neoliberal revolution' in Eastern European ideas was far from being an extremist phenomenon – on the contrary it was based on what was considered the most scientific and advanced social science of the moment. If market arrangements were at its core, that was because the market was at the core of the mainstream thinking in economics. In fact, as one could easily see, by simply following the macroeconomic practices of the region, the ideas embraced in the post Soviet countries were basically the good old combination of Keynesian and neoclassical theories. One should not let oneself be carried along by the rhetoric criticizing 'market fundamentalism' and 'market radicalism'. The spread of economic ideas in Eastern Europe – the 'neoliberal revolution' – was solidly grounded in the core, mainstream economics.

One of the first results of an empirically informed analysis is the dispelling of the myth of a rush to the theories and ideas that are considered in the literature the mark of 'market fundamentalism' – supply side, Austrian market processes, public choice and monetarism – or that a 'neoliberal dogma' took over an unsuspecting population or policymakers. In fact it is even unclear if the majority of Eastern European members of the economics community were initially aware or interested in such distinctions existent within the Western ideas camp. The same is true about the notion that a harsh market neoliberalism was imposed somehow from outside. If 'neoliberal dogmatism' meant embracing aggregate demand notions of Keynesian inspiration and sound business environment standards, under the guidance of the World Bank, the European Union, IMF and UNDP then that is correct. But that is something different from the supply side, public choice takeover claimed by some. Indeed in Eastern Europe those ideas were incorporated after 1989. The 'neoliberal revolution' was at its core a simple realignment with the modern way of seeing and managing the economy. First and foremost was getting on the same page with the Western mainstream thinking in terms of markets and their management. There is nothing radical or fundamentalist in that. As the next chapters will show, the raise of neoliberal ideas was a more complex and tedious process than various authors, more or less ideologically biased, want us to believe it was. When one is focused on the precise ideas diffused, and not on the rhetoric of various critical interpretations of transition and neoliberalism, one thing is clear: the ideas that occupy overwhelmingly the diffusion channels and the minds of diffusion agents were the standard neoclassical synthesis taught in various forms in almost all Western economics departments and not the radical market libertarianism that some either imply or explicitly claim have become the dominant paradigm in the East. Whether the policies implemented (as opposed to ideas diffused) were a form of market radicalism or whether anything like a 'radical market reform experiment' was indeed taking place there is a different issue. The fact is that when one is focusing on the ideas side – more precisely on the theoretical core – the facts are uncontroversial.

This discussion introduces indeed the problem of the varieties of schools of thought and theoretical perspectives that were part of the cluster that accompanied the core 'synthesis' in its diffusion in the East. There is a matter of debate in what measure and how the non-orthodox or dissenting paradigms in economics can be contrasted to the neoclassical economics. As it has already been hinted, many authors argue that there are several schools of thought, or alternative paradigms, in present-day economics. However, there is no consensus about their number or their relationship to the mainstream. Usually, three such schools or paradigms are identified: (neo) Austrian Economics, Post Keynesian Economics, or (neo) Institutional Economics. The other sections of the book will focus on some of them as a vehicle for further exploration of the process studied. Nevertheless, in this section of the book the lion's share of the attention is given to the neo-classical synthesis and the paradigm it came to replace in Eastern Europe: Marxism. And rightly so: they were by far the main contenders.

In a nutshell, the differences between the neoclassical synthesis and Marxism are radical: In the case of the neoclassical research program the hard core affirms individualism, rational behavior of individual economic agents, property ownership and market exchange. In the case of the of the Marxist research programs the hard core affirms the social nature of the individual economic agent instead of individualism, rationality with a social dimension, property ownership and market exchange as social power relations. But this general overview doesn't do justice to the Marxist paradigm, especially as its East European avatar evolved during the twentieth century into a belief system with significant specific features.

East European Marxism was defined by a rather unimaginative, conservative and conventional interpretation of Marx. In the preface to the first German edition of *Capital*, Marx wrote that the ultimate aim of his work was 'to lay bare the economic law of motion of modern society'. None of his extensive writings managed to outline a definitive version of such a law. Therefore the 'scientific revolution' he announced in his work had to be followed by 'normal science' interpreting and systematizing the laws and models often left by him incomplete or only vaguely discernible (Catephores, 1989, p. x). Hence, there is no surprise that various and sometimes divergent interpretations of his work developed in West and East and at one point even within the Eastern countries. Notwithstanding the variations, in the East the conceptual background was everywhere rather similar: a rigid system strongly defined by the early Marxism and its Leninist and Stalinist reinterpretation. That background, bolstered politically and institutionally as it was by the Communist parties, was the reference point, the landmark from which East European economists departed (or became critically engaged with).

Eastern Marxism is best defined and easily and concisely summarized by its vision centered on four 'laws of motion' of capitalism: (i) the law of the falling rate of profit, (ii) the law of the increasing severity of the cyclical crisis, (iii) the law of concentration and centralization of capital and (iv) the law of the increasing misery of the working class (Gillman, 1958). These laws constituted an intermediate level between a more abstract theoretical foundation and the applied and ideological level and as such they were the backbone of Eastern Marxism (Samuelson, 1967). At a deeper level a much more elaborated conceptual and theoretical apparatus was supporting these laws. These theoretical features of Marx's economic model were in fact those that defined in a fundamental way the Marxist paradigm in its Eastern, mainstream interpretation (Junankar, 1982).

Following Junankar's work, these basic building blocks could be summarized as follows: (a) The importance of production. Production is the most important economic process and the key to economic analysis. (b) Competition. Profit maximization by capitalists within a competitive framework leads to movement of capital to sectors with the highest rates of profits, which tends to lead to an equalization of profit rates and bring market prices towards their long-run equilibrium levels. The competitive process contains the seeds of its own destruction: there are inherent forces that lead the system to its antithesis. (c) The economy as a macro system and the inter-relatedness of the different sectors of the economy. Marxist analysis puts a special emphasis on the importance of accumulation (investment), employment and unemployment, etc. and their dynamic structural consequences. (d) Income distribution and classes. Income distribution and especially the laws that govern income distribution between the classes are of primary importance in economics. Classes are defined with respect to the means of production. (e) Labor theory of value and its corollaries. Value is determined by the amount of socially necessary labor embodied. Exploitation is a necessary consequence of capitalism; it is a normal process resulting from the nature of capitalist production and exchange. It is the exploitation of 'surplus value' that provides a pure surplus which is the basis of capitalist profits. The origin and nature of profits are in production, not circulation. (f) Capital accumulation and the falling rate of profit. With capital accumulation goes increasing concentration of capital, to increasing monopolization and centralization. Increasing capital accumulation leads to an increase of the capital/labor ratio that leads to a fall in the rate of profit. (g) Industrial reserve army. Capital accumulation is labor saving and makes labor redundant. This pool of unemployed workers puts a downward pressure on wages. (h) Crises. Crises are a necessary consequence of capitalist production. The 'relations of production' come into conflict with the 'forces of production'. These crises are the way in which the internal contradictions of capitalism were resolved, and these crises would recur with increasing severity (Junankar, 1982, pp. 10–12). As regarding the economics of socialism, Marxist thought was rather confused and initially the Leninist–Stalinist line was embraced wholeheartedly. Latter revisions were suggested but by definition all those revisions represented just departures for the Leninist–Stalinist core. It is important to mention these aspects of the Marxist doctrine as many authors seem to take a rather casual position regarding what was supposed to be really believed and studied by the Eastern European economists before the advent of 'neoliberalism'.

Finally, it is worth mentioning that Marx's analysis stressed the unity of social science and the East European Marxists followed that lead. In this view, economics must be put in its proper social and historical context as it was impossible to study economics in isolation. It is interesting to note that in general the political economy dimension of that feature was over-emphasized in the sense that the unity was defined more as a feature of a core 'political economy' element and less as an interdisciplinary spontaneous phenomenon. In some extreme cases, like the Romanian one, that led even to the banishing of entire disciplines and university departments and to the centralization of research and teaching around the 'political economy' core.

Until close to the collapse of the regime, a model broadly similar to the one described above was supposed to command, in some version or other, the loyalties of most practitioners of Marxism, both in academic teaching or in political life in Eastern Europe. In the measure in which the Marxists were 'normal scientists' (Kuhn, 1962), their research was defined precisely by that model (Catephores, 1989, p. xi). And thus, seen from a purely scientific perspective, the results of 'the Eastern European Mainstream Marxist model' were rather dim. As noted by one of the most astute analysts of the phenomenon:

> Looked at from the point of view of the universal history of economic theory, economics under communism has not produced any spectacular new insights, theorems, laws or controversies which have to be memorized by all students of economics like, for example, the Cambridge controversy, Say's law, the Coase theorem or the Heckscher-Ohlin theory. (Wagener, 1998, p. 24)

This is even true for the contributions concerning the socialist theory or the radical political economy. It shouldn't be a surprise after all that the challenge came very soon. The transition at the level of ideas substantially preceded the social, economic and political transition.

2. Western economic ideas and the fragile hegemony of Marxism: the pre-1989 setting

Despite the fact that officially most East European economists were supposed to share the standard interpretation of Marxism, in reality, the dominance of the Marxist paradigm was not uniform. There were large variations from country to country in both the degree of commitment to the official interpretation and the willingness to elaborate or bypass Marxist doctrine. The comparative overview of the countries of the region offered by the comprehensive national reports on the state of economics in Eastern Europe published by Kaase et al. (2002) reveals that a clear spectrum of positions could be identified: from those that engaged and challenged the paradigm within its own terms and then tried to go beyond it, to those that cohabitated with it either complacently or resentfully subdued. Moreover, as aptly reminded by several scholars, there were also significant differences in the way Marxism–Leninism was approached in the work of each separated economist (Spulber, 1979; Wagener, 2002). As a result, Marxism–Leninism left different imprints on the economic thought of the Soviet period (Gamamikow, 1968; Gabrisch, 1988; Brus and Kazimierz, 1990). As Čekanavičius (2002) explains, first was a dogmatic approach in which the writings of Marx, Engels and Lenin were considered 'the ultimate wisdom in economics', all theories and methodological approaches having to be tested and confirmed with their yardstick; Second was an approach in which honest but naive authors had to fight against the straitjacket of Marxism both to overcome the limits of the Marxist vocabulary unable to capture the complexity of the economic life and to 'avoid transgressing the basic taboos of Marxist–Leninist discourse (e.g. private enterprises, capital, market, etc.)' while still delivering valid economic analysis and policy insights. Finally, there was a 'lip-service approach' in which Marxism–Leninism and the Party documents were quoted in a 'ritualistic way' devoid of any meaning. These 'invocations' were usually placed in the foreword or introduction of each publication: The references 'could take a form of some obscure but relevant quotation from the "holy scripts" of the aforementioned "classics of Marxism–Leninism" – if readily available, and if not then even the general statement that they "deemed the following problem as an important one" usually would do' (Čekanavičius, 2002). Overall, in the case of Balkan and Baltic states (the last being part of the USSR by that time) the practice to pay a routine tribute to Marx, Engels and Lenin and to the latest documents of the Communist Party or speeches of its leaders was more pregnant during the entire period in comparison to Poland, Hungary and even Czechoslovakia.

THE STATE OF MARXISM AS A REIGNING PARADIGM

Both in terms of seriousness of the intellectual commitment to the Marxist paradigm and in terms of the willingness to play the formal tribute to the ideological gods, two basic categories of countries could be identified: First, there were countries like Poland where there was a more serious and systematic intellectual engagement with the paradigm but also a more intense effort towards alternatives. Second, there were those countries like Romania that complacently cohabitated with the paradigm without seriously engaging it but, on the other hand, did not make serious steps in articulating alternative approaches. Between the two extremes lies the entire range of intermediate cases whose diversity could be documented by following the 'The state of three social science disciplines in Central and Eastern Europe' country reports (Kaase et al., 2002).

Seen in the light of that survey, Poland and Hungary stand apart from the rest of the countries in terms of the internal dynamics of the discipline and its impact. In both cases, Marxism defined not only the official language and the academic domain, but also there were underlying dynamics of the intellectual life of the epistemic community that went far beyond the official constraints. That situation materialized at the level of the Marxist paradigm in a strong element of revisionism and reformism (Csaba, 2002; Szamuely and Csaba, 1998; Kowalik, 2002). In the case of Hungary, for instance, that element was institutionalized in The Institute of Economics of the Hungarian Academy of Sciences. The Institute was established from the very beginning by the followers of Imre Nagy, the reformed Communist Party leader and it remained a 'stronghold of reformist-revisionist thinking' for the entire communist period (Csaba, 2002). In Poland, eminent economists in positions of relative visibility became 'institutions' in themselves. In order to understand how that was possible one needs to go back to the pre-communist tradition which was impressive indeed. As the distinguished Polish economist Kowalik (2002) explains, in the 1930s, Poland already had London School of Economics-trained economists, who were modern neoclassical theorists in the full sense of the notion. By that time Oskar Lange had already attempted to 'reconcile the most modern neo-classical theory with Marxism', a clear signal Polish economics was at the cutting edge of the discipline. The degree of integration of the Polish economists into the Western epistemic community of the time was complete: Kalecki for instance as one of Keynes's disciples spent time as a researcher at Cambridge and Oxford, worked in Montreal for the International Labor Organization and then for the UN in New York. Oskar Lange published in German and in English, taught at American universities and become known as a professor at the University of Chicago (Kowalik, 2002). In 1933, Kalecki published a book that anticipated 'the Keynesian revolution' while Lange became known as a key participant in the 'rational calculation debate' with F.A. Hayek and L. von Mises on the economics of socialism. Interestingly enough, Lange and Kalecki returned from the US to Poland (Lange in 1948 and Kalecki in 1955). In what measure their activity might be also considered as an opposition to the official paradigm is a matter of debate. Either way, their work created a legacy of 'revisionism' which has survived over time (Kowalik, 2002).

However, despite their influence, the Soviet-Marxist monopoly in Poland on the public discourse was almost complete by the beginning of the 1950s. As elsewhere, Western mainstream academic economics and even the work of Western Marxists were controlled. Nevertheless, several pre-eminent Polish economists managed to maintain relatively important positions and give a different bearing to the epistemic community in comparison to the majority of other Eastern block countries. For instance both Edward Lipiński and Oskar Lange were forbidden to teach economics but one was named Editor in Chief of the journal *Ekonomista* and Dean at the Warsaw University Economics Department while the other became Rector of the Main School of Planning and Statistics in Warsaw (Kowalik, 2002).

Irrespective of the country or moment, the typical official economics training in the Soviet period followed a pattern that was structured around two core courses of political economy: one on 'the capitalist mode of production', another on 'the socialist economic system'. Čekanavičius (2002) offers an excellent outline of them:

> Both of them presented the basic indoctrination in the Marxism–Leninism, establishing the invisible but not-to-be-crossed-over ideological 'fences'. . . . Education of economists was based on the needs of the existing command-and-control system of economy, emphasizing mainly 'what' (e.g. what sets of indicators are to be used in planning of specific sector) and 'how' (e.g. how are they to be constructed and approved) instead of 'why. The analysis of the existing system was notably shallow as well – probably because going deeper could uproot the shaky theoretical grounds of the official doctrines. (Čekanavičius, 2002, pp. 121–33)

In the Polish case, as well as in the Hungarian and Czech cases, those analyses were at some moment in time rather penetrating and managed to question some basic principles of the system. After Stalin's death, Poland and Hungary were the first communist countries experimenting with liberalization. Nevertheless, the mainstream was still powerful in economic thinking. As noted by Kowalik: 'A paradox of the emergence of revisionism is that its intellectual roots were in the last *pronunciamento* of Joseph Stalin's *The Economic Problems of Socialism in the USSR* (1952). His strong emphasis on the objective character of economic laws in socialism was exploited by Oskar Lange and Włodzimierz Brus to justify the extension of markets' (Kowalik, 2002; Brus, 1961, 1972).

In both Poland and Hungary, professors had some room left to teach Western economic topics if they wished and some were doing it while paying lip service to Marxism (Csaba, 2002; Wagener, 1998). Nevertheless, at least until the end of the 1960s, the critical attitude of the main figures of Polish economics to the Soviet system and Soviet Marxism and to Soviet economics, 'was somehow combined with a continued belief in superiority of the existing and theoretical socialism over capitalism' (Kowalik, 2002). One of the most interesting conceptual developments from a paradigmatic viewpoint was Lange's attempt to create 'a broad theoretical framework that would include non-Marxist economics into the Marxist system', a great 'synthesis of Marxian and Western mainstream economics'. Although he did not accomplish this goal, he managed to popularize many Western concepts and to define a specific school within the Polish and East European context (Kowalik, 2002). Indeed in the last part of 1950s,

> Warsaw was the unquestionable center of intellectual life in Central and Eastern Europe and several schools of thinking could be identified as they grouped around these major personalities. Interestingly enough, besides the Kalecki's and Lange's schools, there was also a school of neo-classical inspiration, the so called (Aleksy) Wakar school, which was arguing for a concept of market socialism based on pure neoclassical (pre-Samuelsonian) foundations. (Kowalik, 2002, pp. 135–49)

Therefore, it is important to note that, in spite of Marxist constraints, both Hungarian and Polish economic research tended to slowly but surely move toward the Western empiricism and formalism. Discussing the issue, Laslo Csaba, a leading Hungarian economist, concluded: 'It is one of the true paradoxes of Hungarian economic thought, how little true Maxism–Leninism, as a seriously taken ideological frame had been shaping research output in the period under scrutiny' (Csaba, 2002). This is indeed interesting as the Marxist takeover erased all non-Marxist thought while pre-war non-Marxist thought was largely non-liberal.

The war related developments crowded out liberalism in favour of generally state-led concepts. Thus the young generation of the 1930s and 1940s, which survived the war, the political purges of 1944–49 and also refrained from emigration, tended to be composed of adherents of the managed economy of one sort or another . . . It is important to underscore that pre-war traditions and insights could thus have a limited impact at best due to the complete purging of the Academy of Sciences and of the universities in 1946–1949 . . . Presence of non-Marxists had been fragmentary and ad-hoc, mostly in the working groups on economic reform and in some privileged places, such as the Institutes of the Academy of Sciences. But even here, personal loyalty or luck, rather than academic excellence shaped survival possibilities. (Csaba, 2002, pp. 83–99)

But the disenchantment, following the 1956 revolution and the failure of the experiment with 'socialism with human face' in 1968 in Prague, led to a self-declared *pragmatism* and 'non-ideological approaches prevailed' (Csaba, 2002). For Csaba that is in a sense in conformity with Hungary's tradition of economic thinking, a pragmatic approach 'interested in *public* finances, *taxation*, and the *economic functions of the state* in general' (Szamuely and Csaba, 1998, p. 182).

The special status of Polish and Hungarian economics during the period was also defined by their impact in the region. The most influential were Włodzimierz Brus's book, *General Problems of Functioning of Socialist Economy* (1961) and Janos Kornai's critique of orthodox theory and of the dysfunctions of the socialist economic system. Both authors define a specific moment in the evolution of the East European economic thought. None of the other countries, with the possible exception of Czechoslovakia, managed to produce something comparable. Both authors were extensively translated abroad. Their work was innovative and many were able to see in it a straightforward blueprint for socialist reforms. Indeed Brus's model of 'planning with incorporated market mechanism' made room for decentralization while the market, instead of being banned, was seen as one among the many economic policy tools available.

The Hungarian reformers were openly acknowledging that one of the sources of inspiration for their 'New Economic Mechanism' implemented in 1968 was in Brus's work, but the Hungarian Kornai went further than Brus's initial views. Kornai's critique of orthodox views was a clear indication of the wave to come. In his work, he criticized fundamental aspects of the standard theoretical framework thus departing even further from Marxism. Also, he introduced a key reformist concept: 'soft constraints' and conceptually bolstered an entire critical line of thinking about the functioning of the Soviet socialist system. This insight offered a fresh look at the socialist system. A different approach to reform was stressed and, in many respects, his work came to define Eastern European economics in the 1980s.

All of the above made Warsaw and Budapest, at various moments in times, the centers of economic thinking of Eastern Europe. An interesting dynamic took place between the two. At the beginning of the 1960s, Warsaw was sometimes called the 'socialist Cambridge' (Kowalik, 2002). The anti-revisionism of 1968 caused a dismantling of Kalecki's school and many economists left the country. Lange died in 1965, Kalecki in 1970, while many other economists, among them Brus, emigrated. Polish Marxist revisionist and reformist economics became less visible and through authors such as Kornai, Hungarian economics gained pre-eminence and started to flourish. Yet all these developments were in fact taking place either outside the Marxist mainstream or eroding it profoundly from inside.

Between the cases of Poland and Hungary on the one hand, and the South Eastern and Baltic cases on the other, stands the Czechoslovakia situation. Czech economics in the pre-war period was rather rich, Czech nationals had achieved higher prominence than the Slovak ones as reflected in the leadership of the three major schools of thought: The neoliberal school was represented by Alois Rašín, the first minister of finance of the independent Czechoslovakia. The second school was represented by Karel Engliš, an 'original economic thinker', the author of a so-called 'teleological theory of national economy' (Turnovec, 2002). The third school, a Keynesian one, was represented by Josef Macek. After a short period of relative freedom between 1945 and 1948, economics was fully subordinated to the Marxist ideology and the leading economists such as Karel Engliš and Josef Macek were persecuted. The very few pro-communist economists (Ludvík Frejka, Josef Goldman, Bedřich Levčík and Eugen Löbl) were leftists who emigrated during the war. They returned to Czechoslovakia in 1945 only to be persecuted in the 1950s – Frejka was executed in 1952, Löbl arrested and condemned to life in prison in 1952, Levčík dismissed from his position, and Goldmann was arrested in 1952 (Turnovec, 2002).

Before the break-up of the Second World War some Slovak economists had emigrated. One of them, Ervin Hexner, had even achieved some visibility in the USA. On the other hand, some Slovak economists (Imrich Karvaš, Rudolf Briška, Július Pázmán and Peter Zat'ko) came to play a controversial role during the period of 1939–1945. After the Second World War many economists left the country (Macek), some did not return (Hexner), some did not continue to publish (Engliš, Karvaš) (Horvart, 2002). Because of the shortage of qualified communist economists, the positions were offered to young people 'the majority of whom had to pass quick courses based on texts prepared by the Party in accordance with the Stalinist doctrine' (Havel et al., 1998 quoted by Horvart, 2002).

As expected, the professional discussion between 1948 and 1989 was dominated by the Marxist jargon. This, as aptly put by Julius Horvart, was 'a veil under which from time to time interesting intellectual contributions occurred'. Horvart divided these discussions and contributions into two. First were discussions dealing with the relationship between the (central) plan and the market. In the Czechoslovak context, that represented, to a large extent, the discussion of the specifics of Slovakia in the Czechoslovak economy. Second, were the efforts to maintain the contact with modern economic theory. As expected, that was more substantial in fields such as econometrics or operation research, following thus the general regional pattern given by the less ideological nature of these fields (Horvart, 2002). On the other hand, Turnovec sees the issue in different terms:

> The development of economic discussion in the Czechoslovakia was always closely related to the political atmosphere in the USSR. The first round of debate started after Stalin death in the mid of 1950s. The reform proposals at that time did not exceed the framework of traditional Marxian political economy, focusing on 'improvement' of the planning mechanisms. The second round of discussion started in the beginning of 1960s, partly as a response to an economic crisis in the Czechoslovakia in the early 1960s, partly under influence of discussions in the USSR (Nemcinov, Novozilov, Kantorovic, Aganbegjan, Liberman, Lisickin) and in other Soviet bloc countries. The general framework of the discussion can be characterized as a 'market socialism doctrine' with some elements of Keynesianism, attacking the state property form, preferring collective or group property design of socialist economy, decentralisation and employing economic interests in 'socialist market mechanism'. (Turnovec, 2002, pp. 50–63)

The 1960s was, in many respects, the most interesting period. Discussing the reform debate of the 1960s, Horwart (2002) divides the participating economists into four groups depending on their views about the relationship between the plan and the market. He reviews the views of Czech economists from the most orthodox conservative to radical liberal (Jaroslav Vejvoda, Ota Šik, Karel Kouba, Oldřich Kýn) pointing out how those definitions apply and make sense only in the context of 1960s. Ota Šik was the most influential economist of the period and his work offered 'the possibility to question the official economic doctrine'. Although most reformers did not reject Marxism, the discussion in the second half of 1960s brought a new approach. That approach was increasingly based on Western neoclassical economics as represented by the studies of Václav Klaus and Lubomír Mlčoch. Most of the participants in the 1960s discussions were expelled from universities and research institutions. Some had to leave the country. Blacklists were created to pre-empt 'reform' economists of having a say in the public debate. As a result of the restrictions and repressions, the Czech economic community was segmented into three different groups:

official, unofficial and exile (Havel et al., 1997 quoted by Turnovec, 2002). There were practically no contacts between the economists active in Czechoslovakia and those economists who left the country in two waves, after 1948 and 1968.

Overall most of the discussions debates and attempts to formulate solutions were concentrated in Prague and no change took place in this respect over the years: from the 1960s to the 1980s, Prague was the center of economic debate. Concerning the Slovak discussion, Adam quoted by Horvart writes:

> Marketisation of the economy had more enthusiastic adherents in the Czech lands than in Slovakia. In the latter, there was some concern that the market might hamper further equating of the economic level in Slovakia with that in the Czech lands. In their outline of the further development of the reform, Slovak economists maintained that 'economic leveling out in Slovakia will be more complicated in a management model based on market relations', and therefore suggested a series of measures to ensure further equalization. (Adam in Horvart, 2002, pp. 168–85)

The translation program was in no way different from other East European countries: These included the usual suspects, Smith, Ricardo, Weber and an interesting exception, Schumpeter. There was also no translation of Western economists active after the Second World War. No basic or intermediate undergraduate Western textbooks were translated into Slovak during the socialist period (Horvart, 2002).

It is noteworthy that in Slovakia the economists were not participating in dissident activities and 'even in the Czech Lands most of the dissidents emerged from non-economist circles'. Economists in Slovakia did not form discussion groups around leading personalities and were less interested in informal unofficial professional or political organizations:

> In the Czech Republic there was a strong group of economists around [future Czech Prime Minister Václav] Klaus, [Tomáš] Ježek and others, who held meetings and taught themselves; . . . Slovakia, on the other hand, lacked that kind of community, and the general level of economic sciences was considerably lower. Some Slovak economists – those who lived in Prague during the 1980s – participated in these Prague discussion circles. (Miklos in Horvart, 2002, pp. 168–85)

It is also important to mention an interesting feature of all East European economic thought already visible in the case of Hungary and Poland: Many economists were involved in one way or the other in the so-called 'critique of bourgeois economic theory'. However, in many cases the 'critique of economics in bourgeois period' was not at all hostile but in fact it was used to keep alive the traditions of the pre-war economic thought. In this context it is very important to stress the role that the pre-communist tradition of economics or, better put, the memory of that tradition, had in defining the intellectual climate for the Marxist paradigm. In many cases, the pre-Second World War economics schools were rather vibrant and they left their imprint on the postwar situation as the Polish case has illustrated. It is difficult to gauge the degree to which the existence of a strong tradition influenced the fate of Marxism in the countries of the region but it is clear that it had some significant impact. In some cases and countries it clearly led to an opening towards the Western paradigm while, in other cases, to precisely the contrary.

In general, in the south-eastern European and Baltic states, the absence or the lack of continuity with pre-war thought had a negative influence on the discipline. In the case of Czechoslovakia, Poland and Hungary, the pre-communist tradition and its 'critique' played a positive role in disseminating the work of the Western economists. However, the university curriculum rarely systematically explored the major contemporary Western economic theories and schools, or for that matter the pre-communist traditions. Almost anywhere in the East, Western economics was avoided, distorted or at best taught in a rather superficial way, and thus had a limited impact on the young generation of economists studying the Western economics under the pretext of its critique.

Different from the previous cases, in Romanian and Bulgarian pre-1989 economics, Marxism–Leninism was the official and unchallenged economic paradigm up to the very end of the regime. One of the specific features of Marxism–Leninism in these countries was its total dogmatism. Compared to other Soviet satellite countries where 'organizational and conceptual alternatives' to the official line of the Communist Party were explored and advanced within the parameters imposed by the official paradigm, Romania and Bulgaria lacked any such attempts (Spulber, 1979). Therefore, the Romanian and Bulgarian Marxism–Leninism had little or no variation from the Party line, and it is hard to identify a 'spectrum' of views and approaches in this respect. Romanian Marxist–Leninist economic thought confined itself to two major objectives closely inspired by the official line: (1) the critique of the 'bourgeois economic thinking' and of the 'Capitalist system' (which in most cases was nothing more than anti-Capitalist propaganda) and (2) the discussion of the proper means for achieving the transition from Capitalism to Socialism and later on to Communism.

Regarding the critique, it is worth mentioning that in the cases of these countries they rarely become vehicles for describing or studying Western economic ideas. In terms of original output, in the case of Romania for instance, the two theoretical areas on which Romanian Marxist economists concentrated their efforts were: the concept of 'economic contradiction' and the idea of economic laws specific to each 'economic system' or 'historical moment'.

Both Romania and Bulgaria were profoundly affected by Stalinism, and the period following continued to bear its imprints. Only during the 1970s (in Romania) and 1980s (in Bulgaria), were there timid discussions on the nature and performance of the system. Those discussions were taking place strictly within the Marxist–Socialist framework. Periodically, almost every five years, new economic arrangements were proposed, all of them with fancy names, destined to solve the 'contradictions' of the Socialist economic system. In the Bulgarian case, these contradictions were more down to earth than in the Romanian one: the contradiction between 'the owner and manager', the 'extensive growth against intensive growth', the tension between workers' and directors' incentives, etc. Analyzing this phenomenon, Dimitrov concludes that 'actually it was more about pseudo changes pseudo-scientifically argued that about searching for solutions' (Dimitrov, 2002).

The 'economic contradictions' played a pivotal part in the Romanian Marxists' worldview as the contradictions were seen as the 'motive power of all social and socio-economic development'. No new contribution to the elaboration of the Hegelian-Marxist dialectical approach implied by the concept was brought up. Nevertheless, it was widely claimed that the Romanian Communist Party, through its economists and indeed through the work of Nicolae Ceauşescu, contributed decisively to the 'development of the theory and analysis of the economic contradictions under contemporary conditions' (Constantinescu, 1973; Nechita, 1986). The idea of economic contradictions in socialism deserves special interest as a typical example of the way official Marxism tried to maintain a façade of intellectual respectability by creating false revisionisms. The basic point was that far from being contradiction free, socialism was ridden by contradictions. That was apparently an unorthodox opinion: those contradictions and the correct modalities of solving them were in fact the source of development and part and parcel of the 'dialectics of building up and developing the socialist economy'. The implication of this idea was that a proper balance had to be maintained between the evolution of the forces of production and the evolution of the relations of production. Given the fact that even in socialism harmonization was not automatically achieved, new relations of production must be discovered in order to accommodate the more rapid progress of the forces (means) of production (Mehedinţiu, 1986). The application of the concept of 'contradiction' was extended also at the global level. Thus, an entire literature on the 'contradictions and crises of the contemporary world economy' emerged. Due to its pre-defined conclusions and the conceptual apparatus involved, this literature was prone to identify crises and contradictions everywhere: from the 'production apparatus structures' to the 'international economic flows' (Dobrotă, 1986, p. 643) everything was in crisis, that could be explained only by the 'materialistic and historical vision' and by 'President Nicolae Ceauşescu's original outlook on the present-day world' (Sută-Selejan, 1986).

However, in Romania there also was a second theoretical idea that might be considered as being of particular interest to the Marxist economists: the idea of special economic laws for each economic system or order. Again, as in the case of 'contradictions', the laws specific to the socialist order were of distinctive interest. The basic point was that there were economic laws proper to the new socialist order. That was correlated not as in the case of Lange's Polish work with the idea of building a new theoretical system but to the idea that orthodox economic theory was confined to an earlier period of human history (that of 'pre-monopolistic' capitalism of eighteenth-century England). It is easy to see what the implications and functions of such a view were: first, it represented a strong ideological weapon against any 'capitalist' critique of the system as it was easy to point out that the capitalists themselves couldn't understand the specific socialist laws at work. Second, it separated the study of the national economy from the study of other (that is Capitalist) economies as the two were allegedly governed by different laws.

In a sense, these developments and the general situation of economics in communist Romania is paradoxical as Romania has a rich tradition of economic thinking. In this respect, the Romanian case is very illustrative and deserves a special note. A wide variety of development theories appeared in Romania during the interwar years, all aiming at the transformation from an underdeveloped peasant society into a modern industrial nation. Among the most influential was the proto-structuralist contribution of Mihail Manoilescu (Love, 1996). Manoilescu's political and economic ideas were both widely discussed in Europe and Latin America and laid the basis for the structuralist theses of Raul Prebisch (Love, 1996). At the end of the 1970s and during the 1980s, Manoilescu's ideas were rediscovered and propagated by the Ceauşescu regime's economists, who emphasized the former's structuralist contribution to Third World economics, ignoring his right-wing corporatism. As Joseph Love, the pre-eminent scholar of the history of Romanian economic thought, put it, his works were not only alleged to be the *fons et origo* of the Latin American school, but Manoilescu was also given credit for the 'deteriorating-terms-of-trade' argument. It has now been renamed the 'Prebisch-Manoilescu effect' – despite the fact that the notion played no role in his work. Thus, the Latin American structuralism and dependency theory were appropriated and indigenized to meet the ideological needs of Ceaușescu's Romania, a 'developing social-ist country' whose leader saw it at the ideological forefront of the Third World.

In spite of this potentially relevant legacy during communism, the sole feature of the pre-war Romanian school preserved as a continuity element with the postwar period was its historical orientation, an orientation shaped by the beginning of the century by the influence of the German Historical School. In contrast, the strongest and most viable element of the pre-communist tradition was probably statistical analysis for the Bulgarians. Oscar Anderson worked in Bulgaria for more than two decades and left his mark. An entire generation of statisticians, with doctoral degrees from the most prestigious European and American universities (Kiril Popov, Prokopi Kiranov, Ivan Stefanov, Anastas Totev) was emerg-ing. This tradition survived in Bulgaria but, given the ideological con-straints, never managed to flourish. It is also noteworthy that the emerging strong agrarian-peasant tradition inspired by Ceaianov, and represented by authors like Virgil Madgearu in Romania and Alexander Stamboliski in Bulgaria, had never been really employed or recycled by the communists in spite of its many left and left of center elements. Instead, an unalloyed Stalinism was preferred as a hard core for its economic paradigm.

Specific to Bulgaria and Romania (and even more valid for the Baltic states) was the fact that there was virtually no public opposition in eco-nomics, either in terms of criticizing the Party policy or of suggesting organizational alternatives in or outside the system.

> Due to the established after 1948, total control over the social activity there existed no possibility of publishing an opinion of economists with opposi-tion attitudes. It was forbidden to disseminate in the country articles and books of Bulgarian authors-oppositionists, published abroad. (Dimitrov, 2002, pp. 34–48)

In both countries, all discussions were presented by their authors as an attempt to improve the socialist economic system or as 'directed towards technical problems solving, which do not have anything in common with politics' (Dimitrov, 2002). In Romania, for instance, except a couple of arti-cles published in the mid-1980s and some timid calling into question of the plan parameters imposed by the Party upon the National Council of Planning, 'nothing of any significance' happened. In the last years of com-munism existed a growing antipathy to the program of excessive consump-tion reduction, a reduction due in part to the reimbursement of the external debt and in part to the general economic collapse of the regime (Aligica, 2002). But again, that wasn't made public and thus wasn't publicly known until after 1989.

It is well understood today that economists, as any other professionals or intellectuals, were under huge pressure from both the Party and the political police. In Romania, the sole economic theory journal was banned and its publication stopped in the 1970s after it published a debate on Romania's economic development strategy (among the participants were reformist economists like Igor Lemnij, Vasile Pilat and Tiberiu Schatelles). Economists were banned or fired from their institutions if they voiced opinions or tried to criticize even at a minimal level the regime's views or policies (Igor Lemnij, Alex Olteanu, Sorin Covrig) and in some cases (Daniel Dăianu and Vasile Pilat) softer, but no less effective, pressure was put on them (Dăianu, 1999). Some left the country while others were marginalized. However, in a small number of places, economists continued to try to keep alive a meaningful economic conversation (Dăianu, 1999).

Similarly, in Bulgaria, Marxism–Leninism dominated over the economic science during the entire Communist period. No critical views were allowed. There were two timid exceptions. In the first case during 1948–49, Minister of Finance Ivan Stefanov supported the idea of preservation of a planned economy but suggested an opening to the European countries' markets. He was fired and transferred to the Bulgarian Academy of Sciences. In a typical Stalinist trial only months later he was sentenced to lifelong imprisonment. The second, two decades later, was a somewhat broader discussion on the issue of market socialism. Overall, the Bulgarian and Romanian discussions had never achieved the intensity and profundity of those in Central Eastern Europe and the contagion with which Marxist revisionism spread from those countries never managed to create a critical mass there (Aligica, 2002; Dimitrov, 2002).

Quite unsurprisingly, similar trends were visible in the Baltic states (by that time part of the USSR) where Marxism–Leninism was indeed the sole legitimate way of doing economics. In the Baltic states, the situation of the discipline was strongly determined by the fact that those countries were under direct Soviet administration. After the Second World War, when they were incorporated into USSR, the education and research system was subordinated to the Soviet education and research system. Marxism–Leninism was thus not only the framework of economic education but also for science in general. For instance, a World Bank study indicates that in Latvia during the postwar period, in all universities, irrespective of whether they were teaching natural or social sciences, about 20 per cent of the teaching content was ideology – history of the Communist Party, materialist-dialectic philosophy, and Marxism–Leninism (World Bank, 1996). In a similar vein, a Baltic economist notes that:

Marxism–Leninism was a mandatory subject if a person wanted to get a graduate degree. No matter which field was chosen by applicant for scientific career, all persons had to pass so-called 'exams for candidate minimum', among which there were also dialectic and historical materialism (developed from the Marxism–Leninism ideology), for economic disciplines also history of Communist Party and political economy. References to Karl Marx, Frederick Engels, and Vladimir Lenin, as well as Party documents and quotation of current political leaders were mandatory constituents in preamble of every single research paper. This requirement could be fulfilled in routine manner, as far as any deeper motivation of relevance of selected citations to the research topic was not a requirement. Marxism–Leninism theory could not be criticized, therefore it was not subjected to creative and critical investigation and further development. (Karnite, 2002, pp. 102–17)

That situation is typical. In the Baltic states' case, not only did Leninist and Stalinist Marxism enjoy an absolute dominance, but in some cases even the institutional infrastructure of the discipline was challenged and undermined. That happened in a context in which those very institutional foundations were rather fragile from the very beginning. For instance, the studies of economics in Lithuania had to be started in the 1920s virtually from zero after 120 years of annexation by the Russian empire and the forced closure of Vilnius University. Economists were lacking – the first program in economics took off in 1924 at Vytautas Magnus University in Kaunas (Čekanavičius, 2002). Nevertheless, Lithuania had its own prominent economists. They and their followers basically introduced modern economics, 'lithuanizing' economic terms and concepts, teaching the discipline in universities and initiating the first Lithuanian economic journals. But as Čekanavičius (2002) notes, all these developments were interrupted by the Soviet occupation when Marxism–Leninism was imposed as the official paradigm. Thus, contrary to some of the Central East European cases, no extension of the pre-war traditions in the communist period existed. The tradition was too fragile to be able to penetrate decisively the Marxist–Leninist monolith.

The independent Faculty of Economics of the University of Tartu Estonia is a second illustrative case in point for the way the institutional infrastructure of the discipline was put under continuous pressure in the Baltic States. The Faculty of Economics of the University of Tartu opened in 1938, only to be suspended after the war. The teaching of economics was re-established only in 1954, and 'even then only on a very small scale' and part of a program offered by the Faculty of Law. In the second half of the 1960s, some progress was possible and mathematical economics was introduced. Moreover the Faculty of Economics was re-established in 1968. As a result of the changes in the political situation in the second half of the 1980s, the disciplines taught at the Faculty of Economics and curricula were slightly updated (Karnite, 2002). It is interesting to note that only in 1989 was an international economics specialization introduced at the Faculty of Economics. However, irrespective the development of mathematical economics or the teaching of international issues, the truth is that they had a limited impact in introducing Western, neoclassical synthesis concepts in the region. Indeed, it was only after 1990 that the dissemination of ideas and their institutionalization started in the Baltic States (Karnite, 2002; Čekanavičius, 2002).

Quite unsurprisingly, the state of the research was similarly dire. Although strongly institutionalized, institutionalization was more a means to control than to support analytical, critical or creative thinking. The result, in terms of research output, is eloquently described by one of the leading young economists from the region:

> Another notable feature of the time was the 'reiterative reproduction' of one's publication in slightly modified versions (either in Russian or Lithuanian) in various journals, collections of papers or – especially popular method – collections of conference thesis. What counted (and, actually, still does) for your academic career was mainly the *number* of publications – and this manifested itself in a huge numbers and volumes of 'science' produced each year. Needless to add that the overwhelming majority (would be safe to put the figure at least 96%) of it was 'indigenous publications' published within the Soviet Union, some of the rest – in the COMECON countries, and probably just about one percent – in the Western journals and collections of papers. (Čekanavičius, 2002, pp. 121–33)

The difference between the Central European and the Baltic states is one of degree, not of nature. Nevertheless, that difference of degree (and it was indeed a large one) meant a lot for the rhythm and timing of the paradigm change process. Thus, to sum up, pre-1988 Marxism in Eastern Europe was heterogeneous not only from country to country but also from organization to organization and from economist to economist. Overall, the basic parameter was the official approach obsessed with the ideological 'purity'. As Čekanavičius (2002) put it, the Western thought was roughly equated to propaganda or patent errors of vision and conceptualization and was feared for its 'spoiling influence' on weak minds lacking a 'proper ideological training'. Nevertheless, in spite of this effort, that influence became increasingly important as years passed. By 1989, the Marxist paradigm was a barren rhetorical and ideological edifice that collapsed officially the very moment its political support faltered. By that time, according to some accounts, the paradigm change had already taken place. Moreover, by other accounts, the new political conditions were a facilitating condition but not a sufficient condition of paradigm shift: 'Disappearance of ideological constraints was welcome and many . . . economists hastened to disavow their allegiance to Marxism. However, quite a different issue was to decide *what* exactly economic paradigm they do adhere now' (Čekanavičius, 2002).

THE PACE AND CHANNELS OF WESTERN INFLUENCE

The answer to the question whether a paradigm change has taken place or not in a specific field depends very much on the operational definition given to what such a change might entail. In Eastern European economic thought a long and slow process of change indeed took place and in some cases its beginnings could be traced back to the mid-1960s. The facts are rather evident although their interpretation might be controversial. Identifying the tipping point is largely an exercise in interpretation. This study avoids a discussion about the precise moment of paradigm change, a discussion that seems to engender a mere terminological dispute. Instead, it traces and documents the process of change outlining some of the main aspects of that process starting with the incipient or residual influence of the Western thought and ending with the radical institutional reform of the discipline in the 1990s.

That process of transformation is extremely complex and the magnitude of change and the difficulties it encountered are hard to overstate. That is especially true as those difficulties also meant very concrete personal challenges to each and every economics teacher or researcher living beyond the Iron Curtain:

> Previous knowledge of the planned economy became mostly useless and one had to start anew from studying the essentials of economic processes in a market economy . . . The economists lacked basic knowledge of disciplines that describe the behaviour of a firm that operates in a market economy environment, such as corporate finance, management, accounting etc. In a somewhat better situation were scientists who had in the Soviet times specialized in empirical methods and statistics, but they also had to apply familiar methods of analysis to a new object. As the economic system and its treatment changed, economic terminology changed also. The whole system of economic terminology needed to be revised and changed . . . [National language] terminology was completely missing in many areas of economics or was insufficient. It was also necessary to adopt methodological changes, completely new concepts emerged, such as marginal analysis, opportunity costs, general equilibrium, welfare economics, etc. (Püss, 2002, pp. 65–76)

Discussing the rhythm and timing of change, it is tempting to divide the process into three stages: an incipient period during which the influence of Western thought was mostly indirect and strongly resisted or resented by the authorities; a period of rapid transformation at the end of the 1980s and beginning of the 1990s, defined by a visible radical change in economic discourse, publications, research and teaching; and finally there was a rapid and deep process of institutional reform and development leading to the complete institutionalization of the new, Western paradigm. Nevertheless, the temptation to over-simplify things should be resisted. These three stages were neither synchronic nor similar in all countries. There were differences in lengths, starting moments, intensity (quality and quantity of exposure to the Western thought) and rhythm of change. Moreover, in several countries, the second stage started only in the mid-1990s. Thus, a careful overview of the entire region reveals that the dominance of Marxist paradigm was not uniform and a specter of positions as regarding the Western penetration and influence could be identified.

In the case of Hungary and Poland, the Western influence was most visible and pervasive. The paradoxes of Hungarian economic thought, as defined by Csaba was: 'How little true Maxism–Leninism, as a seriously taken ideological frame had been shaping research output in the period under scrutiny' (Csaba, 2002). According to him, the relative liberalization, the study abroad stages, the contacts with foreign scholars, and the translation of Western economics created a long and increasingly stronger trend in Hungarian economics towards integration into the international epistemic community. Almost all Eastern European countries initiated translations of the political economy classics at one point or another. Nevertheless, a few of them, including Hungary, were able to sustain their projects over the years. The series was started by a Hungarian edition of Keynes' *General Theory* in 1965 and in a very atypical way for a Soviet block country followed by the publication of economics Nobel Prize winners. Besides Max Weber's or Alexander Gerschenkron's works, Milton Friedman, Tobin, Hicks, and Shultz became available over years. The 'relative free access to libraries' facilitated the update with Western theories. Thus in applied fields, such as finance, management and marketing, the Western approach set the standards long before the collapse of the Soviet Empire. The significant role played in Eastern Europe by the so-called 'criticism of bourgeoisie thought' as a source of information on Western economics developments has already been noted. The criticism of bourgeoisie economics was, in the case of Hungary and Poland, a successful vehicle for disseminating Western ideas. By the beginning of the 1960s in Hungary, the university curriculum contained an extensive, though critical, presentation of major Western contemporary economic schools (Csaba, 2002).

After 1956, Poland was relatively open to the West and Polish scholars visited and even studied at Western universities, especially in the United States. A new climate was created in which Western economic ideas could find their way to the epistemic community. In the first phase, the reopening to Western ideas came through the publications of Western Marxist economists such as Maurice Dobb, Paul Swezy, Paul Baran, Rosa Luxemburg, Rudolf Hilferding, Karl Kautsky and Antonio Gramsci (Kowalik, 2002). These publications were used in teaching and as bibliographical sources for the study of capitalism. The situation of what was called 'bourgeois economics' raised more problems but it was still better than in other parts of Eastern Europe. Besides Keynes's *General Theory*, there were translations of several authors, such as Joan Robinson, Kenneth Galbraith, Nicholas Kaldor, Evsey Domar, Gunnar Myrdal, Vassily Leontief and Joseph Schumpeter. Paul Samuelson's synthesis was published in 1959 (Kowalik, 2000). As elsewhere in the East, the economists were allowed to study and publish econometrics and cybernetics, fields considered ideologically neutral and thus not dangerous for the regime. In Polish universities, professors had some freedom to teach Western economic theories. Some economists, Kowalik notes in his review of Polish economics, were taking advantage of that freedom and introduced micro and macro notions. However, the works critical to Soviet socialism were forbidden. Even authors sympathetic to socialism but not sharing the Soviet official view on economy, such as E.H. Carr, R.W. Davis or Alec Nove were prohibited. Given the fact that those authors were illegal it is not at all a surprise that the works of F. Hayek, L. Mises and M. Friedman were banned.

Lazlo Csaba's conclusion that in Hungary the influence of Western economics was much broader and deeper than direct reference to academic writings would have suggested is noteworthy (Csaba, 2002). This point most probably applies to Poland too, and offers a better understanding of the sources of the relatively higher disciplinary standards existent in those countries in comparison to the other members of the Eastern block. During the 1980s, the convergence with Western standards became clearer and clearer. That was clearly materialized in teaching: for instance, in 1986 the Budapest University of Economics socialist political economy courses were replaced by standard macroeconomics and microeconomics. Moreover, the school dropped the reference to Karl Marx from its name, as reported by Csaba (2002). Also it is interesting to note that several standard Western textbooks were translated even before 1989. The Samuelson–Nordhaus text was translated in 1987. Nevertheless, classroom use of the textbook seems to have been limited. According to the same Csaba, overall, gradual but clear changes in teaching took place though the changes were more intense in microeconomics where Western standards diffused more rapidly than in macroeconomics. Also, as elsewhere in Eastern Europe, econometrics, cybernetics and operational research were at the forefront of the diffusion process. In fact, the difference between the diffusion rate of theoretical and analytical ideas on the one hand and the formal and quantitative methods on the other was so large that we could speak of a two-speed or two-level diffusion process.

In spite of the differences in the way the demise of the socialist regimes took place in both Poland and Hungary, the transition at the level of economic ideas was in both cases long, gradual and smooth. Hungary's revolution was 'negotiated' and the same is true about the economic transition (Csaba, 2002). In Poland, the systemic changes took place rather differently. Poland abolished the communist political system peacefully, but after a 'long and bitter internal struggle', then it 'pioneered a rapid transition to market economy' (Kowalik, 2002). It is reasonable to think that economic ideas had an impact on the rhythm and nature of these events but the impact of events on the rhythm and speed of paradigm change seems to be limited.

The two-speed process of diffusion (theoretical and analytic vs. formal and quantitative) was at work in Czechoslovakia too. As noted by Julius Horvart, the contact with the advancements of the economic theory in the West 'was more functional on formal quantitative side where considerable advancement was achieved in econometrics, operation research and mathematical foundation of modern economic theory'. The official university textbook on dynamic modeling edited by Adam Laščiak contained 'sophisticated treatment of mathematics for graduate macroeconomics and optimization as well as the review of different macroeconomic and sectorial models used in the Czech and Slovak Republic during the socialist period' (Horvart, 2002). However, he notes, their impact on the general public and on policy making was minor. This view is confirmed by Turnovec:

> It is interesting that the only part of economic science which never lost contact with international development was operations research and econometrics: on the one hand highly formalised mathematical methodology was out of limits of understanding of ideological supervisors, on the other hand the philosophy of 'the theory of optimal functioning of socialist economy', imported from Moscow, was successfully used by mathematically oriented economists to justify some intellectually interesting programs of quantitative economic research. (Turnovec, 2002, pp. 50–63)

Western economic thought was not well represented in the textbooks and was taught in rather sketchy ways. Translations included Smith, Ricardo, Weber and Schumpeter but it is noteworthy that 'no basic or intermediate undergraduate Western textbooks were translated into Slovak during the socialist period'. As in the rest of the Eastern Europe, the so-called 'critique of bourgeoisie economic theory' was a major diffusion vehicle, while economic history and the history of economic ideas became bastions preserving the memory of professional economic research standards. Similarly to Hungary and Poland, Czechoslovakia had several waves of debates on the 'improving of the command system'. The first was in the 1950s when questions about the nature of planning were raised. But Poland and Hungary were far ahead in terms of criticism of the system and reformist ideas (Havel et al., 1998). Nevertheless, by the beginning of the 1960s, the criticism was stronger in Czechoslovakia than anywhere else in the Eastern block because the 'systemic weaknesses such as waste and mis-allocation of resources were particularly felt in the highly industrialized Czech economy' (Turnovec, 2002). Thus, Czechoslovak economics enjoyed its brief moment of pre-eminence between 1965 and 1968 when 'the closest understanding and most mutual impacts appeared among Czechoslovak, Polish and Hungarian reform minded scholars' (Havel et al., 1998, p. 219). They converged on the idea of market socialism and together were pretty close in creating a critical mass in changing the dynamics of economics in the Eastern block. The 1968 events changed that and the 1970s and 1980s came to be considered 'a period during which the development of Czech economic thought was abruptly discontinued and teaching seriously dis-torted' (Havel et al., 1998). During that period, the unusually large number of Czechoslovak economists in exile provided a vital link with the Western thought (Turnovec, 2002).

Quite unsurprisingly, the impact of Western economic literature in Bulgaria and Romania was rather limited due to the restricted contact. Dimitrov reviews the situation succinctly:

> The access to the Western books and journals was supervised. The books and the journals were divided into two groups. The first group was defined as ideo-logically dangerous and the access to it was based on a special authorization. The access to the other Western books and journals was based on registration. Not until the 80s the most considerable part of the Western economic literature was given an open and free access but in specialized reading rooms. (Dimitrov, 2002, pp. 34–48)

It is needless to say which economics books were defined as 'ideologically dangerous'. Thus, an element of commonality in the Balkan countries (a commonality they share with the Baltics and that distinguishes them from the East Central European countries) was that Western theories were made available only for certain people who were employed in so-called 'special', 'restricted' or 'closed' research topics. In these countries, the dissemina-tion of Western theories, and even the survival of the memory of classical economics took place in a more indirect way – through criticism of the weaknesses of bourgeois theories in comparison to the strength of Marxism–Leninism. In a similar way the information on the organizational experiments of Central-European countries or former Yugoslavia was obtained and disscussed; that is through the description made by those economists enjoying the privilege of being informed and having the right to comment on the information.

As far as the classic authors were concerned, Romania never managed to get a set of translations of the standard economics classic texts published. A series of translations was initiated by the Romanian Academy with only David Ricardo, Adam Smith, Friederich List and John Maynard Keynes being published before the series was brought to an end (Aligica, 2002). In a similar way, the translations into Bulgarian were limited to the same usual authors. The access to original editions was limited with the sole exception of econometrics. Until 1980, not a single book written by a Western economist had been translated into Bulgarian. Only between 1981 and 1984 were the works of Adam Smith, David Ricardo and the usual suspects published. Also, between 1981 and 1989, a dozen or so management books were translated but most of them were popularizations having no scientific or theoretic value (Dimitrov, 2002).

Due to both international political reasons (Romania's attempt to enlist to the Non-Aligned block and to affirm itself as one of its leaders) and to the new-found affinity of the Romanian communist regime for Manoilescu's work, there was a wide opening towards Third World structuralism, dependency and world system paradigms, and the Western literature concerned with the problems of the least developed countries. As has already been mentioned, pivotal to this effort was the special attention that was granted to the Romanian inter-war economist, Mihail Manoilescu, whose attempt to refute the Ricardian theory of international trade (the law of comparative advantage) had some international echo at the time and largely influenced the policies adopted by several South-American countries in the 1960s (Nechita, 1993). The interest in development economics was accompanied by the Romanians joining other underdeveloped countries' theorists in analyzing the asymmetric relations center periphery and calling for a new international economic order (Nicolae-Văleanu, 1986; Mecu, 1973; Dijmărescu et al., 1977). Nevertheless, the level of dissemination and understanding of these non-orthodox schools was rather limited as the translations of key works like those of Immanuel Wallerstein, Celso Furtado or other ECLA School authors had to wait until after 1989.

Interestingly enough, the Western debate on global environmental, natural resources, and population problems (including global warming and climate change, resource depletion and unconventional energy sources in the context of continuous population growth, etc.) had found a strong echo in the pre-1989 Romanian economics community. In fact, at one point in the 1980s it seemed that the Romanian economists were more involved in dealing with global issues than with any domestic or theoretical problems, a fact that served the regime too well to be considered a mere accident. It is also interesting to note that, in general, the Western academics and scholarly economists were not translated or studied. Among the Western contemporary writers only J.K. Galbraith managed to find his way to the Romanian public. It is worth mentioning that Alvin Toffler and John Naisbit were considered top Western economists in Romania in the 1980s (Aligica, 2002).

In spite of the affluence of 'airport economics' and 'global problems' literature there was still a niche within which more scholarly and technical work from the West was absorbed. Due to obvious policy concerns at the practical level, a special emphasis was put on operational research, quantitative techniques and system dynamics research in relation to the planification of the economy. This line of interests was not openly undermined by the Party's officials as long as it did not exceed certain limits or touch certain taboos. In Romania, these kinds of books were translated and published mainly by the Editura Științifică și Enciclopedică from Bucharest, where authors like L.V. Kantorovici, Oscar Lange, W. Leontief, Francoise Perroux, K. Lancaster and even Janos Kornai were translated (Aligica, 2002). In Bulgaria, a 'Laboratory on Economic Modeling' was established at the Economic Institute of the Bulgarian Academy of Science and 'Economic modeling' and 'Econometrics' started to be taught in universities during the 1960s. In this context, in which the economists were free riding on the non-ideological nature of mathematics, it was possible to get in touch with and disseminate the results of Western developments in operational research, macroeconomic statistics, production and operation programming.

In the Baltic States, the dynamics of the epistemic community and the paradigm change were strongly affected by the complete isolation of social sciences in the Soviet Union. The academic literature was published only in Russian. To make things worse it was exceedingly ideological. Only several Moscow universities had access to foreign literature. Thus updated information on the developments in economics was in fact unavailable. In the case of Lithuania, Čekanavičius notes that just a very limited number of Western economic journals (e.g. *Econometrica, Operations Research*) 'in discontinued series, with missing volumes', were available in libraries. He very succinctly and vividly described the predicament of the Baltic economist during the period:

If some Lithuanian economist were keen enough to keep in touch with the Western developments in his profession, he would have to visit Moscow libraries, e.g. library of INION (Russian abbreviation of the Institute of Scientific

Research of Social Sciences). However, access to the stocks of these libraries was restricted – one has to obtain permission to use them. Another possibility – which had materialized in the last decade of the Soviet regime and was available only to the highest ranking Lithuanian economists – was to order copies of selected papers and articles from the Western journals to be received by mail from the aforementioned Institute. (Čekanavičius, 2002, pp. 121–33)

The contact with Western science and academic community was truly reactivated only in the 1990s. Yet, the number of contacts with the West was very limited in the beginning of transition. Later their number increased. Besides social and political isolation, another obstacle was language. It is very important to stress how important, in the case of the Baltic states, was the fact that the main language of science in the Soviet Union was Russian. As a consequence, the learning of other foreign languages was neglected. That led to an inability to follow the developments in English and take advantage of the limited bibliographical access allowed by the system. Nevertheless, as aptly put by one Baltic economist, 'the iron curtain in economics was never totally impenetrable': Western books and articles were 'occasionally translated'. Also, a glimpse on what was going on in Western economics was given by the aforementioned 'critiques of the contemporary bourgeois economic thought'. Finally, mathematical economics was a major conduit of Western ideas. That was facilitated on the one hand by the fact that mathematical economics had an established tradition in Soviet economics (e.g. L. Kantorovich, V. Novozhilov, V. Nemchinov, N. Petrakov) and on the other hand, by the fact that mathematical models did not directly challenge the official doctrines or openly undermine Marxism (Čekanavičius, 2002; Karnite, 2002; Puss, 2002).

Having said that, it is nevertheless true that 'in the Soviet period the mainstream of Baltic economics was mostly out of direct touch with Western academic thought, closer contacts with the latter being rather accidental and always under the shadow of ideological suspicion' (Čekanavičius, 2002). And that applied equally to the economics education system and the research institutions. The structural change of those institutions under the pressure of larger political transformations was in the entirety of Eastern Europe the signal that the paradigm change process was entering its decisive stage.

3. The remarkable path to primacy of Western economic ideas: change and institutionalization after 1989

Although the process of change of economic ideas in Eastern Europe started incrementally, was slow and had begun long before 1989, that year is probably the most likely date to mark the crucial moment of 'paradigm shift' in the ex-Soviet space (Spulber, 1997; Boettke, 1993). The Kaase, Sparschuh and Wenninger (2002) survey of the field reinforces the notion that around that date, a critical mass was created and the change in ideas and beliefs became manifest and materialized in radical political and economic changes. The case of Poland is exemplary in the chronology of the shift of ideas. The Polish developments became a reference point for the reformers in almost the entire post-communist Europe and as such had a great impact on the way reform was thought of in other countries of the Soviet block in the 1990s. The pressure of changes in the political and economic ideas started long before 1981. In 1981, the 'Solidarity' program 'Self-Governing Republic' was promoting economic reforms, although all of them were defined 'within the limits of the general framework of a market socialist economy' (Kowalik, 2002). And although they 'were not challenging directly either state property or the domination of the Communist party', they were a clear signal that the general climate of opinion regarding economic problems and solutions had changed. The Round Table negotiations and the final Agreement pushed the process into an even more radical direction. The Agreement outlined a much more radical, 'new economic order'. As the Polish economist Kowalik, a witness to those developments, notes, the Agreement was a clear break with the past:

> It is true, that in the line of thinking of old socialist and right-wing communists, the negotiators agreed to strengthen self-management at the factory level. But several other statements were innovative. They declared: abandonment of administrative planning in favor of steering the economy by mainly economic levers, a far reaching liberalization of prices, a possibility of privatization of state firms, constitutionally guaranteed, equal treatment of different forms of ownership and even creation within two years the Warsaw Stock Exchange. Thus, we may justly say that the Round Table Agreement outlined a really new socio-economic order. (Kowalik, 2002, pp. 135–49)

However, the Round Table Agreements were just the beginning. The real irreversible and formal break with the residues of the old paradigm came a couple of months after the elections. Then, the Round Table Agreement was 'abruptly substituted' by a 'radical reform program known as the Balcerowicz Plan'. The plan was ratified by parliament and at that moment the paradigm change, incomplete as it was, became a social and political reality (Kowalik, 2002).

In a similar way in Hungary, 1990 was the moment when the de facto demise of the Marxist paradigm become a *de jure* reality in economics. During the entire previous decade, covert ideological differences slowly but steadily surfaced and pro-market radical reform views became more and more vocal. By 1990, the economic situation was of such a nature that it was difficult to stop the neoclassical, neoliberal discourse and solutions to rule the agenda:

> Indebtedness of the country was so severe, that it constrained the room for experimentation by the new elite. With the exception of some queer émigrés, nobody had advocated radically dissimilar economic policies. There were, of course, *differences* in terms of speed, sequence, distributional consequences and the like, but *not in the fundamentals* of the underlying strategy. (Csaba, 2002, pp. 83–99)

Needless to say, by then those fundamentals were of a clear and firm neo-classical nature with changes become rapidly visible at the level of teaching. The translation of several standard Western textbooks (following the Samuelson–Nordhaus volumes already translated in 1987) were the beginning signs of the transformation. Despite the fact that their use remained limited, they were a clear signal that the paradigm shift had reached a tipping point. International economics seems to be a critical test for the degree and depth of the process of paradigmatic shift in East European economics. In Hungary, international economics continued to be dominated by the neo-Marxist approaches, but 'a growing body of descriptive material on the European Union' came to increasingly influence and change the field (Csaba, 2002).

In terms of teaching, other noteworthy symptoms manifested initially in Hungary, Poland and the Czech Republic, and later all over Eastern Europe. First was the increasing importance of business management that soon came to dominate economics. Then was the unprecedented expansion of the university and college programs and degrees in economics or economics related disciplines. Most new faculties and programs were built on inherited political economy departments or former Marxism–Leninism institutes. In the case of Hungary for instance, that implied that 'although several universities hired former dissidents and specialists, most hired the same old people'. Commenting on those evolutions, the same Csaba is keen to note that: 'The negotiated revolution in Hungary allowed for limited changes, with no purges or the like. Leading ideologues of the *ancien régime* could enjoy renewed tenures and late retirements in a large number of cases (even without necessarily converting themselves to national-conservative activists)' (Csaba, 2002).

Therefore, the change wasn't as radical as might have been expected as the paradigm change was paralleled and substantiated by a change of elites that at its turn was *gradual*. The elite change was strongly affected by 'switchovers to politics and business', a phenomenon familiar in the whole of Eastern Europe. This phenomenon is significant enough to deserve a special note. Čekanavičius, discussing the Lithuanian case, makes in this respect a comment pertinent for the entire post-Soviet space:

> Faculties of academic institutions themselves suffered quite a lot of painful losses of bright minds both to the Government and to the private business sector. This internal 'brain drain' (. . .) and was strongly stimulated by the vivid disparity of salaries in those sectors and in academics. The clear insufficiency of the academic salaries for making a decent living forced many of those faculty members who still stuck to the academics to have second and sometimes even third 'full time' jobs elsewhere. (. . .) Thus, many of them became just kind of a 'hangers-on' who rush into their classes, deliver outdated material to the students, occasionally write down some shallow paper, and collect their meager pay (which is by many regarded just as a kind of 'job security' payment). (Čekanavičius, 2002, pp. 121–33)

But the incremental nature of the change of professional elites in Eastern Europe also had some notable exceptions. In the Czech case, according to Turnovec (2002), the new elite seemed to have appeared overnight out of several groups of researchers related to the Economics Institute and the Institute of Forecasting, together with university professors, 'underground' economists, exile economists and even 'some more enlightened members of the old establishment'. Given the rigid ideological constraints of the Czechoslovak Marxist regime, the change of the climate of ideas was dramatic. Only a few months before November 1989, the 'ideological taboos stopped being obeyed'. That would not have happened without the Communists' power erosion. The Institute of Forecasting and the Institute of Economics of the Academy 'became main platforms of the debate on reform' (Havel et. al, 1998). The economists from exile played a decisive role by contributing to the increased access to economic literature, and to the economic education and research reform projects, they offered scholarships and fellowships, and organized fundraising to support the development of the infrastructure of the discipline. An exceptional role was played by Jan Svejnar, while economists like Josef Brada, Zdeněk Drábek, Karel

Kánský, Jan Kmenta, Jiří Kosta, Oldřich Kýn, Luděk Rychetník, Jiří Sláma, George Staller and Milan Zelený actively participated in initiatives on the same lines (Turnovec, 2002).

On the other hand, as reported by Julius Horvart, the cooperation of older and younger generations that 'characterizes the normal functioning of an epistemic community' was not a norm in the Slovak Republic. He offers an excellent example of this phenomenon noting the discontinuity characterizing the history of economics epistemic community in Slovakia:

> A generation of economists, who matured before socialism, may have provided the first pillars of economic education and economic theory making of high standard, however this group of economists had not continued in their academic career after the socialist revolution. The generation of economists who matured during the socialist period did not create a Slovak economic school and some (most) of their intellectual endeavor lost its value at the beginning of the 1990s after the collapse of socialist order. Thus, we witness a peculiar situation: in the 1950s, to some extent also in the early 1970s, as well as in the early 1990s young generation of economists rose to high government and academic position because the older competitors were compromised by the previous regime. (Horvart, 2002, pp. 168–85)

After 1989, visible change took place in the public discourse on economic affairs in Bulgaria and Romania but the measure in which the new vocabulary derived from a deeper paradigm change was rather limited. The elite change process started only in 1989. Therefore, immediately after 1989, the slow change of the professional and academic elite resulted in limited changes of paradigm apart from the drop of the Marxist themes and language. It was an otherwise easy thing to do, given the fact that in Romania and Bulgaria Marxism has never been the main research topic, but rather a password for related topics, such as development economics, international relations, etc.

In the view of most Romanian reformist economists, at the Academy of Economic Studies Bucharest (the main Romanian economics institution and a token for any change in the Romanian economic science) there was no paradigm change until the mid-1990s. Until then the Academy went through only a language or discourse shift. After 1995, there were increasingly clear signals that a critical mass was getting closer to making a real change but the moment was still far away. A similar interpretation has been exposed on the Bulgarian side by Mitko Dimitrov who differentiates between two periods in the process of paradigm change – until 1994–95 and after. The first period was characterized by a 'massive invasion' of translations and an explosion of publications. He notes that in many cases, especially from the older-generation professors, who did not master foreign languages, 'an imitative replacement of terms' and the use of 'market language', without practically changing their approach. During the second period as a whole, there was an improvement of the situation although the 'characteristic phenomena of the first period' still existed (Dimitrov, 2002).

Indeed illustrative for the situation noticed by Dimitrov was the mimetic adoption of the Western economic theory from the mainstream textbooks, with Paul Samuelson (often in its French translation) being the most quoted. It is interesting to focus as an example on the first post-1989 original textbook published by the Bucharest Academy of Economic Studies for many reasons including the great influence the Academy has on the modal type of Romanian economist due to its large number of students (more than 5000 students being enrolled each academic year in day-courses, with half of them receiving state subsidies) and also for the fact that it offers a clear illustration of the muddle specific to the transitional state of the discipline. The first textbook was written by a group from the economics department of the Academy of Economic Studies (Dobrotă, 1993). It had as one of the main sources of inspiration Samuelson's text-book (quoted or mentioned as a reference point in more than half the chapters of the book, almost 50 per cent times more the French translation than the English edition), but also Gilbert Abraham-Frois and Paul Heyne; both of them being so pre-eminent because they were the first Western textbooks translated and thus more accessible to the Bucharest Academy professors. Michel Didier's *Regulile jocului* (*Les regles du jeu*), a French textbook that fortuitously was translated into Romanian in 1994 is also an important source of inspiration. J.M. Keynes is also quoted frequently as is the economic historian Ferdinand Braudel (his work was translated into Romanian in 1988). As late as 1995, the avatars of the textbook of the Economics Department of the Academy of Economic Studies (Catedra de Economie Politică, *Economie Politică*, Ed. Economică, 1995) still drew heavily on Samuelson, Abraham-Frois and the aforementioned textbooks.

For anybody familiar with the Western textbook market it is obvious that the authors of the text displayed a rather eclectic and not very deep exposure to the current economics literature. That reveals that if a paradigm change is likely to take place, it has a long way to go until it becomes manifest at this leading south-east European teaching institution. Nevertheless, change took place, too: a larger variety of economics or political economy books were translated and the narrowness and dilettantism of the pre-1989 publishing policy in this regard became, in many respects, a thing of the past. Key economics books and authors were made available to the Romanian public although their use in classrooms or in public discourse was rather limited.

As already mentioned, in Bulgaria and Romania the elite change process only started in 1989. Despite the efforts, this evolution was by its very nature a lengthy one and the new generation less constrained by the legacies of the past was only starting to gain ground in the recent decade. Leading reformist economists like Costea Munteanu in Romania or Rumen Avramov in Bulgaria consider that we could speak of a real generational change only in ten to 15 years from now. In this respect, one may consider it a process driven by a natural demographic replacement process. The current economics elite is heterogeneous and fractured. Its scholarly status is difficult to evaluate by Western standards. Members of the elite maintain academic or research affiliations either as professors at the main universities or as advisers at the National Bank. They are also affiliated to research institutes, the National Academy research centers, the multinational institutions and, in a lesser measure, to other private or public institutions. The change of the elite was more visible at the policy and decision-making level, with the academy being rather conservative, although as mentioned before, the change of generations brought some new developments there, too. The National Bank and the ministerial offices were taken over by younger economists, but in many cases these young economists lacked a proper training and they displayed a rather questionable ability to use the 'economically correct' jargon without fully understanding its meaning (Wagener, 2002; Aligica, 2002).

The paradigm change symptoms, although less dramatic than in Central Europe, became evident in Baltic states at the beginning of the 1990s, too. Western books were translated and 'Socialist Political Economy' gave way to 'Basics of Economic Theory' and even to microeconomics and macroeconomics. With the collapse of the Soviet Union and independence, the contacts with the international research community resumed. In general, the changes in the Baltic states were pretty much on the same lines as in southeast Europe. In both cases, as it will be documented in the next section of the chapter, the role of the Western assistance deserves a special note as the inspiration and guidance coming from international organizations (the World Bank, The International Monetary Fund, European Commission) played a decisive role. The European Union through its PHARE and TEMPUS programs, the Soros Foundation (Open Society) and the Civic Education Project were crucial in the whole of Eastern Europe. To these, in the case of the Baltic states, the pan-Baltic and long-term EuroFaculty project, the Baltic Economic Management Training Project (financed by the Canadian International Development Agency) and other specific region-focused initiatives were added creating a critical mass.

A signal of the changes was in this region as elsewhere the emergence of business administration and management as fields increasingly separated from the economics. On the other hand, it is worth mentioning that many observers of the regional evolutions noted that the reforms 'swept away' the program of mathematical economics. The official reason was realignment to the Western standards in which all economics is mathematic; therefore there is no need for separate mathematical economics departments. But the same authors suspect that the real reason might have more to do with its relevance for the transition period or its ability to make clear that relevance to the public (Horvart, 2002; Čekanavičius, 2002).

The change in the professional elite in all these countries was mainly due to 'natural' reasons, but at various moments this process was speeded up by 'soft' administrative measures. In Bulgaria and Romania, institutes and research centers were closed down, and the former Communist Party's appointees to university top administration were in some cases replaced. In this respect, the Bulgarians went further than the Romanians. For instance, they introduced an institutional accreditation system as well as an attestation system for lecturers and researchers, which facilitated the process of natural change of the professional elite (Dimitrov, 2002). In Romania, in spite of the efforts of reform-minded minister level officials, the older generation continued to control the institutional system and to manipulate the attestation process in its own interest (Aligica, 2002).

The case of the Baltic states is in most respects similar to the Balkan ones. The situation is well summarized by Čekanavičius with reference to the Baltic states and more specifically to Lithuania but his point is valid (with country-specific minor adaptations) for the whole of Eastern Europe:

> In many cases changes in the study programs were of a rather 'cosmetic' nature, Western-like titles masking the low quality contents of the course. The 'new' economics is still done and the new programs of economic studies are still served mostly by the same old staff. It is a sad truth that the formal academic titles and seniority is often regarded as superior to the scholarly achievement (. . .) Thus the change of elites in economics was rather insignificant, as the 'old-timers' firmly held their privileged positions (. . .) and the emerging new generation of economists (often with an education in the West), faced with too thorny path in academics and too succulent career temptations outside it, did not particularly aspire to overtake them. (Čekanavičius, 2002, pp. 121–33)

To sum up, the paradigm change has been strongly related to the change at the level of professional elites. As aptly summarized by Püss, the elite change had different sources: 'Ideological' (most deans, directors of economic institutions, chairs, etc. were communists, and were forced to resign leadership after 1990); 'financial' and 'practical' (dramatic cuts of funding in research institutions while the transforming economy offered researchers numerous better jobs in business and administration or top political positions); 'organizational' (some institutes were closed) (Püss, 2002). However, irrespective of the sources of elite change, while discussing the relationship between paradigm change/change of elites on the one hand and individual economists on the other hand it is important to keep in mind the human aspect of the phenomenon. It is easy to condemn and judge the 'resistance to change' but it is worth considering the lives of the people involved in this process. They were first of all people that built a career or at least made their living by tinkering with 'Socialist or Marxist Economics'. Even when well intended, their lifelong efforts were rather frustrating. It is difficult to over-state the degree of confusion associated with the process of paradigm change for these researchers and teachers. Facing a new and unfamiliar conceptual universe pressed on them by changes that were threatening their jobs, social status and identity, they were forced to adjust rapidly. Even when doing their best, the task and the effort to keep up was daunting:

> It was not known which research topics had great potential and which had already far advanced. There was the danger of getting involved in areas in which problem set-ups and directions of research had become so specific that it would have been very hard to contribute on an international level without being familiar with earlier literature. (Püss, 2001, pp. 65–76)

All these created incontestable personal dramas. The situation started to improve when they began to participate in international research groups, and the systematic international effort to support them stepped up. Nevertheless the efforts, frustrations, and personal dramas involved in this transition process shouldn't be overlooked when analyzed under the neutral and impersonal notions of 'elite replacement' or 'elite change'.

THE INSTITUTIONALIZATION PROCESS

The last phase of the paradigm change process was associated with an increasingly stronger process of institutionalization. While in the initial phases personal contacts, translations and fragile curricular reforms were typical, in the later stages the institutional structure and infrastructure came to play a major role. A 1993 World Bank study on the state of eco-nomics in the Baltic states sums up very well the situation not only for the entire Baltic region but in large measure for the entire post-communist Europe:

> Important fields of study in a market economy either do not exist or are oriented in the wrong direction. Programs improperly oriented include economics, busi-ness, law, agriculture, and several fields of technology. Economics and manage-ment, in particular, need a complete overhaul. Moreover, owing to . . . isolation

from outside development, university teaching and scientific research have become seriously outdated. Lacking ready access to professional networks and literature, many teachers and researchers have fallen well behind developments by their colleagues in the West. Staff, teaching programs, libraries and textbooks, and laboratory equipment are not as up-to-date as they need to be in a competitive market economy. (World Bank, 1993, p. 181)

In all countries, universities were major playing grounds for the institutionalization of the paradigm change. An overview of the region reveals the typical pattern distinguishing East Central European countries from South East European and Baltic states. As reported by Csaba, in terms of institutional success, in spite of their progress, the Hungarian 'private universities and private research institutions have remained the exception'. Only the Central European University, funded by George Soros, and the Pázmány and Károli Universities, funded by the Roman Catholic and Reformed Calvinist churches, seem to be solid enough. Notwithstanding their rapid development, or maybe precisely because of that, very few of the new programs reached even 'minimal professional standards'. A typical example of what happened to many state institutions is Budapest Technical University which, while trying to bolster and enlarge their economics and management curricula, failed to renew and expand its faculty with young, modern-economics-trained professionals. In fact, it only managed to re-employ the 'losers of various power twists and turns of the other Universities, much less, however, in creating a supply response of new, previously non-tested talent conquering the pages of leading academic journals nationally and internationally alike' (Csaba, 2000).

In Poland after 1990, the number of faculty-level economics programs grew to more than 20: 15 public universities, the so-called Economic Academies (Wrocław, Łódz, Katowice and Warsaw), and the Lublin Catholic University. During the 1990s, about 230 tertiary-level private schools emerged, most of them being economics or business schools. However, only a few were meeting minimal academic standards. A majority of them had 'very high staff/professors ratio, usually lacked reliable libraries, and were short of space and other facilities' (Kowalik, 2002). If this is the case with countries like Hungary, Poland and the Czech Republic it is not a surprise that in the rest of the region the situation is, in the best case, similar.

In the Slovakian situation, the only attempt to establish a thorough graduate economics department was the Professional Program in Applied Economics at the Academia Istropolitana. The attempt failed. Most students left Slovakia to study abroad, especially in Prague (CERGE-EI), Budapest (CEU) and US. The case of Academia Istropolitana in Bratislava is very interesting as yet another typical situation specific to the process of institutionalization of economics in the post-communist period. Academia Istropolitana was originally intended to be a university-type institution but as Horvart notes:

> Since this concept run to some legal barriers a group of scholars tried to create an elite graduate training school. Finally, Academia Istropolitana was founded on inter-governmental agreements with support of different governments, foundations, and partially was financed by state budget. In 1994 Academia Istropolitana started the Professional Program in Applied Economics. The problems of the legal status of Academia Istropolitana further increased, which led some scholars to found Academia Istropolitana Nova as an independent graduate institution in October 1996. The Professional Program in Applied Economics was organized in cooperation with the University of Technology in Vienna, and the University of Pittsburgh. The generous grant from the Ministry of Foreign Affairs of Austria helped to finance this program. PPAE had students from more than ten countries, some of them continue currently in doctoral programs in Tilburg, Louisiana, Calgary and Pittsburgh. Its lecturers included economists from Technical University of Wien, Central European University in Budapest, Charles University in Prague, Comenius University, University of Bonn, University of Pittsburgh, and Slovak Academy of Sciences. (Horvart, 2002, pp. 168–85)

The Comenius University's cooperation with the University of Pittsburgh is illustrative of the most ambitious post-communist programs in the region. The University of Pittsburgh started by inviting lecturers of the Institute of Applied Mathematics to 'participate in the first four semesters of the Ph.D. economics program in Pittsburgh'. As a result of that, some of the Slovak participants ended up with a Pittsburgh University MA in economics. Some continued their studies and earned a doctoral degree (Horvart, 2002).

The major Slovak institutions of undergraduate education in economics are the University of Economics in Bratislava and the Comenius University in Bratislava. It is interesting to note that an undergraduate program of economic and financial mathematics was initiated by the Institute of Applied Mathematics of the Faculty of Mathematics and Physics. In parallel, a business administration program started in 1991 at the newly created Faculty of Management and in 1993 the Institute of Applied Mathematics of the College of Mathematics and Physics of the Comenius University started the master's program in Economic and Financial Mathematics. The list of higher education organizations offering economics courses includes the Matej Bel University in Banská Bystrica, the Agricultural University in Nitra, the University of Trencín, the University of Zilina, the Faculty of Business Management of the Bratislava University of Economics in Košice and the Technical University in Košice. Many of these programs were created only in the 1990s (Horvart, 2002).

In the Czech Republic, as elsewhere, the institutional reform of the system of higher education, including economic education, was a priority after 1989: 'The easier part of reform was re-establishment of basic attributes of university education: academic freedom and university self-administration. The more difficult part of the reform – restructuring of study curricula – required more time, but the significant changes in this respect are observable' (Turnovec, 2002). New viable programs emerged. One of the most successful initiatives has been the Center for Economic Research and Graduate Education (CERGE) of Charles University, designed as an international Ph.D. programme in theoretical and applied economics. The Center was initiated through a joint effort of Charles University in Prague, Pittsburgh University, USAID and the European Union in 1991, an effort coordinated by Jan Svejnar, a US based economist of Czech origin. In the Czech Republic, as elsewhere, the reform of research institutions had a mixed success. The Academy of Sciences managed to withhold the shock of transformation, although in an adjusted form. Its economics component, the Institute of Economics of the Academy, was dissolved in 1993 and Jan Svejnar was called to create the new Economics Institute. The new institute, comments Turnovec (2002), now looks more like a department of economics at a good American university.

In Bulgaria and Romania the higher education system and with it the teaching of economics underwent considerable changes. The existing economic universities (in Sofia, Varna and Svishtov in Bulgaria and in Bucharest, Cluj, Craiova, Timisoara and Iasi in Romania) modernized their structures and started restructuring their curricula. A Western model of education system was introduced – Bachelor, Master and Doctor. National Agencies for Evaluation and Accreditation, having the task of assessing the extent to which the universities, faculties, departments and curricula satisfy higher education standards, were established in both countries. In Bulgaria, new programs in economics were created at seven universities: three new private universities with strong economics majors and four new private colleges specialized in economics. In Romania, the number of teaching units rose sharply too: 15 state education and 33 private universities or colleges with an economics chair or faculty (Dimitrov, 2002; Aligica, 2002).

In the Baltic states, the changes were materializing into new institutional structures too. Departments of economics or business administration were established at nearly every university. Given the Soviet period background in the Baltic states, the institutionalization of economics in teaching centers is most visible and the explosion of new or refurbished programs has been spectacular. By the end of the 1990s, 11 institutions in Lithuania offered university degrees in economics, and/or business administration. Among them were the Vilnius Faculty of Economics, the Vilnius University International Business School, the Vilnius Faculty of Business Management, the Faculty of Economics and Management, Vytautas Magnus University and the International School of Management (established jointly with Norwegian School of Management, Oslo) in Kaunas. In Estonia's case, the independent Faculty of Economics of the University of Tartu, the Faculty of Economics and Social Sciences of the Estonian Agricultural University and the Faculty of Economics and Business Administration of Tallinn Technical University were the leading players in the process of economics higher education reform. Similarly, the number of institutions offering study programs in business and economics in Latvia expanded. Among them were the Latvian University, the Stockholm School of Economics in Riga, the School of Business Administration 'Turiba', the Banking College of Higher Education, the Riga International College of Economics and Business Administration, the Vidzeme College of Higher Education in Valmiera and the Ventspils College. It is true that the quality of the work done in these institutions is not always up to professional standards, at least to the standards of the expert engaged in the GESIS evaluation (Čekanavičius, 2002), but the trend toward institutional structural consolidation is obvious.

It is difficult to generalize about economic research in Eastern Europe as the differences between countries are rather substantial. However, the general trend was toward the institutionalization of Western economics after 1990. Overall, in the whole of Eastern Europe there was a clear reorientation towards applied research. There seems to be a direct relationship between the advancement of the paradigm change, the restructuring of the old research centers and the rise of the policy-oriented and applied research agenda. Csaba documents this trend as regarding the Hungarian case in a very telling way:

> While institutions of the Academy of Sciences had to be merged and 'consolidated', i.e. downsized, they basically keep on by self-financing, i.e. on case by case project financing by their members. Applied economics research institutions, such as Financial Research Inc, Kopint-Datorg Economic Research or GKI Economic Research Institute have been pushed increasingly (next to exclusively) towards business consultancy, with some of the long time members still devoting some of their time and energy to research as a private hobby. Cooperation with western institutions were helpful as bridging solutions to individual headaches, not, however for creating a new structure for funding research. Other new institutions, such as the Institute for Economic Growth, or the TREND Forecast Group, are thinly veiled party think-tanks, employing a couple of analysts, and – naturally – not proving terribly ambitious in terms of measurable academic achievement. (Csaba, 2000, pp. 83–99)

The dynamics and structure of the professional organizations vary from country to country. In this respect, the economics community in Hungary presents a very interesting situation. On the one hand, many Hungarian economists are well integrated in the life and activities of the Western professional organizations. Examples abound: János Kornai was elected president of the Econometric Society in 1978, and to the Presidency of the European Economic Association in 1987; József Bognár, a member of the Club of Rome, and Béla Csikós-Nagy were founders of the International Economic Association, 'an institution that served as a bridge between East and West'; András Bródy was an editor of Economic Systems Research; Ivan T. Berend was Vice President of the International Association of Economic Historians between 1986 and 1994; etc. (Csaba, 2000). On the other hand, it is interesting to contrast this impressive international record with the minimal, if any, performance of the domestic professional associations of various sorts, as criticized by Csaba 'as primarily social and regional events with some policy flavor, not academic fora'.

The instituionalization of this aspect of the discipline is different in the Polish case, where the think tanks, professional associations and research centers have been rather active and influential. According to Kowalik, in Poland, almost all traditional universities do some economics research. In terms of the publication of research, a couple of Institutes and Committees belonging to the Polish Academy of Sciences continue to play an important role: the Institute of Economics (focused on different aspects of transformation of Polish economy and the competitiveness of the Polish enterprises in the perspective of the European Union accession) and the Committee of Futures Studies 'Poland 2000 Plus' (Kowalik, 2002).

The Polish case is also very interesting for the strong institutionalization of the pro-market, neoclassical approach. Starting in the early 1990s, several very influential private neoliberal think tanks were created. The Institute of Research on Market Economy was created by the Gdańsk group of economists associated with the Congress of Democratic Liberals. The Adam Smith Research Center was founded in Warsaw in 1989 as 'an independent, non-profit, non-partisan institution devoted to the development of a free market economy, democratic system and free and virtuous society'. Noteworthy is the fact that on its Advisory Board are Armen Alchian and James Buchanan. The Carl Menger Research Group, supported by the liberal Friedrich Naumann Stiftung was the institutional expression of a group of scholars developing and applying ideas of the Austrian school. The Centre for Social and Economic Analysis (CASE), which managed to achieve a rather influential role in politics and economic policies, deserves a special note. Kowalik notes that Leszek Balcerowicz and Marek Dąbrowski 'imprinted strongly on the direction and character of research' and that due to them 'CASE enjoys probably exceptionally high possibilities of fund raising'. It is important to note that this think tank has been unique among the Eastern European think tanks because it has also functioned abroad through its three foreign chapters (in Ukraine, Georgia, Kyrgyzstan) which were advising foreign post-communist governments (Kowalik, 2002).

The economists active in the aforementioned private research centers created Towarzystwo Ekonomistów Polskich (Society of Polish Economists) which is a 'neoliberal organization, an intellectual alternative to the old Polskie Towarzystwo Ekonomiczne' (Polish Economic Society). The latter had about 7000 members while the first had about 200 members. The competition between the two has been very tense and had unmistakable ideological and political dimensions. In this respect Kowalik notes that:

> At all congresses and statutory conventions of the Polish Economic Association, starting with one in Autumn 1989 the dominant attitude towards neo-liberal policy was highly critical. The Warsaw Main School of Economics and Łódź University's economic faculty apparently dominated by the neo-liberal current are rather an exceptions. Both serve as the main source for economic rulers (of 9 finance ministers 5 were from Warsaw Main School and 3 from Łódź University). This division between small, but powerful and well organized currents of economists belonging to the neo-liberal school, and much more numerous economists of social democratic orientation and close to traditional (social) liberalism which stems from ideas of J.S. Mill, J.M. Keynes and his Cambridge followers (like Joan Robinson) explains why the Polish transformation process has engaged that many American economists. (Kowalik, 2002, pp. 135–49)

In the Czech case, the initial radical reform plan failed. As has already been mentioned a new Economics Institute was established at the Academy of Sciences (Turnovec, 2002). Initially, the Academy of Sciences had three economic research institutes: the Institute of Economics, the Institute of Forecasting and the Social-economic Institute. In 1992, these three institutes were disbanded and one new Economics Institute emerged instead. The new Economics Institute was established 'of a rather different design' looking more like 'a department of economics at a good American university' stressing publications in prestigious journals (Turnovec, 2002). During the same period, not only the Academy related but also other units of economic research were disbanded: the Central Institute of National Economic Research, the Research Institute of Ministry of Finance, the Institute of Economic Policy, the Institute of Economic Sciences at Charles University and the Economic Institute of Czech National Bank. Summarizing these changes, one author concluded that if the country had about 1000 economic researchers 12 years ago, now it has only several dozen (Havel, quoted by Turnovec, 2002).

In Slovakia, the Institute of Slovak and World Economics was the successor of the Institute of Legal and Economic Sciences of the Slovak Academy of Sciences, which was founded in 1949 and was supposed to be the most prestigious research center. According to Horvart, this institute was reorganized in several steps and is financed mainly through projects from the Scientific Grant Agency of Slovakia, EU Phare projects and UN projects. Other institutes providing economic research are the Institute for Forecasting and the Institute of Informatics and Statistics (established as a result of an agreement between Czechoslovakia and the Development Program of the United Nations). As in all other countries in the region, a series of non-governmental institutions and think tanks, which monitor and analyze the economic, political and social developments, were established in the 1990s. For instance, a group of 'economists and social scientists with liberal values established the Center for Economic and Social Analysis, better known as M.E.S.A. 10'. Many of its members 'served in key executive and legislative bodies in the first years of economic reforms' (Horvart, 2002).

As in the entire region, in Bulgaria and Romania the National Academy of Science was the main official research center before 1989. Thus, it was no surprise that after 1989 the National Academies were at the center of the institutional reform of the discipline. The Bulgarian Academy of Science was radically restructured. The Institute for Socialist Integration was closed down and the Economic Institute was restructured and went through an 'institutional accreditation and employees' attestation' process. One of the consequences was that the number of the researcher-economists at the Bulgarian Academy of Science was reduced by 75 per cent (Dimitrov, 2002). Similar changes took place in Romania, although the number of economists employed did not diminish as radically. In general, the research institutes that were related to the government underwent considerable changes. The party training and research centers were closed down. Many ministries had their own research units which were discontinued or privatized.

That change generated counter-reactions and the tensions between generations soon took an institutional form. In the Romanian case, the history of the post-1989 institutional evolutions in the realm of economics could be reduced to the story of the competition between two institutions or professional societies. There were two new professional organizations established at the beginning of the 1990s. The first is the General Association of the Economists of Romania, AGER, established in 1990 as an umbrella for the older-generation economists. It considered itself the heir of the inter-war organization with the same name (founded in 1913) and among its members were most of the pre-eminent economists of the time: Virgil Madgearu, V. Slăvescu, Constantin Tașcă and Mihail Manoilescu. The Association lacked a scholarly journal. The official publication of the organization was a daily economic newspaper, *Economistul* (started in 1990, but issued as a daily only from 1998), but it is also associated with *Adevărul Economic*, a weekly newspaper. The organization established its own publishing house, Ed. Economică, specializing in economic literature, mainly Academy of Economic Studies undergraduate textbooks. The leader of this group was the late N.N. Constantinescu. The other organization, The Romanian Society of Economy – SOREC – had a more reformist and liberal orientation. The organization's main publication is *Oeconomica*, an academic publication with 4–5 issues a year. SOREC has a close relationship with the newly established Center for Economic Policies, CEROPE, a center that is correctly seen as its think tank. The frictions between these two define and explain many aspects of the dynamics of Romanian epistemic community. It is unlikely that the tensions will end other than by generational change. This evolution is by its very nature a lengthy one. Leading reformists consider that we could speak of a real generational change only ten to 15 years from now.

In the Baltic states too, the changes brought about new institutional structures. As has already been mentioned, departments of economics or business administration were established at nearly every university. In the case of research, the situation was even more radical. The case of Latvia is exemplary: In Latvia before 1990, economic research was indeed structured in the Soviet style: the Academy of Sciences with its typical network of 15 (in this case) research institutes was pivotal but economic research was also carried out in universities (Latvian University, Riga Politechnical Institute, Agriculture Academy in Jelgava) and several specialized research units belonging to ministries. International cooperation in the research area was closed within the borders of Soviet Union and universities did not play a major role in economic research (Karnite, 2002).

The reform in Latvian science dates back to 1990 with the creation of the Latvian Science Council, and took off in 1992, when the Danish Research Council (on the request of the Latvian Council of Science) carried out an evaluation of the research system of Latvia. Economics was the subject of one of the 19 expert panels that examined the economic research institutions and suggested restructuring measures. Among them were: Riga Technical University, Latvian Agriculture University, Daugavpils Pedagogical University and Valmiera College. The new research infrastructure also consists of a number of small research institutes within Latvian University; the Institute of Economics, Latvian Academy of Science, and several private institutes or consultant companies.

The pace of change was similar in Lithuania. As in most cases, the decisive changes took place at the center of the system. The Lithuanian Institute of the Planning and Economic Research was disbanded, together with the State Planning Committee. A new research institution was formed, the Institute of Economics and Privatization. Besides the universities, several other institutions that were involved in economic research went through structural transformations: the Institute of Economics, located in Vilnius; the Lithuanian Institute of Agrarian Economics, Vilnius and the Banking Policy Department of the Bank of Lithuania. To these should be added the Lithuanian Department of Statistics, the Economic Research Team of Vilnius Bank and the Lithuanian Institute of the Free Market Economy, a private non-profit institution (Čekanavičius, 2002).

In the case of Estonia, the central institution was the Estonian Institute of Economics that traditionally had the leading role in conducting and coordinating economic research. The post-communist reforms introduced a rather interesting system organized around topic-oriented groups. According to Püss (2002), between 1995 and 1997, there were four major groups focused on: social development and social policy (social development and social policy in Estonia in the period of transition); economic integration (adaptation of the Estonian economy to the integration processes in Europe); institutional changes (formation of market mechanisms and institutions); and economics of natural and energy resources (economic problems of the use of local natural resources). After 1998, two research groups were formed: one focused on natural and energy resources economics and another one on institutional development (The Theory and Practice of Harmonizing the Social and Market Economy Institutions in Estonia's Accession to the European Union) (Püss, 2002).

Overall, the institutionalization of the Western paradigm seems to have been completed by the end of the decade in the whole of Eastern Europe. Although the East European epistemic community is far from mastering neoclassical theory and methodology, it is clear that a serious and systematic effort in that direction has been made and the necessary institutional framework has been created. The West substantially supported that effort. A decisive factor determining the process was the massive institutional and financial assistance given by international organizations, Western governments, EU and Western countries-based NGOs. Many of the aforementioned institutional developments couldn't have taken place without Western contributions and support. In order to offer a view of the range and scale of their contribution, a couple of illustrations of the international institutions' efforts should be given.

INTERNATIONAL INSTITUTIONS

One of the most active players in supporting the institutionalization of the new political economy paradigm in Eastern Europe was the World Bank. However, the World Bank's contribution to the institutionalization of the new political economy paradigm should be seen first and foremost as part of its broader contribution to the education system reform in the region. Taking as a starting point the idea that education was 'a key growth sector' and that the generation trained under the Soviet system was ill prepared for a competitive market economy, the World Bank put a special emphasis on the reform of higher education and of the research infrastructure.

Consequently, the Bank supported the governments of the region to improve the capacity of the education system to face 'the demands for new professional and managerial skills required by a market economy' and thus specific projects' objectives had implicitly and explicitly to deal with the change of the economic ideas. Two areas were deemed as priority: improving the capacity of the individual institutions to develop the new undergraduate and continuing education programs demanded by the transition to a market economy; and developing the kind of postgraduate education and research training needed to supply the next generation of academic staff, and the professionals with advanced training in the new fields demanded by the transition to a market economy.

Besides that, within the World Bank a special institutional structure was created to deal precisely with the transfer of new economic ideas. The World Bank Institute was created to teach 'the economics of poverty reduction and sustainable development'. The World Bank Institute's work program included training, development-related seminars, workshops, and courses, policy consultations and the creation and support of 'knowledge networks' related to international economic and social development. Topics addressed such themes as economic policy, governance and regulation, human development and the environment. For instance, the Macroeconomics and Policy Assessment Skills program was typical for the economics the World Bank disseminated. As declared by the World Bank, both objectives of the program were to increase the Western modern economics capabilities of policymakers, academics, Bank staff, staff from other international organizations and other development practitioners, to analyze current issues in macroeconomic management, and 'to build relevant analytical and practical skills in the area of policy assessment in government institutions, multilateral organizations, universities, and other research-oriented institutions'.

In a similar way, a distinct program focused on the 'market-based solutions for long-term investment and growth' was another example of a source of dissemination of Western ideas. That program was an example of the applied level initiatives that focused on the country's specific economic and political institutions (security of property rights, credibility of government commitments, rule of law, regime stability, contract enforcement, corporate governance, regulatory structure and democracy). The program has introduced the newest theoretical ideas of Western political economy and has shared 'knowledge and best practices on institutional capacity building as well as expertise in promoting long-term growth and poverty alleviation'. Finally the World Bank has been a generous sponsor of economic research throughout the entire period. The selection and funding of different research projects has represented a supplementary channel through which the Bank has bolstered the spread of Western economics in the region. Many projects were supported through the country funds. However the Bank also had central resources that were made available to local researchers.

Far less action on the research support line has been taken by the European equivalent of the World Bank, the European Bank for Reconstruction and Development. The European Bank for Reconstruction and Development was established in 1991, after communism's failure to provide financial support for the private sector to Central and Eastern Europe and ex-Soviet countries. The European Bank for Reconstruction and Development provided project financing for banks, industries and businesses, and supported privatization, restructuring state-owned firms and improvement of municipal services and bolstered the business environment. Recently it has been considered the largest single investor in the region mobilizing significant foreign direct investment beyond its own financing. In spite of its involvement in the region, the European Bank has focused more on traditional banking activities and less on the economics of paradigm change. Its projects and infrastructure to support the paradigm change in economics were rather weak compared to that of the World Bank. Research was conducted and disseminated, a scholarly journal on economics of transition was published but the breath and impact in this respect were far from matching the World Bank's impact. This should not be a surprise as the European Bank for Reconstruction and Development had explicit objectives and policy targets in the area of transportation, agribusiness, property operation energy and natural resources but no economics or education policy. This guiding principle was continued through the entire period. In 1999, the bank concluded that the region has changed substantially in the years since it formulated its initial operational priorities. Accordingly, the Bank carried out a strategic review of these priorities. The result was a new set of operational priorities for the medium term but no priority in intellectual infrastructure or economic ideas dissemination was introduced.

In this respect, the International Monetary Fund situation is substantially different. In the case of the International Monetary Fund, as in the case of the World Bank, the analytical and cognitive infrastructure became an explicit part of its organizational mission. That was even formally defined in the official documents as 'technical assistance'. The objective of IMF technical assistance, as described in its Articles of Agreement was 'to contribute to the development of the productive resources of member countries by enhancing the effectiveness of economic policy and financial policy'. The International Monetary Fund fulfilled this objective by providing support to capacity building and policy design. In other words, it helped countries strengthen their human and institutional capacity, as a means to improve the quality of policy-making, and gave advice on how to design and implement effective macroeconomic and structural policies.

Thus, 'technical assistance' was one of the benefits of International Monetary Fund membership. It complemented and enhanced the International Monetary Fund's other two key forms of assistance, surveillance and lending. Technical assistance was normally provided free of charge and in Eastern Europe took several forms. These included staff missions from headquarters; the placement of experts for periods ranging from a few months to a few years; the preparation of technical and diagnostic reports; the delivery of training courses, seminars and workshops; and the on-line provision of advice and support from headquarters. The activity was deemed so important that technical assistance and training was delivered not only from its headquarters in Washington, DC but also from the regionally based centers.

In addition to training offered at headquarters, the International Monetary Fund also offered courses and seminars through overseas regional institutes and programs. There were four regional training centers and one of them, the Joint Vienna Institute (located in Austria), was playing an important role for Eastern Europe. The Vienna International Monetary Fund Institute was established with the goal to provide training in economic management to officials of the Fund's member countries and was designed as a cooperative venture of six international organizations: Bank of International Settlements, European Bank for Reconstruction and Development, International Bank for Reconstruction and Development, the International Monetary Fund, the Organisation for Economic Cooperation and Development, the World Trade Organization and the Government of Austria. Its explicit role was to 'supply, through training' support for 'the national efforts of the countries of Central and Eastern Europe, and the countries that were formerly republics of the USSR, in making the transition from centrally planned to market based economies'. Indeed, during the transition period, it provided training for officials of

Central and Eastern European countries, and the former Soviet Union. The target groups for these courses were primarily the public officials and training officers from ministries of finance, economy and central banks; the economic advisers to governments; and the private sector executives. The institute offered courses helping to build economic, financial programming, and statistical skills that in IMF's view were the basic building blocks for good macroeconomic management. Lecturers were well-known experts from prestigious universities and research institutions worldwide and the majority of courses and seminars were in macroeconomics, econometrics and finance. Finally, IMF financially supported some research done by the economists of the region on the same macroeconomics and econometric issues.

The UN contribution to the spread of neoliberal economic ideas may come as a surprise for those that consider the UN as the repository or at least an enabler of an alternative economic paradigm. The UN input to the economic paradigm change away from Marxism was given through two institutional structures: the United Nations Development Programme and UNESCO. The latter contributed to the higher education reform and as such has complemented the World Bank and European Union efforts. The UNDP activity in this respect was even more interesting. The United Nations Development Programme defines itself as the 'UN's global development network, advocating for change and connecting countries to knowledge, experience and resources'. During the transition period, this organization had a series of noteworthy initiatives both in the areas of economics dissemination and applied economic research. The goal was to 'employ policy analysis techniques to improve the policy approach to issues such as democratic governance, poverty reduction, energy and environment, areas that have a significant economics component'. In 1997, in order to increase the impact of the national bureaus, UNDP's Regional Bureau for Europe and the Commonwealth of Independent States established the Regional Support Center in Bratislava. This was correlated with the launching of UNDP's first regional cooperation framework for Europe and the Commonwealth of Independent States – a series of interrelated programs, specifically based on UNDP's programming priorities and available to all 30 countries in the region.

The Bratislava Regional Support Center took over the management of these programs, together with the responsibility for 'certain training and support functions for the whole region'. Related to it, in 1999, a Regional Knowledge Facility was created, as a service for 'sharing of information and knowledge through its development assistance programmes in East Europe and the CIS'. The facility was developed to serve not only the needs of the UNDP regional Country Offices in the region but also of 'all development practitioners and interested institutions in the region'. It had the function of centralization and coordination of knowledge specialized expertise, information on the staff, experts, institutions, projects, reports, best practices and others through a referral database. The UNDP attempt in this respect was very bold as it could be seen as nothing less than an attempt to create an 'economic development' virtual epistemic community. To make the idea operational a set of thematic networks and resource groups was built. Two types of networks were created – one linking the staff of UNDP and the second linking experts and institutions who are not part of UNDP but with 'prominent recognition in the region'. These networks were meant to 'support pragmatic consultations in all the thematic areas' and were active in the area of governance, poverty reduction, environment management, sustainable development, etc. To sum up, this UNDP initiative deserves a special note as a significant attempt to create a new institutional basis for the Eastern Europe epistemic community as a whole, i.e. not just on a country basis.

Finally, the European Union's contributions to the economic paradigm change and the consolidation of an East European institutional infrastructure for economic policy have been manifold. In this respect, besides the training of Eastern European officials and bureaucrats, probably the most important impact of the EU was in the area of higher education. The trans-European cooperation scheme for higher education was, in this case, crucial. Tempus Phare was part of the overall program of the European Union for the economic and social restructuring of the countries in Central and Eastern Europe and started in 1990 as 'an instrument to contribute to the restructuring and adaptation of the Partner countries' higher education systems'. Funding was provided through Phare Action Programmes, the individual amounts per country being a result of negotiations between the European Commission and the 'Partner Countries'. That program provided 'financial grants for co-operation projects between higher education establishments in the EU and the Partner States in priority areas which are defined by the Partner States' authorities and the European Commission and which are in line with the overall socio-economic reform process of these countries' (European Commission, 2002).

The Tempus program encouraged institutions in the EU member states and the partner countries to engage in cooperation through the establishment of 'consortia' and to implement joint European projects. Tempus also provided individual mobility grants to individuals working in higher education institutions to help them work on certain specified activities in other countries. Among the many areas, it included important assistance for modernizing economic departments, for creating new programs and schools and for 'disseminating economic thinking and skills'. Of further relevance was the Socrates program, an education program aimed at 'an increase of mobility for students in higher education' and to promote 'broad and intensive cooperation between institutions at all levels of education in every member state through the mobility of teaching staff'. It also aimed at the institutional homogenization of the area by encouraging the academic recognition of diplomas and periods of study, in particular through the introduction of academic credits and modules aimed at facilitating such recognition at Community level. Also, the EU gave significant support for the development of research infrastructures in East European countries. The emerging European framework acknowledged from the onset the status of East European countries' researchers as members of the research community.

Finally, the mobility issue: one of the worst challenges for the East European economists was their isolation from their Eastern and Western colleagues. The EU took concrete steps to induce the member states to remove all obstacles to free movement within the Community for students, teachers and trainers. That was materialized in the Recommendation of the European Parliament and the Council of 10, July 2001 on mobility within the Community for students, persons undergoing training, young volunteers, teachers and trainers and that will have an important impact in the future on East European students and economists, too.

CONCLUSIONS

The overview of the process of the spread of Western economic ideas in Eastern Europe offers a panorama of diversity and complexity. However there are several significant observations emerging that cut across the national and contextual specificities. For instance, the overview reconfirms the discrepancy between on the one hand the group of countries where there was a more serious and systematic intellectual engagement with the Marxist paradigm but also a more intense effort towards alternatives and more openness towards the Western ideas, and, on the other hand, those countries that complacently cohabited with Marxism without seriously engaging it but then again did not make serious steps in articulating or importing alternative approaches. Besides that, an entire set of themes comes out as pivotal in understanding the process of economic ideas change and, as such, each of them deserves a separate investigation: the role of pre-communist traditions in facilitating or impeding the alternatives to the official Marxist paradigm; the presence of eminent economists as a crucial factor for the strength and dynamics of the national epistemic communities; the existence and extent of the political and cultural liberalization

period as a factor facilitating ideas diffusion; the crucial role of direct contacts and participation in the Western epistemic community; the role of
political dissidents and dissidence in general; the pivotal function of
'central institutions' such as the National Academies of Science both in the
communist period and the post-communist change process; the paradoxical importance of the criticism of the bourgeoisie theory as a vehicle for
ideas diffusion and paradigm challenge and change; the key role played by
the book translation programs and their utility as reliable indicators of the
degree of openness and vitality of the epistemic communities; the existence
of a two-speed diffusion (theoretical and analytic vs. formal and quantitative) with mathematical economics as a main outlet contact with the
Western thinking; the incapacity of mathematical economics to become
either a challenge to the domination of Marxism or a source of paradigm
change; the political element as a key catalyst of ideas and their dynamics;
the disappearance of mathematical economics as an institutionalized discipline after 1990 and the explosion of applied programs (management,
finance, etc.); the slowness of the elite change process and the imbalanced
competition with business and government for economic talent; and the
decisive role of the international community in institutionalizing the new
paradigm.

   If one is to speak about a 'neoliberal revolution' in Eastern Europe then
the 1989 watershed was far from a concluding point. In fact, the process
continued while in a very interesting way, the neoclassical ideas came to be
challenged by the very economic and political reality they engendered. The
transition experience forced the new ruling paradigm to adjust to the many
unanticipated evolutions in the region and thus new approaches, many of
them of heterodox origins, came to be reconsidered. Hence a sensible
overview should not leave the impression that once Marxism was replaced,
the march of neoclassical–neoliberal ideas stabilized in an absolutely
unchallenged and unmovable position. In fact, as will be discussed in detail
in the third section of this study, a new dynamics was set into motion, a
dynamics that while accepting the neoliberal tenet regarding the central role
of markets, question important assumptions of neoclassical economics in
the light of the policy experience. However for now it is important to note
this key fact: the dominant position neoclassical ideas had in the process of
spread and change of economic ideas in Eastern Europe in the period
before and after the 1989 political transformations.

   An empirical overview of the myriad of 'basic facts' defining the process
of spread of economic ideas dispels the notion that a radical doctrine
described as 'market fundamentalism' took over the whole of Eastern
Europe after 1989 and that a homogenous group of 'market doctrinaires'
managed to impose something called 'radical neoliberalism'. As one could

see, the process of ideas change was more complex and multifaceted than that. But it is not just a matter of acknowledging the complexity of the phenomenon. The very idea that something called 'market fundamentalism' was at the core of the transformation of economic ideas in Eastern Europe doesn't look to be factually accurate. At the core of the process were simply the standard neoclassical Western ideas. And calling the doctrine dominant in most Western academic and research institutions 'radical' is indeed an option but probably it is not the most constructive way to describe it. The radical features claimed to be identified by the authors denouncing the 'neoliberal hegemony' in Eastern Europe may be indeed in the eyes of the beholder. But amid this dance of subjective perceptions one thing is clear. These features consisted basically of what was taught in all Western universities. One has to repeat again and again that what was called the 'neoliberal revolution' of ideas was a very complex phenomenon. But in the end what happened in Eastern Europe may be read in a simple key: a pragmatic alignment to what was perceived by the East as workable ideas coming from the countries that succeeded where the East failed. From there to the notion of an ideological coup or to the notion that economic ideas were somehow imposed on reluctant victims is a long way. The story of such an imposition is indeed the story of the way socialist ideas got a grip on the region. But what is true for the 'socialist revolution' is not true for the 'neoliberal revolution'. Yet, for some reason the myth of 'market fundamentalism' dictating over the transition from communism seems to be more resilient to facts than one may expect. Nothing illustrates better this problem than the preoccupation with the issue of 'shock therapy'.

The most important fact to note is that the 'shock therapy' vs. 'gradualism' debate was less a debate about political economy paradigms but a debate on strategy. In other words, there are two dimensions of the debates generated by the transition experience, related but still different: a debate on strategy, more precisely a debate on the speed and intensity of change and a debate on the theories and models inspiring and supporting the strategic views. The bottom line is that it is possible to argue for or against any of the two strategic positions both from within the neoclassical framework or from outside.

Radical, shock therapy policy also known as 'one stroke' or a 'big bang' was usually considered a 'neoliberal' strategy (Aslund, 2002; Kornai, 1990; Lipton and Sachs, 1990; Wei, 1997). Usually five dimensions were simultaneously identified: stabilization, price liberalization, privatization of state-owned enterprises, promotion of the private sector and trade liberalization. The strategic objective was to shape every aspect of the economy as closely as possible to the free market model. The arguments stressed the importance of a move towards the market in clear strategic terms (McKinnon, 1991;

Dewatripont and Roland, 1995; Benham and Merithew, 1995; Hausner et al., 1995). First, a big-bang approach provides a critical mass of privatized entities in the economy efficiency of the privatized firms; increases the credibility of a reform; doesn't give time to reform opponents to organize themselves and resist; does not generate an inter-temporal speculation (goods hoarding) and finally, a big-bang approach brings the benefits more quickly. There is an internal logic required by the relationships between these aspects. As Lipton and Sachs put it,

> [T]he transition process is a seamless web. Structural reforms cannot work without a working price system; a working price system cannot be put in place without ending excess demand and creating a convertible currency; and a credit squeeze and tight macroeconomic policy cannot be sustained unless prices are realistic, so that there is a rational basis for deciding which firms should be allowed to close. At the same time, for real structural adjustment to take place under the pressure of tight demand, the macroeconomic shock must be accompanied by other measures, including selling off state assets, freeing up the private sector. (Lipton and Sachs, 1990, p. 99)

As a critic of that approach noted, behind this view there is also the implicit understanding that these different dimensions 'can change in more or less the same speed, or at least that the lagging behind of any particular aspect would not be so serious as to disrupt the whole package'. In this regard, it appears to be an extension of the 'new classical counter-revolution' in Western economics. 'By assuming rapid and smooth adjustment of economic institutions and structures, together with the behavior of rational expectations, this strand posits that instantaneous market clearing can be achieved' (Lo, 1995, p. 81). That view has thus a clear basis in the neoclassical paradigm.

Yet, conversely, gradualism has been argued with neoclassical tools, too. A group of neoclassical mainstream Western economists, primarily Gerard Roland, Mathias Dewatripont, Phillipe Aghion and Olivier Blanchard, have developed an extensive theoretical literature of neoclassical inspiration on the political economy of gradualism in transition. That approach is facilitated by the very definition they give to gradualism that implies only a strategic difference in implementation from shock therapy. A gradualist approach to reform is defined as 'a sequential implementation of minimum bangs':

> A simultaneous implementation of a minimum set of reforms that can be implemented independent of other reforms without failure. Conceptually, we can distinguish a gradualist from a piecemeal approach. The latter simply implements different parts of a reform package in many steps without regard to the possible 'strong interdependence' among them. In contrast, a gradualist approach

assigns different parts of a reform program into groups. Within each group, there is strong interdependence. Across groups, there is no strong interdependence. Reforms within the same group are better implemented simultaneously. For the type of massive and fundamental changes that have to take place in the former centrally planned economics, there are likely many blocks of reforms. Within each block there is 'strong interdependence', so that a minimum bang is the best strategy. (Wei, 1997, p. 1236)

Armored with this important distinction, the typical arguments for a gradualist approach to reform have been mostly couched in neoclassical theory-consistent terms and pointing to the typical reform objectives: a gradualist approach avoids excessive cost, especially for the government budget, avoids an excessive reduction in living standards at the start of a reform, it allows trial and error and mid-course adjustment, it helps a government to gain incremental credibility and finally, it may allow for 'divide and rule' tactics when compensation for the losers from reform is costly. Thus, seen from this perspective, the debate was more or less within the neoclassical paradigm.

But as time went by, the 'big bang' versus 'gradualism' debate came to be seen as a more general, and theoretical, competition between two different strands in economic theory, namely the orthodox neoclassical framework and a heterodox one. While the neoclassical side was a constant, some viewed the contender as an evolutionary theory, others as institutionalist one. For instance, Lo, following Murrell (1992) and Olson (1992) saw the difference as one between the evolutionary perspective and the neoclassical mainstream:

The difference involves both the spheres of focus and the underlying assumptions about real world economic development. In contrast to the neo-classical emphasis on the market as an allocative mechanism, the evolutionary approach focuses on its role in generating innovations. Instead of assuming substitutability of productive inputs, the evolutionary writers emphasize the system-specificity of economic information and the widespread existence of linkage effects, hence the need for forming specific institutions and expectations for the proper functioning of any economic system. This latter aspect, in particular, provides a forceful explanation for the economic depression of the Eastern bloc under big bang: i.e., the programmes, while destroying the old institutions and expectations, cannot bring into place new ones because the formation of the new is inevitably a time-consuming process. (Lo, 1997, p. 1236)

But as the supporters of the evolutionary approach themselves acknowledged, 'it is far from definitive that the evolutionary perspective must be a hostile rival to the central arguments of the big bang approach'. To confuse things even more, it should be noted that although usually gradualism may be supported by non-orthodox, evolutionary views, that is not a rule.

Among the non-orthodox economists, Austrian theorists inspired by the evolutionary thought of Hayek were among the most adamant pro-shock therapy supporters, so the line is not clear even in this respect. To make things even worse, even the evolutionary views come in many respects to be absorbed in the neoclassical framework, broadly defined, through evolutionary game theory. In other words, both shock therapy and gradualism could be and have been argued from both neoclassical and alternative perspectives. The idea of grouping on the one hand shock therapy and neoclassical economics and calling them neoliberal and on the other hand gradualism and non-orthodox views and calling them 'alternatives to neoliberalism' is not very fruitful and, in the context of this study, instead of illuminating the discussion, is confusing it. The discussion about paradigm change and the measure in which the transition experience affected economic thought should be kept, at least in a first stage of analysis, as much as is possible distinct from the strategy debate. In this respect, one thing is clear: the neoliberal revolution in Eastern Europe was led, was defined and consisted of mainly 'neoclassical synthesis' ideas. The genuine and most basic cleavage, the division of historical significance was between Marxism and Western neoclassical ideas, between pro-market views and its adversaries. That is enough to make clear that the nature of changes was more profound and important than the focus on the distinction 'gradualism vs. big bang' strategies implies.

To sum up, the debates on economic strategy although indicative of the dynamics of the 'neoliberal revolution in ideas' in Eastern Europe are not the best and most profound indicators of the magnitude and nature of the changes. The main elements of a political economy school of thought are a general theory, a normative perspective, and a corresponding strategy and policy technology (Solo, 1991, pp. 75–8). One should not confuse a debate on strategy and policy technology with the core elements. Those that take the policy and strategy position advocated by one side in such a debate as the core and epitome of the radical changes in Eastern Europe are obviously free to label things as they please. Yet this kind of labeling misses an essential part of the phenomenon and misleads the analysis. The 'neoliberal revolution' in Eastern Europe was an ampler and more profound phenomenon than that labeling implies.

On the other hand, as has already been mentioned, it may be the case that the debate on strategy may change the very foundation of the neoclassical paradigm and challenge the liberal views. In Eastern Europe, the debate was indeed important as it tested the boundaries and limits of the neoclassical paradigm. The question is: how far? Neoclassical economics received a clear impetus for change. Interestingly enough, it looks as if immediately after its triumph in Eastern Europe over Marxism, the neoclassical synthesis came to be challenged by the very economic and political realities it engendered. But in what measure the challenges and the pressure put by the transition process on the mainstream economic theory will lead to a new paradigm change and in what measure will that be in a 'market fundamentalist' direction, remains, as the last chapter of this book will try to show, an open question.

PART II

Frameworks for analyzing and understanding the spread of economic ideas

Coats and Colander start their 1989 book, *The Spread of Economic Ideas*, by asking the question why, given the importance of ideas, the process and institutions by which economic ideas are spread and changed were not studied. One of the main reasons was, they wrote, the fact that 'the concepts are vague, the institutions hazy and the process messy'. But then they added that the difficulty of the subject was not the only reason for its neglect. According to mainstream social sciences, the issue 'was a non-subject'. The standard theories and methodologies assume that the best ideas necessarily win out and therefore the sole significant issue was not how ideas spread, but rather how to disseminate 'sound' ideas. Yet during the last decade, this naive view lost its clout. Once new theoretical approaches have gained legitimacy, and once the positivist obsession with purist methodological prescriptions lost ground, the processes by which ideas spread has increasingly become a subject of interest as these new approaches allow for the key distinction between the 'best ideas' and those that 'win out'. And as Coats and Collander (1989, p. 2) put it, 'as soon as one accepts this distinction, the dissemination process becomes an integral part of the discipline's subject matter'.

This section of the book will further explore the issue of the spread of economic ideas in Eastern Europe by looking at a series of theories and conceptual frameworks that could illuminate in an analytically informed way the demise of Marxism and the rise of neoliberal political economy ideas after the fall of Communism. The challenge of framing the phenomenon for analytical purposes is obvious. Our understanding of its nature and dynamics is conditioned by the conceptual framework applied. Framing the case is the first and crucial step. What is the Eastern European case in question a case of? Is it a case of 'diffusion' or a case of 'market-place of ideas' at work? What way of framing it captures best its most relevant features? Is it a standard 'growth of knowledge', 'paradigm-shift' case, or does framing it as a conversion from one secular belief-system to another capture better the nature of the process? How far could a 'rational choice' theory go in setting light on the empirical reality? The section explores an array of theoretical and conceptual lenses as well as their potential to reveal key dimensions, processes and mechanisms at work in the phenomena investigated. It is hoped that this strategy will offer sharper insights and create the premises for building complementary interpretations, while articulating a basis for further, more elaborated and more focused analyses. Although the approach embraced recognizes the importance of producing general laws and theoretical propositions, the idea of putting together a 'general theory of the spread of neoliberal ideas' or the goal of extracting from the empirical reality 'the laws of diffusion of neoliberalism' are not objectives of interest for the current investigation. Instead, the goal is to look at the specific historical phenomenon and to identify in an analytically informed way some of its most significant dimensions, helping thus our understanding of it.

Summing up, this section is an attempt to chart a set of different frameworks, models and theories considered of potential relevance for our understanding of the case and by doing that, to implicitly test their usefulness in analyzing and interpreting the phenomenon in question. Some of these theories and frameworks prove to be more useful then others, some reveal their limits faster than others, while some offer only a false promise leading to obvious dead ends. Overall, as the result of this exercise of going through a catalog of successive theoretical lenses with the Eastern European case in mind, a deeper understanding of the case may emerge, while the unity of the logic of the line of reasoning moving from one theoretical lens to another may be able to bring a hidden unity in this seeming exercise in eclecticism.

4. Frameworks for analysis and interpretation: diffusion, marketplace of ideas and growth of knowledge

The rise of neoliberalism, broadly defined as a complex of policies, ideas and institutional changes, was discussed in the literature of the past decades from many perspectives. Usually the empirical illustration used in the attempt to explain the process was either the case of Western advanced democracies or the case of Latin America. The Eastern European front of the neoliberal revolution was usually taken for granted and the causes, drivers and stages of the process of ideas change were seen as evident and in no need of further explanation. That is the reason why when discussing the dynamics of neoliberal ideas in Eastern Europe one has to heavily rely on the Latin American literature as a reference point. Making a virtue out of necessity we consider that the discussion of the Latin America case could reveal significant insights on the causal mechanisms assumed to be at work, mechanisms that might also have been operating in Eastern Europe.

With that assumption in mind we hope that inventories of explanations for neoliberal reforms given by scholars of economic policy in Latin America like the list produced by Jack Knight (2002, p. 32) may offer at least some clues for the European case. Knight lists among the most prominent explanations: The pressure from international financial organizations that forced politicians to adopt neoliberal reforms (Stallings, 1992); The very fact that the diffusion of neoliberal economic ideas 'reached Latin America at an especially important time'– a moment that made it easy for the government officials to adopt them (Kahler, 1990); The state's efforts to 'further the interests of the capitalist class' (Veltmeyer et al. 1997); The severity of the economic crisis and the fact that political leaders had no choice but to adopt neoliberal reforms (Naim, 1993) as a last-resort electoral strategy to remain in office (Przeworski, 1991); a more or less clear understanding of the governments that, in order to enhance aggregate economic growth, 'the "shock" strategy was more efficient than more gradual approaches' (Morales and Sachs, 1989; Lipton and Sachs, 1990). Finally the spread of neoliberalism was explained as the result of political competition among domestic capitalists and various forms of demonstration effects associated with it (Conaghan and Malloy, 1994).

As Knight (2002, p. 32) noted, the diversity of these explanations is daunting: some treat the neoliberal programs as 'intentional reform efforts, highlighting the role of preferences in the determination of these changes', while others 'emphasize the importance of contextual factors, such as international pressure and competition', while yet others 'emphasize the importance of the diffusion of ideas, a factor that can influence both the preferences and beliefs of the relevant actors' (Knight, 2002, p. 32). The mere overview of this list shows that not all these explanations travel well from Latin America to Eastern Europe. But all these explanations imply at their turn more abstract theoretical frameworks (such has rational choice, institutionalism, structuralism, etc.) that may be relevant to the Eastern European case despite the differences between it and the Latin American developments.

By focusing mostly on the economic element of the neoliberal cluster of ideas, values and institutional and policy designs, one could narrow down the array of analytical avenues to those that are explicitly dealing with the dynamics of ideas, belief systems and mental models, i.e. with the core epistemic element given by economic theory. Even after this refocus, the range of competing and complementary types of frameworks available remains rather large. The reason is simple: the multiple levels and facets of the phenomenon in point. Each type of theoretical framework captures and emphasizes one or another of these dimensions. Some are explicitly used and defined in the literature; others are just implicit. In conjunction they convey the sense of a multifaceted perspective. A first typology contrasts explanations that focus on the domestic arena as the place of the key determinants of the changes of economic ideas as opposed to those that focus on the impact of external forces or the pressure of the international environment (Goldstein and Keohane, 1993; Campbell and Pedersen, 2001). At their turn, the approaches concentrating on external forces may be seen in two ways. On the one hand are those that look at the process in a mechanical way – as a specific deterministic dynamics set into motion by relative prices, international trade patterns or exogenous shocks that impose specific economic ideas as a response. On the other hand are those that see the process more or less as an interdependent phenomenon based on diffusion. Simmons, Dobbin and Garrett (2006) describe this interdependence as a 'dynamic process whereby decisions in Country A are systematically conditioned by prior choices made in Country B (sometimes mediated by international actor C)'. In this respect, 'diffusion can involve a broad range of mechanisms from the hyper-rational and materially-based to processes more common to cultural anthropology (social scripts and the like)'. The distinction between the two approaches is clear: 'diffusion, so defined, explicitly excludes independent decision-making' (Simmons et al. 2006).

Another set of approaches concentrates on economics as a scientific discipline and a necessary core element of the neoliberal belief system, the assumption being that a change at the core leads to a change of the entire system. One could introduce a distinction between two major schools of thought on the problem of scientific ideas selection. The first assumes that theories and their frameworks are ultimately reducible to singular or basic statements and that these basic statements are the ultimate building block of the scientific enterprise because they are the bases for deciding whether a theory is testable empirically. The second directs attention out from the propositional content of scientific theories to the social and historical dimension elements. Thus one could develop explanations analyzing the internal dynamics of the discipline, and explanations looking at factors external to the disciplinary boundary. To that, one may add the distinction between the 'internal history of science' and the 'external history of science' introduced by Kuhn's (1962) philosophy of science. The internal history of science involves those evolutions that can be reconstructed through the application of criteria of scientific rationality. The external dimension of science covers those episodes not subject to 'rational reconstruction'. Thus, social and political considerations could be legitimately invoked to account for developments pertaining to the external history of science that do not conform to the standards of scientific rationality.

Another relevant framework distinguishes between frameworks that focus on the 'material factors' as opposed to 'ideational factors' – such as the Marxist or class-based theories that relegate to a minor role the internal dynamics of ideas but look instead at the role of material forces, property structures and means of production as drivers of the 'ideological superstructure'. In a similar way, one could distinguish between rational factors determining the change in belief systems as opposed to non-rational factors and one need not look for the help of psychoanalytical theories to identify such factors (Glass and Johnson, 1989). Yet another typology may be built around key social theories. One could thus develop rational choice, neo-institutionalism explanatory accounts, may apply sociological institutionalism and discursive institutionalism, or may look at critical juncture explanations and path-dependent analysis (Campbell and Pedersen, 2001). Finally one may follow Simmons, Dobbin and Garrett (2006) in an even more focused taxonomy of the possible mechanisms that may be employed to explain the international diffusion of neoliberal ideas and practices. First are coercive processes explanations – explanations that involve 'material (and sometimes non-material) pressures exercised in a hierarchical manner' – by implication, from this perspective the changes in ideas and policy are 'less than fully voluntary'. The second type of explanations involve economic competition, i.e. pressures from markets that make capital and economic activity move between states and administrative units 'creating incentives for governments to respond to policy innovations elsewhere in kind'. Third are the learning models that look at policy innovation as a function of 'new information gleaned from observing and interpreting the effects of policy experiments by other governments'. Finally are social emulation processes that involve 'less rational and more subjective imitative processes based on a less rationally based logic of appropriateness' (Simmons et al. 2006).

These are just some of the ways in which the literature dealing with the spread of neoliberalism has tried to frame the explanations of this phenomenon. As Knight (2002) put it, by 'focusing on the different mechanisms that form the basis of the alternative approaches', we realize that 'the approaches that are usually described as conflicting are, in fact, often complementary'. For instance, the relationship between the rational choice approach, historical institutionalism and the epistemic communities approach is edifying in this respect. Rational choice models build on the relationship between the preferences and interests of social actors and the effects of social institutions and that 'highlights the importance of identifying the social mechanisms that affect the formation of individual and social beliefs, preferences and interest'. At its turn the epistemic community explanations (Haas, 1992) provide one solution to the problem of belief formation by emphasizing the role of governmental learning and how scientific knowledge and groups of experts can 'substantially affect the knowledge base of state policy decision making'. Finally, historical institutionalism (Pierson, 1994) is emphasizing the historical processes 'by which actors come to have their economic and political preferences'. To sum up, although the diversity of the approaches to the problem of the spread of neoliberal ideas is daunting, it is clear that this diversity seems to be mostly one of complementary approaches as opposed to one riddled with competitive tensions.

Even a cursory literature review such as the above one makes clear the fact that how ideas, interests and institutions interact and how ideas spread and change is not at all easy to capture in a single straightforward conceptual framework. The difficulties are increased by the great role played by contextual and historical factors and the intrinsic volatility of the phenomenon in question: 'the spread of economic ideas is messy; no single model will suffice' (Coats and Colander, 1989). There is no surprise therefore that each of these approaches has its own strengths and specific limits. Nevertheless, all of them, each in its own way, is important in illuminating the complex facets of the phenomenon. Each of them, even in their failure to explain, manages to help and guide our understanding. Taken as a whole, they demonstrate the need of an eclectic and flexible approach, an approach that is required by the very nature of the phenomenon studied. This section tries to incorporate that lesson.

THE 'MARKETPLACE OF IDEAS' CONSIDERED

The most intuitive and common explanation given to the victory of Western ideas over the Marxist-socialist one is framed in terms of the 'marketplace of ideas'. From its perspective there is no substantial difference between the market for goods and the market for ideas. Superior goods and superior ideas survive the test of the marketplace. New entrants are constantly trying to win as large a share of the marketplace as possible. Some of them fail, some of them succeed. In this view, the paradigm change in Eastern Europe is the final result of a century-long global competition between ideas. Finally, one set of ideas won in a 'natural' way. That was due to the fact that the 'consumers' of ideas, having a choice, decided that one set was better. People from Eastern Europe compared the choices and liked one over another. The triumph of the market was thus double: in the 'market of ideas' where ideas about market were triumphant and in society at large where the institutions of the market were restored.

The question is: is it meaningful to try to analyze the spread of ideas (and more precisely of political-economic ideas) in terms of a market model? Is it possible? Is there a social phenomenon that could be soundly described as an 'ideas market'? If the answer is yes, that could lead us to a very handy analytical framework because the explanation could be arranged around the market model and thus all relevant explanatory variables could be rounded up in a coherent way. In order to do that, all one has to do is to articulate the appropriate model and then apply it. In other words that means that one needs to determine if the market of ideas metaphor could be translated into a model. Then even if that translation is possible, it remains to be seen what kind of market is the market of political-economic ideas and even more precisely, what kind of market was the one in which the Marxist and Western economics competed. Market imperfections lead to specific institutional arrangements. It may be the case that those imperfections and arrangements could be more relevant for the explanation than the market process itself. Consequently, an inquiry of this type should start with an exploration of the limits of applicability of the very concept of a marketplace of ideas.[1]

The answer starts with the analysis of the 'information good' as an object of economic transactions. The first is very simple and straightforward.

From its perspective the 'marketplace of ideas' argument sounds like a restatement in a market-inspired language of the commonsensical robust notion that the attributes or qualities of the object diffused are the key factor in the object's rejection or retention. The Western economic ideas fared better on all or at least on a majority of the attributes. And this is the end of the story. Nothing like supply, demand, equilibrium, etc., concepts that we usually associate with the market model-inspired analysis, need to enter the picture. The second is more sophisticated and requires a rather extensive elaboration. The argument starts with the analysis of the 'information good' as an object of economic transactions. Focusing on properties that seem to cause difficulties for market transactions, one could determine in what measure social science products like 'paradigms' or schools of thought are amenable to a market model.

Three features are relevant for this analysis: First, information (ideas, knowledge) is an experience good: information must be experienced before its quality and content gets known. Second, it has the feature of returns to scale: information typically has a high fixed cost of production but a low marginal cost of reproduction. Finally, information goods are normally non-rival and non-excludable, in other words are public goods. All these features impose a specific institutional structure necessary to make them tradable. As Varian (2000) explains, the experience-good feature of information goods generates an entire array of social and economic practices that are used to overcome it. Previewing, reputation and reviews are among the most important and the fact that they have developed into a pivotal institution in the growth and diffusion of science and that they have survived in spite of all their critics is a testimony of the fact that those practices meet the critical function of evaluating the experience-good information. The returns to scale feature generates another set of problems and solutions. Information is costly to produce and cheap to reproduce. Moreover, the fixed costs incurred producing information goods are not just fixed but also 'sunk' costs. They must be 'incurred prior to production and more often than not are not recoverable'. Consequently, according to Varian (2000), the market structure for most information goods seems to be one of a non-competitive market. Finally, information goods regularly have public goods features (are non-rival and non-excludable). Non-rivalry denotes that 'consumption' of an idea or information by a person doesn't diminish the 'amount' available to other people. Non-excludability denotes that one person cannot exclude another person from 'consuming' an idea or information. Non-rivalry is an inherent property of the information good. On the other hand excludability depends, in large measure, on the institutional arrangements and the legal system (Varian, 2000). In many cases these arrangements are rather complicated, increasing even further the complexity of the institutional structure encapsulating the trade and circulation of information and ideas.

The translation of the 'market for ideas' metaphor in a corresponding model is even more complicated by the existence of the so-called 'network externalities'. Network externalities emerge when the demand for a product depends in part on the number of existing users. Selection of an idea may depend mainly on a network of people using it and less on the market competitions. The more users there are, the better for the selection or diffusion of a technology or good. The implication of all of the above for the notion of marketplace of ideas was very well pointed up by Oomes (1998). 'If this metaphor is to be more than a metaphor', the market for ideas 'should be thought of, first of all, as a market for scientific articles, and secondly, as being governed by a citation mechanism'. That is to say that

> . . . just as a price mechanism is needed in commodity markets to induce firms to supply those commodities that they expect consumers to be willing to buy, a citation mechanism is needed in science to induce scientists to supply those articles that they expect other scientists to be willing to cite. This, however, implies the existence of network externalities in science: the benefits associated with belonging to a network of scientists who share the same paradigm increase with the size of that network, because it increases the chance of being published and being cited. (Oomes, 1998, pp. 2–3)

Exploring the implications and consequences of network externalities, Oomes developed several formal models in which the paradigm choice of scientists was affected not only by the search for truth but also to a certain extent by their concern with obtaining 'social status' (defined in terms of publications, citations etc.). His conclusion was that in the absence of social status considerations 'the distribution of scientific articles is shown to converge to "truth", in the sense that observationally equivalent paradigms are given equal weight'. Nevertheless, when social status plays a role 'the probability that a scientist adopts a given paradigm increases with the average support for this paradigm by other scientists'. The consequence is that 'under certain conditions these network externalities can speed up scientific progress, they also can lead a discipline to become locked into a suboptimal paradigm, thus implying a market failure' (Oomes, 1998, pp. 2–3). That is to say that the problem of the 'market for ideas' is much more complicated than one may have initially expected. The next chapter will further elaborate some of these institutional aspects. For now it is important to note that in this view, the 'marketplace of ideas', if it exists, is functioning on different parameters from those defined by the standard model.

To sum up, the institutional architecture around the information goods transfer of what may be called the 'marketplace for ideas' is very complex.

The problems and their institutional implications are even more complicated in the case of a specific category of ideas, the social sciences, schools of thought or the political economy belief systems that this book is interested in. It seems that any conceptual elaboration of the market metaphor for ideas in general and even more, for social scientific ideas in particular, leads sooner or later either to the acceptance of a persistent market failure situation or to the allocation of a rather marginal role for the market model in the general scheme of things. As Wible aptly put it:

> The significance of the marketplace of ideas is that it is tantamount to an admission of the irrelevance of the commercial marketplace to science. The marketplace of ideas is a metaphor which simultaneously denies the relevance of commercial markets and thereby implicitly asserts the noncommercial market character of the organizational structures of central importance to science. The metaphor 'marketplace of ideas' is an institutionally nonspecific way to generically assert the noncommercial, self-regulative character of science. (Wible, 1994, p. 181)

Thus the problem is the very applicability of the market theories. That applicability to the problem of the political and economic ideas or, even more precisely, to the social science products is riddled with challenges. The magnitude of the deviations from the simple competitive markets used as a foil by the standard economics is evident. But setting thus aside the question of whether the East–West dynamics of ideas is properly described as a 'market competition', the basic problem is the limited measure in which the market model in itself is applicable to a specific type of information/ideas – the social science products or even more precisely to the political and economic ideas.

In these circumstances, it is mandatory to explore other ways to model and analyze the processes related to the dynamics of scientific and political economy. Although invoking the marketplace of ideas has been a tempting and handy way of explaining the change of ideas in the Soviet space, looking at the Eastern European developments through the lenses of the 'marketplace of ideas' model doesn't seem to have a very powerful potential besides the compelling metaphor conveyed by the notion itself. That is why even when addressing the problem in explicit market terms, authors like J. Wagener use supply and demand to structure the analysis but never go as far as to claim that a real market process was at work in the Eastern European ideas change process (Wagener in Kaase, Sparschuh and Weinninger, 2002). It seems that one may retain the metaphor for its power to convey the meaning of change but one needs to look for alternative ways of building explanatory frameworks. The simple but robust diffusion theory offers a promising alternative.

THE DIFFUSION THEORY FRAMEWORK AND ITS LIMITS

Diffusion research investigates the factors determining the adoption of a specific item (be it object or idea) among members of a particular adopter group (Rogers, 1995, 5).[2] There is no clear-cut, unified and comprehensive theory of diffusion. Instead, there are a large number of concepts and theories, from a wide variety of disciplines, each focusing on a different element of the innovation–diffusion process such as: the innovation itself, communication or transmission channels, time, and the nature of the social system into which the innovation is being introduced (Rogers, 1995). These concepts and theories merge to create a meta-theory or theoretical framework for the study of diffusion processes. The framework has as a pivot the 'innovation decision process theory' and focuses on the distinct stages of the diffusion process: knowledge (exposure to the existence of the item and understanding of its functions); persuasion (the forming of a favorable attitude to it); decision (commitment to its adoption); implementation (putting it to use); and confirmation (reinforcement based on positive outcomes from it) (Rogers, 1995).[3] Important roles in the diffusion process include: opinion leaders (who have relatively frequent informal influence over the behavior of others); change agents (who positively influence innovation decisions, by mediating between the change agency and the relevant social system); change aides (who complement the change agent, by having more intensive contacts with the targets, and who have less competence credibility but more safety or trustworthiness credibility). Innovation decisions may be optional (the person or organization has a real opportunity to adopt or reject the idea), collective (the decision is reached by consensus among the members of a system), or authority-based (the decision is imposed by another person or organization which possesses requisite power, status or technical expertise). Another important building block of diffusion theory research is the 'rate of adoption' theory. From this perspective, an innovation goes through a period of slow, gradual growth before going through a period of rapid growth. Following the period of rapid growth, the innovation's rate of adoption will gradually stabilize and eventually decline (Rogers, 1995).

As it becomes clear even after a cursory overview, diffusion theory offers a relatively viable descriptive framework although there may be doubts about its ability to reveal the underlying mechanisms and forces of diffusion and about the extent to which it can generate robust explanatory frameworks. Nonetheless, it should be added that irrespective of the inherent limits (whether a result of the object studied or of the theoretical apparatus itself) there are substantial gains to be obtained from the application of the diffusion framework to the case of the spread of economic ideas and the demise of the Marxist paradigm in Eastern Europe. A brief review of the case in the light of some elements of that framework would illustrate that point.

In terms of the characteristics of the object of diffusion, the ideas diffused and the ideas discontinued or rejected, it is noteworthy that the two (neoclassical and Marxist) had, at least initially, the same epistemic credibility, as they were recognized as equal-footing competing paradigms. Their success or lack of success was not affected by any initial asymmetry of status. However in time one could notice an increasing asymmetry favorable to Western ideas based on their increasing scientific legitimacy. Time is undeniably an important variable in diffusion research but also a very problematic one. Even when one deals with less volatile diffusion items than 'ideas' are, the literature makes clear that there is 'no clear cut diffusion across a population of one isolated element at a time but instead a gradual erosion and accumulation that takes place within a framework of continued social and technological change' (Hagerstrand, 1988, p. 228).[4] Despite these difficulties one can identify several stages in the diffusion of Western ideas to Eastern Europe: after a period of aggressive Stalinism there followed an incipient period during which the influence of Western thought was mostly indirectly trickling in while strongly resisted or resented by the authorities; a period of rapid transformation at the end of the 1980s and beginning of the 1990s, defined by a visible radical change in economic discourse, publications, research and teaching; and finally there was a rapid and deep process of institutional reform and development leading to the complete institutionalization of the of the new, Western paradigm. However, these three stages were not similar in all countries and there were substantial differences in lengths, starting moments, intensity and rhythm of change. Moreover, in several countries (the Baltics) the second stage started only in the mid-1990s. It is also noteworthy that the legacy of the past, the strength of the repressive measures of the regime and the vigour of the revolts or reform movements were very powerful forces determining the timetable of the ideas change.

As regarding the channels of diffusion, the publications had a significant role even before 1989 although the national production was heavily Marxist. However, paying lip service to Marxism–Leninism and to the Party documents was increasingly a routine that redeemed the innovative or subversive ideas introduced for publication through the back door. As years went by, the practice to pay a routine tribute to Marx, Engels, Lenin and to the latest documents of the Communist Party was more evident in the Balkan and Baltic states in comparison to Poland, Hungary and, in a lesser measure, Czechoslovakia. In a similar way the quantity of 'subversive content' grew. The access to foreign literature was restricted, with a very limited number of Western economic journals 'in discontinued series, with missing volumes' available in libraries. However, again the Central European economists were somewhat better in this respect than their counterparts. In a similar way, translations were limited: more in Poland and Hungary and very few in Romania and the Baltics. Not only regular publications but also paradigmatic works were not translated. For instance, the Paul Samuelson textbook was translated even in the 1960s in Poland while it was never translated into Romanian. Overall translations were not the major channel of ideas diffusion that they were supposed to be. Only after 1989 did translations regain their function. In countries like Romania and Bulgaria, the number of books translated expanded, rising by an estimated factor of ten.

Many economists were involved in one way or another in the so-called 'critique of bourgeois economic theory' and it is interesting to note that in many cases the 'critique of bourgeois economic theory' joined by the 'critique of economics in bourgeois period' were used by many to keep updated with the Western developments or keep alive the traditions of the pre-war economic thought. In many cases, the pre-Second World War economics schools were rather vibrant and they left their imprint on the postwar situation. In this context, of critical importance was the role that the pre-communist tradition of economics, or better put, the memory of that tradition, had in defining the intellectual climate for the Marxist paradigm and as a facilitating condition for the diffusion of Western ideas.

After 1989, the situation changed radically and all barriers existent in the channels ensuring the flow of ideas were released. In addition to the increase in the volume of the flows, the number of channels multiplied and the old network and institutions were integrated in the powerful machine created by Western fundraising. With the important financial support from Western institutions and the Western epistemic community, the universities were taken over and became centers of neoclassical ideas. A network of think tanks, some of them embedded very well in transnational associations, developed and furthered the neoclassical agenda. Very soon the entire institutional structure came under the influence of the neoclassically inclined economists who were very active diffusion agents even if many of them did not have a sound mastery of the paradigm. That increased exponentially the impact of the ideas not only in the epistemic community but also in the policy-making circle. Media were also affected by this change. Rarely, if ever, before 1989 was mass media a channel of diffusion of Western economics ideas. However, after 1989 it has started to play an important role. The role was not direct but one of disseminating the policy dimensions of the neoclassical agenda and couching it in standard mainstream terms. That made media economic analysis a source of support of the paradigm change.

In terms of institutional channels universities were, as expected, major diffusion nodes in the institutional network of channels of diffusion. However, their role in accelerating or slowing the change was differentiated not only from country to country but also from university to university. Although once hit by the Western and international institutions' wave of adjustment funds, all were factors of promoting the agenda of change. It is noteworthy that in Balkan and Baltic states the universities were less dynamic and even after 1989 were an impediment to radical change in the epistemic community. However in the conceptual map of the diffusion of economic ideas in Eastern Europe, universities are major nodes both before and after 1989. That is not true of the think tanks. Think tanks were almost non-existent before 1989 and they exploded after that, becoming sometimes a challenge to the more conservative academic institutions. When it comes to the direct channels of international institutional contacts, the difference before and after 1989 is radical in the sense that they were restricted and monitored before and encouraged and sponsored after. The strong institutionalization of ties through cooperation and exchange programs became a widespread phenomenon especially under various EU programs. Interpersonal channels and contacts were closely following the institutional ones after 1989. They stepped up and created the cement of a truly international network integrating many Eastern European scholars. However, the number of participants varied. While in countries like Romania, for instance, the number has been very limited, the economists from Poland, Hungary and the Czech Republic are very well embedded in the international epistemic community.

As regarding adopter categories, the existence of very pre-eminent opinion leaders and change agents in some countries and their absence in others is noteworthy, Poland, the Czech Republic and Hungary being again the ones benefiting from the existence of such significant social actors. Their role was extremely important and any account of the way the diffusion took place should take them into account because their influence went well beyond national borders. However, the success of the neoclassical paradigm would not have been possible irrespective of the stature of its promoters had the paradigm in itself not had some intrinsic winning features.[5] One can say that the adoption process of the Western economic ideas was clearly shaped by the fact that several perceived attributes clearly played in favor of the neoclassical synthesis. First was the relative advantage given by the fact that it was perceived to be better than Marxism both in epistemological and in policy making terms. Diffusion scholars have found relative advantage to be a very accurate predictor of an innovation's rate of adoption (Rogers, 1995). Relative advantage indicates the benefits and the costs resulting from adoption of an innovation. The components of relative advantage include the degree of profitability, low initial cost, a decrease in discomfort, social prestige, the savings in time and effort and the immediacy of the reward (Rogers, 1995). If before 1989 the diffusion took place against the relative advantage after 1989, on almost all these dimensions, the Western economic ideas seems to have fared much better than Marxism because all costs were overshadowed by the fact that once the language if not the essence of neoclassicism was absorbed, the adapters were able to integrate rapidly in the international circuit, with all benefits, material and non-material emerging from that. Second was compatibility, a relative consistency with the values and needs of the social category that made the economics epistemic community. Finally, was the trialability (the degree to which it can be experimented with on a limited basis: the 'economic way of thinking' advocated by the Western approach being a very powerful analytical tool applicable to all sorts of daily situations.

All these features contributed not only to the diffusion and retention of the Western ideas but also to a very high rate of adoption. The limited statistics available generate a certain degree of ambiguity in any quantitative estimations. However, it is safe to say that the adoption stepped up immediately after 1989 and then came to stabilize at the end of the decade. However, there were different comparative rates of adoption in East European countries and a hypothesis on the correlations between pre-war traditions, distance from normative center, pre-1989 diffusion, elite change and the rate of adoption might work in terms of explaining the differentials.

While discussing the case from a diffusion process perspective the effects of incentives should not be forgotten. That is mandatory because some voices have suggested that the remarkable raise of Western ideas in the East may be the result of mainly the financial resources employed for that goal by the West. That is indeed a legitimate point. In addition to the intrinsic winning features of the Western ideas, many change agencies awarded clear incentives or subsidies to Eastern economists to speed up the rate of adoption. The main function of an incentive for adopters is to increase the degree of relative advantage of the new idea. Incentives are direct or indirect payments. In this context it is interesting to note the adopter versus diffuser incentives problem. Incentives may be paid either directly to an adopter, or to another individual to persuade an adopter. The adopter incentives increased the relative advantage of Western ideas, and diffuser incentives increased their observability. In the case of neoclassical diffusion in Eastern Europe the system worked in both ways but with an emphasis on diffuser. There is also a noteworthy trade-off resulting from the use of incentives by the West. Although incentives increase the rate of adoption, the quality of such adoption may be relatively low. If individuals adopt ideas partly in order to obtain an incentive, there is relatively less reason to go beyond a mere symbolic and superficial adoption. That is even truer when one is discussing the East European case. That concern was voiced by many authors dealing with the issue of paradigm change in Eastern Europe when they complained about the superficiality of adoption and questioned the degree of understanding of and commitment to the new paradigm. To sum up, the incentives offered affected not so much the direction but the rate of adoption. Moreover they did that at a cost.

Finally, two elements of relevance that deserve to be mentioned are the centralization (decentralization) of the diffusion systems and the creation of new networks of diffusion. In a centralized system, an innovation originates from some expert source that diffuses it to potential adopters. That is a 'center-periphery model' because the innovation originates from a centralized source and then the individuals adopt it as passive accepters. In decentralized diffusion systems, the innovation originates from different sources and then diffuses via horizontal networks. In such diffusion systems, adopters make many decisions and may serve as their own change agents. In the case of the spread of Western economic ideas in Eastern Europe, the diffusion took place in a centralized way. At the top were several Western centers of diffusion, then the universities, opinion leaders, or top experts, and from there to the rest of the Eastern European epistemic community via think tanks, personal and institutional interactions, publications, etc. One of the most important decisions in diffusion processes is whether to create a new network of diffusion agencies or to utilize an already existing one. The spread of economic ideas in Eastern Europe was facilitated because the existing distribution network created by the old regime and consisting of a series of academic centers linked together in national systems was actually used in a spontaneous way by the diffusers. Thus by utilizing the existing network, the new paradigm had coverage over the range of all crucial locations included in the network. However, new institutional elements were injected at strategic points by the pro-Western diffusers in the existing network of diffusion channels. That was basically done through the new think tanks that were very effectively used to step up and bolster the process.

In summary, even before 1989, Marxism was no longer a viable option for the epistemic communities in Eastern Europe. However, there was no sign of an alternative paradigm close to being generally adopted and no indication in the epistemic community that it was anywhere close to a takeover by another paradigm. It was mainly the intellectual rottenness and vacuity of Marxism that explains the extraordinarily efficient way in which the Western epistemic communities promoted neoclassical and neoliberal ideas through the very networks of the Marxists after 1989. Other factors involving the incentives and the existing epistemic networks in place may add up to explain how neoclassical economics become the reigning paradigm there after 1989, in less than one decade. As becomes clearer even after this brief overview, diffusion theory offers a viable descriptive framework. Yet, although it enlightens important factors related to the studied phenomenon it has clear limits. It provides an excellent device for the heuristics of the relevant facts and elements of the process studied but for those wanting an analytical big picture is less effective in illuminating at a deeper level the processes through which those facts, factors and elements interconnect. For that, it needs additional theoretical resources, from complementary perspectives. Minute investigations at the level of deeper underlying mechanisms and forces of diffusion and change seem to be required. Also given the diversity of cases, paths and processes involved, it is necessary to be more specific about the mechanisms that lead to the spread, adoption and acceptance of one set of ideas and the decay, rejection and demise of the other in each separate case. Finally, the analytical contribution of large overarching conceptual frameworks approaching the phenomenon at the macro-level seems to be necessary.

The fact is that when dealing with belief systems such as a political economy paradigm, the challenges of their study are not only a function of the limits of diffusion theory but also of the case itself. Or more exactly, of the key components that the case consists of: Belief systems as diffusion objects raise special operational challenges. Being items with 'only a software component' they have a very low degree of observability; their spread, their shape and their margins are difficult to trace (Rogers, 1995, p. 13). In this respect, an inquiry on paradigms couldn't be a mere replication or imitation of a standard approach but an attempt to extend it to an area not much explored and very unlikely to be amenable to the standard approach. Another problem is the temporal-historical nature of the process. The impossibility to trace step-by-step the process through time via longitudinal surveys is a general problem with diffusion studies that focus on long run processes such as our case that covers several decades. Finally, the international magnitude of the process adds a new dimension of complexity to the project. Evolutions in nine European countries imply the existence of different cultures, traditions and institutions and different adjustment processes of and to the ideas in point. This no doubt makes the task exponentially more difficult.

But the most fundamental challenge is the result of the fact that one is dealing with a very special and complex kind of 'diffusion object': ideas about social order. Just drawing nodes and counting units on a map to build diffusion curves is not enough to understand the phenomenon in question.

We are dealing after all with mental models, paradigms, worldviews. They are complex and intellectually sophisticated clusters of concepts, arguments and visions. As such, their study always needs a distinctive focus on the conceptual universe constructed by the epistemic community. Approaches are needed from perspectives that penetrate beyond the surface and that open up the black box of the shared conceptual universe that ultimately defines and circumscribes any epistemic community and school of thought. It is important to keep in mind that ultimately the unity of the social and institutional processes associated with an epistemic community and its dynamics comes from the conceptual and argumentative universe its members share. To sum up, the tracking and study of the specific diffusion processes, agents and networks illuminated by the diffusion theory framework is a promising research direction. Even as superficial an application of the framework as the one sketched above puts us in the position to get a glimpse of the pattern emerging and the kind of insights one could get out of that. However one needs to approach the topic at different levels and focus at more aggregate levels through which the phenomenon is captured in broader and more coherent and unitary ways. To understand the deeper mechanisms and processes, one needs to incorporate the insights given by diffusion theory but also to go beyond it.

PARADIGMS AND BELIEF SYSTEMS

The philosophy of science literature trying to answer the question of why scientific ideas change and how scientific progress takes place comes next to the 'marketplace of ideas' metaphor and 'diffusion theory' as one of the most intuitively appealing approaches to the problem of the rise of neoliberalism in Eastern Europe. Two major schools of thought define this so-called 'growth of knowledge' literature, each supporting a different view on the problem of scientific ideas selection. The first looks at ideas as separated units and focuses on the verification/falsification of their propositional content. The second looks at ideas as clusters and paradigms – systems that have their own endogenous dynamics involving not just the adjustment to the empirical reality but also a series of contextual and social factors. Together these two schools offer two related yet different frameworks for interpretation of the Eastern European spread and change of economic ideas.

From the perspective of the first school, a theory or a hypothesis is tentatively accepted as true until it is shown to be false. One needs to refute it empirically, that is to test it by experience. Science and schools of thought progress by trial and error, conjecture, and refutations where imaginative and bold conjectures are controlled by systematic tests (Popper, 1963). As science progresses, so theories should become increasingly falsifiable and consequently have more content and be more informative. The family of verificationist–falsificationist approaches is almost exclusively focused on the propositional content. As such, due to its relative simplicity, it is a very tempting alternative. If one takes that route, the 'internal history' of a scientific discipline or school of thought (and for that matter the progress from Marxism to neoclassical economics) should be self-explanatory. No reference to extra-scientific social or political factors is required to explain why the internal history of science (in this case economics) developed as it did. Marxism retired and neoclassical economics gained ground because that was written in the logic of scientific progress.

Could the replacement of Marxism in Eastern Europe by neoclassical economics be explained this way? Is the verificationist–falsificationist 'adjustment to the scientific facts' the answer? In a sense one is tempted to say that such a process indeed took place in the Eastern European case. Yet on a deeper level, this is more of a metaphorical interpretation than a realistic description. Indeed ideas that were deficient on scientific standards were rejected while other ideas, which had behind them the scientific legitimacy of an international epistemic community, were adopted. But does that mean that the process of interplay between theories and empirical reality described by the literature was really at work in this instance? The 'atomist' view of scientific dynamics in which theories and their frameworks are ultimately reducible to singular or basic statements just to be falsified, has a very limited explanatory potential for the case in point. In the case of Eastern Europe, if a 'falsification' happened, that was primarily outside the scientific community and more at the level of practical policy consequences than at the level of theory testing.

Moreover, what is the meaning of 'falsification' and 'adjusting to facts' when one comes to discuss the Marxist school of thought? Is there any evidence of a gradual transmutation, proposition by proposition, conjecture by conjecture, of Marxism into neoclassical economics? Any 'internal history of science' based on a falsificationist, 'atomist' view of scientific dynamics would be hard-pressed to develop an adequate empirical-data-based analytical narrative fit to this specific case. To track the changes in political economy ideas and mental models to bits and pieces of theory falsified through scientific methods is far from being encouraged by the existing evidence of the Eastern European process.

Thus we are left with the second approach that points to a broader range of factors and processes and the question of if it is a better fit with the existing evidence. The work of Kuhn and Lakatos directed attention out from the propositional content of scientific theories to the broader social and historical dimension of the change process. The dynamics of scientific ideas takes place, according to this second school, differently in function of the state of the 'paradigm' (Kuhn, 1962, pp. 43, 52, 66).[6] In *The Structure of Scientific Revolutions* (1962), Kuhn defines 'paradigm' as a set of beliefs (Kuhn, 1962, pp. 4, 2, 17), a way of seeing (Kuhn, 1962, pp. 117–21), an organizing principle governing perception (Kuhn, 1962, p. 120), an entire theoretical worldview, a series of laws, a methodological recipe and a set of fundamental values (Kuhn, 1962). Paradigm change process has a different logic from the hypothesis testing and the play of conjectures and refutations of the verificationist–falsificationist approach. These authors point out that the history of science exemplified few or no decisions in accordance the confirmationism or falsificationism standards. They could be viable as normative standards but not as explanations for the real historical dynamics of ideas. Therefore one should not lose the perspective by looking at small elements, bits and pieces of theory and their change. Instead, the solution is to renounce the micro-level as the source of the basic unit, and thus rely on a larger unit, what was called 'the paradigm' (Kuhn, 1962, pp. 10–11). During normal science, the paradigm is neither questioned nor seriously tested. But once anomalies and flagrant contradictions and puzzles accumulate, the epistemic community enters into crisis, which pushes the paradigm into a revolutionary phase during which its basic principles and its contenders are questioned and the role of factors other than the pure logic of scientific rationality are the drivers. The routine puzzle or problem-solving ceases until a new paradigm establishes dominance.

This approach opens up several possible interpretations of the East European change of economic ideas, emphasizing sociological and socio-psychological processes that diverge in many respects from the standard logic of the scientific rationality path.[7] Although not precluding reason, this approach departs clearly from the rationality implicit in the verificationist–falsificationist approach. Indeed, as will be extensively discussed in the next chapter, one could go further: Using as a source of inspiration Kuhn's suggestions, one may claim that the paradigm change is essentially achieved through persuasion and conversion and that in many respects it is not reasonable but a matter of intuition. This indeed is a very challenging proposition. However, for now one need not go so far. The point is that the case of the Eastern European paradigm shift in political economy is a hard case for the theories in the 'growth of knowledge' tradition and those that want to use them to give an account of the ways things evolved in Eastern Europe. Yet, all in all, the paradigm shift perspective seems to have got a very interesting illustration with this case. The empirical constraints pressed the Marxist system either to change and to get in line with observed facts or to reinterpret the facts to fit them into the system. Unable to go beyond its self-imposed ideological shackles, Marxism in Eastern Europe tried to work in the latter direction. As a result, it produced contradictions, anomalies and a distortion of reality that had the opposite effect and that played a crucial role in undermining the entire paradigm. It is clear that the encounter with facts may have led the Eastern European economists in many directions. However, it is clear that while it led them to dismissal of Marxism, no obvious alternative emerged based purely or mainly on the falsificationist procedures. Although neoclassical ideas trickled in, starting in the 1960s, no radical change took place until the 1989 transformation. Thus, the epistemic choice process was not a simple choice between this and that tested hypothesis but a more complicated process involving competing interpretations, the contemplation of the relations between theories and their practical implications and also a very important social, political and economic factor. Post factum we are inclined to believe that the replacement of Marxism with neoclassical ideas was inevitable. Yet neither the internal or the external approaches to this episode of the history of social sciences justify this belief of ours.

Following the logic of this argument to its conclusions raises some problems. Kuhn goes as far as to suggest that such paradigm transitions occur not through deliberation and interpretation but rather through a Gestalt switch characterized by relatively sudden intuitive convictions, a sort of religious conversion (Kuhn 1962, p. 123). The problem is that, followed to its final implications, this view leaves out any process logic other than that of context, accident and path dependency. The hypothetical implication for the analysis of the East European situation is that there was no overall, general logic in the process. The evolutions could be traced back to the effects of a series of cumulated decisions or path-dependent developments. And therefore there are very few if any analytical or explanatory avenues left once that statement is made and the specific diffusion and change channels are traced. This is definitely not an entirely satisfying avenue for those that want to find more powerful patterns in social order. Additional perspectives, still rooted in the Kuhnian tradition but amenable to be applied to the political economy ideas changes in Eastern Europe, are available. Before making further steps in their direction, a brief summing-up is in order.

One takes out of this discussion a sense of the salience of several important issues: First that one may get an enhanced understanding of the spread of economic ideas if one looks more at systems of ideas than isolated propositions. The ideas studied are in fact *entire systems* which are not necessarily consisting of pure justified true beliefs or beliefs on their way to justification through the scientific method. Second, the dynamics of these systems of beliefs is determined not only by internal factors but also by external ones.[8]

An enhanced perspective on the problem of ideas spread and change emerges thus slowly, a perspective that is rooted but goes beyond the more popular and intuitive approaches. The basic unit of analysis is clearly defined as a 'system of ideas'. The propositions of such a system are subject to two forms of constraint: rational constraints (pertaining to the internal organization of the system) and empirical constraints (pertaining to the system's relation to observed facts) (Richter, 1972, p. 47). The existence of rational and empirical constraints is a general feature of any belief system. Although these constraints are salient in the case of science, they are present in various degrees in any such system. Rational constraints determine its dynamics in the direction of maintaining the internal coherence, logical consistency and mutual reinforcement of its propositions. On the other hand, the empirical constraints determine its dynamics in the direction of maintaining the factual plausibility–compatibility with the perceived or accepted facts and the capacity to explain them. The rational constraints may demand internal changes in the system (eliminating some propositions or elements of it) or may involve the differentiation of the system into competing variants. The empirical constraints may involve 'the changing of the system to bring it in line with the observed facts' but also may lead to 'reinterpreting the facts to fit to the system'. Empirical and rational constraints may emerge naturally through long-term evolutionary processes, or artificially through deliberate arrangements or institutional construction by particular individuals (Richter, 1972, p. 47).

At the same time, the story of how a belief comes to be accepted by the community, and thus to become a 'mental model' or 'cultural belief system', is more complicated than the story of triumph of the intrinsic truth of the propositions out of which the system is made of an ongoing adjustment to logical and rational constraints followed by a triumphant march to dominance through markets and networks. In the past, many genuine scientific systems were displaced or rejected. In other words, just as most cultural knowledge systems are not scientific, so many scientific systems are not cultural in the sense that because they are not accepted by communities or societies, they are not 'cultural knowledge systems' (Richter, 1972, pp. 46–8). From that emerges a legitimate question: The problem is not only what makes a cultural knowledge system scientific but also what makes a scientific belief system culturally acceptable, within the framework of the society.

These recalibrations of the problem have important corollaries. For instance one of the key points is that interpretation matters. The logical constraints and the empirical constraints may involve changing a system to bring it in line with its own internal structure or with the observed facts. But equally valid, the process of change may involve reinterpreting the facts to fit them into the system to cultural contexts using cultural symbols, metaphors and cognitive frameworks (Richter, 1972, p. 45). Therefore, *interpretation* and all the psychological and cultural factors determining it seems crucial. To sum up, the encounter with the facts may lead the beliefs about economic order in many directions, while the intellectual forces that are driving the change are many. And there is no doubt that for the political economy belief systems, the reinterpretation of facts is as important as the adjustment to facts. At the pure intellectual level, not only falsification or verification but also interpretation could be a major mechanism in the process. Once liberated from the shackles of standard epistemological views, with their obsession with the adjustment to the facts of atomized propositions, entire new horizons are opened up.

CONCLUSIONS

Where does this discussion does lead us in our investigation of the Eastern European dynamics of ideas? The key point is that the popular, 'common sense' frameworks almost intuitively applied to the case as guides to our understanding, have significant limitations. Yet, all share a core element, a very simple component that has a strong appeal and a non-negligible explanatory power: be it labeled 'adjustment to facts', 'falsification/ verification', 'incentives' and 'perceived attributes', 'exchange' and 'market adaptation', or even 'paradigm shift', all these refer back to an ultimate element of calculation or adaptive rationality that as a result of the interplay with the empirical reality generates change in the nature and spread of ideas or ideas systems. In some sense, one gets the impression that one is confronted with varieties of the same, very simple theme. However this simple theme is slippery and hard to capture in one concept.

At the same time, the more one looks at the case through diverse theoretical lenses, the more one has the feeling that above this core element grows a very complex architecture in which interpretation, norms and values, accidents, social and economic factors play an important role in shaping the rhythm and the direction of ideas change. Suddenly, once this 'systemic' dimension is added, things become less unambiguous and more puzzling. Simple explanations, initially apparently so powerful, seem all of a sudden insufficient. Factors that looked to be such clear and straightforward drivers of the spread and change of ideas are obscured, and now new and more difficult to grasp factors creep into center stage. Confronted with all that, one may opt for either of two approaches. One may go with the simpler version: 'Marxism was a bad (incorrect, inefficient, false, etc.) idea. It was rational to have it discarded and replaced with better ideas. And that is what happened in Eastern Europe.' On the other hand, one also may take the more complex path. Unpacking the complex architecture of meanings, interpretations, accidents, circumstantial rationalities and functions may reveal facets and processes that illuminate in profound ways the phenomenon. Some may think that one should limit oneself to the simple path. And they may be right. For some purposes that may be sufficient. Yet, in a study like this book, one is bound to at least explore some of the alternatives that emphasize more complex views and facets of the phenomenon of interest.

NOTES

1. The idea of a marketplace for ideas could be traced back to and bears the imprint of John Milton's *Areopagitica* (Wible, 1998, p. 137). Milton supported the view that truth will result from a free and open encounter of opposing ideas and that authorities' intervention in the form of censorship or other regulations will lead to the protection of error and falsehood. Its contemporary contours owe as much to its liberal restatement by Ronald Coase and the Austrian Economics as to the new emerging field of economics of information. Coase's article, 'The market for goods and the market for ideas' (1995) challenges the distinction between the market for goods and the market for ideas. 'There is no fundamental difference between these two markets and in deciding on public policy with regard to them we need to take into account the same considerations' (Coase, 1973, p. 389). Coase's article is typical for the standard use of the 'marketplace for ideas' notion. In other words, it is policy-oriented and the notion of an ideas market is not further defined or modeled. The interest of the Austrian School of economics derived and materialized especially from its interest in the problem of the 'uses of knowledge in society' (Hayek, 1974; Machlup, 1962). But their conclusions regarding its applicability were moving more in the direction of a theory of self-governing processes than in the direction of the standard view of the market. However, all these do not mean that the metaphor couldn't be conceptualized. The neoclassical-economics-inspired economics of information is a case in point.
2. Some authors restrict the term diffusion to the spontaneous, unplanned spread of new ideas, and use the concept of 'dissemination' for diffusion that is directed and managed (Rogers, 1995, p. 7). The specific difference from other social communication or transmission processes is the newness of the item transmitted. 'It matters little so far as human behavior is concerned whether or not an idea is objectively new as measured by the lapse of time since its first use or discovery. The perceived newness of the idea for the individual determines his or her reaction to it' (Rogers, 1995, p. 11).
3. The 'individual innovativeness theory' (Rogers, 1995) maintains that individuals who are predisposed to being innovative will adopt an innovation earlier than those who are less predisposed. This theory illustrates its point by a bell-shaped distribution of individual innovativeness. Also, it estimates the percentage of potential adapters falling into each category. Innovators are the risk takers and pioneers in adopting an innovation. Earlier adopters tend to be more educated, have higher social status and upward social mobility, have greater empathy, less dogmatism, greater intelligence, more contact with other people, greater exposure to both mass media and interpersonal communications channels to engage in more active information seeking, a greater ability to cope with uncertainty and risk and higher aspirations. At the other end of the curve are the Laggards who resist adopting an innovation until rather late in the diffusion process.

4. Thus, a double fuzziness (ontological and temporal) and a methodological problem of determining the temporal boundaries of the process studied: 'Sometime we may state immediately and with precision that a certain person or organization has adapted a new item. This does not mean we know when the innovator began to think about the invention or about adopting a new idea' (Hagerstrand, 1988, p. 218).

5. In diffusion theory, that could be defined in terms of the Theory of Perceived Attributes that deals with the basic features of the innovation or diffused item (Rogers, 1995). From this perspective, the potential adopters judge an innovation based on their perceptions of its attributes. These five attributes are: relative advantage (the degree to which it is perceived to be better than what it supersedes); compatibility (consistency with existing values, past experiences and needs); complexity (difficulty of understanding and use); trialability (the degree to which it can be experimented with on a limited basis); observability (the visibility of its results). In other words, the rate of diffusion increases if potential adopters perceive that the innovation: can be tried on a limited basis before adoption; offers observable results; has an advantage relative to other innovations (or the status quo); is not overly complex; and is compatible with existing practices and values.

6. Lakatos's work further developed Kuhn's theory. The key concept in his view is the research program (Lakatos and Musgrave, 1970; Lakatos, 1978). A research has a hard core (the features of the theories that are essential for membership in the research program), a protective belt (the features that may be altered), a negative heuristic (an injunction not to change the hard core) and the positive heuristic (a plan for modifying the protective belt). The dynamics of scientific ideas is explained by focusing on how the protective belt is altered in order to make the program more realistic.

7. The work of Kuhn, Lakatos and their followers elaborated the distinction between the 'internal history of science' and the 'external history of science'. The internal history of science involves those evolutions that can be reconstructed through the application of criteria of scientific rationality. The external dimension of science covers those episodes not subject to 'rational reconstruction'. Thus, social and political considerations could be legitimately invoked to account for developments pertaining to the external history of science.

8. It seems that the most productive approaches to the 'sphere of ideas' usually start by defining and analyzing its units of observation and analysis in a holistic or systemic manner. Indeed, traditionally the study of the dynamics of ideas has been more inclined to be focused on clusters or systems of beliefs rather than on isolated propositional entities. The fact that the propositions making up a cultural knowledge (or belief) system are not randomly connected is significant. These 'systems' are so-called because there are certain patterns, structures or forms that define them. It is an observable reality that 'randomized collections of propositions are characteristically not culturally established, while knowledge systems which are non-randomly patterned are found in all cultures' (Richter, 1972, p. 45). A belief (or cultural knowledge) system is from this perspective any set of ideas prevailing in a given culture or subculture which provides a way of organizing information about the world or about any aspect of it. It includes worldviews, philosophies, theologies, political ideologies and scientific theories (Richter, 1972, p. 43). Given this definition it is clear that a scientific system (or paradigm) is just a specific variant of the belief systems class and in many respects it is similar to any other system of its class. As any similar beliefs system, the 'scientific' one does not achieve and maintain cultural acceptance automatically by the mere power of its 'scientific method' and logic.

5. Frameworks for analysis and interpretation: from personal commitment to functional rationality

Even a brief look at the literature dealing with the issue of neoliberalism reveals that some of the most tempting ways of discussing the spread and change of pro-market economic ideas are those based on the assumption that the rationality of the standard logic of science is only slightly relevant and the role of deliberation and interpretation is secondary or even marginal in the change of such economic belief systems or paradigms. One doesn't need to espouse a sophisticated social theory to develop such an interpretation. For instance, such claims are made systematically by those that suggest that the spread of neoliberal ideas was the result of indoctrination or the induction of a form of 'false consciousness'. The argument is simple: the 'interests' of a 'class' (i.e. the 'capitalists') are cloaked in an economic ideology that gets accepted by the rest of the society not so much by logic and empirical validation but by other psychological mechanisms.

However, setting aside the cogence of an argument involving the doings of an abstract 'capitalist class' able to mount sustained and devastating mass-level, 'false-consciousness'-creating ideological operations in the heart of the Soviet part of the world, this type of argument is often asserted but rarely presented in explicit forms conceptualizing coherently the process claimed to be at work and never convincingly illustrated in detailed empirical case studies. One has to look for better grounded starting points for the discussion of the Eastern European developments. That is, one has to look beyond the literature playing variations on the theme of debunking economics (or neoliberal economics) as an ideology of the exploiters. As the previous chapter made clear, the conjecture that suggests that factors alien to scientific rationality may play a central role in phenomena like the neoliberal revolution in ideas in Eastern Europe is too significant and plausible to be neglected. Yet, to take off, the discussion needs more than to merely recognize the significance of the challenge. A more consistent basis for this discussion may be given by the literature on 'the growth of knowledge' and scientific beliefs, already touched upon in the previous chapters.

Probably the closest thing to an attempt to intellectually engage such processes in a serious way is to go back to the Kuhnian analysis of scientific beliefs systems.

Paradoxical as it may seem, the strongest thesis regarding the a-rational basis of the adoption of (scientific) belief systems has its sources in the work of a philosopher of science. In an interesting twist, Kuhn's work ends up arguing that it is impossible to switch to a new paradigm gradually, by following logical steps (Kuhn, 1962, p. 150). Because it is a transition between incommensurables, the transition between competing paradigms 'cannot be made a step at a time, forced by logic and neutral experience'. That is to say that competing paradigms such as Marxism and neoliberal economics in Eastern Europe are by their very nature incommensurable. The competition cannot be settled by scientific means – i.e. critical rationality or experiments. The paradigms are talking different languages, and they live in different worlds. Due to that, 'the choice is not and cannot be determined merely by the evaluative procedures characteristic of normal science, for these depend in part upon a particular paradigm, and that paradigm is at issue'. In a debate about paradigm choice, 'each group uses its own paradigm to argue in that paradigm's defense'. Hence a circularity. Yet, 'whatever its force, the status of the circular argument is only that of persuasion. It cannot be made logically, or even probabilistically compelling, for those who refuse to step into the circle' (Kuhn, 1962, p. 94). As a consequence, other non-scientific factors must play a part in determining which paradigm a community opts for. But none of these, Kuhn claims, is logically compelling. A decision to adopt a new paradigm is not a matter of acknowledging a proof: 'A decision of this kind can only be made on faith' (Kuhn, 1962, p. 158). Irrespective of the nature of those factors, the paradigm change requires a 'gestalt switch' something akin to a religious conversion. From this perspective the competition between Marxism and Western ideas in Eastern Europe could not be realistically represented by 'market models' or as a sort of battle that can be resolved by proof (Kuhn, 1962, p. 148).

In some of his writings, Kuhn applies the metaphor of language (combined with the conceptual apparatus he built around the notion of paradigm) as his model of science. Scientific beliefs systems could be better understood if the functioning of science is considered somewhat akin to a natural language. This introduces into the discussion issues such as vocabulary, understanding, learning and, most important, translation. Words do not come in isolation and are not learned in isolation but must be seen within the whole structure of language and the linguistic relations they established as well as the ways that system refers to the world. Scientific theories have the same relationship to each other as language systems have. If that is the case, then the move from one paradigm to another is analogous to moving from one natural language to another. Therefore, the incommensurability problem is if not solved, then at least alleviated because languages are not incomparable. But the crucial point for the argument is that learning foreign languages does not require critical thinking. The standard procedure does not require any analytical or logical sophistication: it is just learning words and their meaning. The consequence of this lexical view of paradigm change is that the lexicon containing the key concepts of a paradigm (or belief system) and its inculcation becomes crucial for the transition process. Again, critical rationality is relegated to a secondary position.[1] Revolutionary science is even more inimical to critical thought than normal science. Ultimately, it is conversion or persuasion and not rational critical thought which wins the day (Kuhn, 1962, p. 150).

The implications of this position for the analysis of the East European situation are rather interesting. First, the question seems to be rather simple: How has the new 'language' of Western neoclassical economics been learned in Eastern Europe? How was the lexicon diffused? The answer should be in a sense the return to a diffusion theory framework coupled with an attempt towards a careful historical reconstruction of the moments and stages of the process. From this standpoint, the objective would be to trace as many lexical and 'disciplinary items' as possible to see how they create a critical mass. At each moment in time the paradigm will be imperfectly assimilated at an aggregate level. But each lexical element and each new trainer and trainee added are new pieces in the slow move towards total paradigm change. Even if aggregately the ideal model of the paradigm is not attained and may never be attained in its purity, every new diffusion channel and every new institutional structure created are a step forward in the paradigm change process. The reasons for each move are specific or contextual. Overall, the pattern emerging is that of a paradigm change but there is no overall, general logic in the process, just the effects of a series of cumulated micro-level decisions or accidents. If one is able to identify an overarching cause, that cause would be located at a level of such generality that is ultimately irrelevant in operational terms for the analysis of the specific micro-level dynamics.

If that is the case then one can easily say that the neoclassical lexicon has been widely diffused in Eastern Europe and that a critical mass has already been created. However, there are very few if any analytical or explanatory avenues left once that statement is made and the diffusion channels are traced, chartered and described, a task that has already been sketched in the previous chapters of the study. The question is: could one do more using these insights than try to explain the reasons and processes related to the paradigm shift by looking directly at the countless ways the spread of the lexicon and 'disciplinary traits' of the paradigms in question takes place?

In a study exploring precisely the paradigm competition in economics, Glass and Johnson articulate a very interesting alternative of pushing this line of analysis out of the relative dead-end. They take as a starting point the by now familiar criticism of the notion that the appraisal of an economic school of thought (i.e. its comparison with other schools of thought) as well as the recourse to critical rationality are the key elements in paradigm change. As the explanatory contents do not overlap, the comparison of research programs becomes a very complicated endeavor.[2] They note that the commensurability problem is exponentially complicated by the fact that the rival research programs contain in their hard cores statements which have very different normative elements, and entail very different social and political implications. As Glass and Johnson explain, the neoclassical and Marxist research programs have very different, distinctive hard cores:

> Each distinctive hard core represents a distinctive, conjectural world picture (or metaphysics). In other words, since the statements (or basic assumptions or hypotheses) contained in each distinctive hard core make claims or assertions about the fundamental nature of the economic situation (or domain) under investigation, these statements provide what is known as a conjectural or speculative world picture. Thus, the unfalsifiable, distinctive hard core of ... a research program can be viewed as providing an unfalsifiable, conjectural world picture. This means we can now speak of the hard core of the orthodox research program as providing one conjectural world picture and the hard core of the Marxist research program as providing another, very different, conjectural world picture. (Glass and Johnson, 1989, p. 130)

The worldviews underlying a research program will affect the theory construction within the research program, 'in the sense that although it will not provide detailed guidance about the exact form that any theory should take', each specific theory will 'not only be constructed around but will also imply the fundamental set of statements constituting this distinctive world picture' (Glass and Johnson, 1989, p. 131).

Important as this conjectural hard core world picture is, note Glass and Johnson, one should not forget that the practice of an epistemic community is not fully bounded by it. The existence of a hard core world picture does not mean that every economics researcher, working within a given research program (a) views the program's hard core as the true representation of the world; (b) believes that all theory development and economic analysis should be based exclusively on this specific metaphysics; (c) believes that all economic policy recommendations should be based only on the theories and economic analysis generated by this specific metaphysics (Glass and Johnson, 1989, pp. 131–5). That important clarification introduces a series of important distinctions. Based on them one could introduce the issue of the *personal commitment* of the researcher as distinct from the institutional or contextual professional obligations.

> It may well be that some economics researchers, working within a given research programme, are personally committed to the specific metaphysics underlying that research programme . . . However, it is important to recognize that economics researchers, working within a given research programme, are not automatically, and necessarily, personally committed to the specific metaphysics underlying that research programme. Rather, it is possible to work within a given research program without believing that its specific metaphysics constitutes the basic structure which should underlie all theory construction, economic analysis and policy recommendations. (Glass and Johnson, 1989, p. 132)

The two authors go on to make the point that in practice *commitment* is separated from the daily routine and procedures of an epistemic community. And if we take this view, it becomes clear that it is possible for economists to provide a Marxist analysis without necessarily being personally committed to the Marxist world picture. In other words, it is quite possible that someone could be working within the Marxist paradigm, to generate and test theories, without automatically being personally committed to the hard core Marxist worldview. The application of the standard methodological procedures, the logical deduction, and the implementation of epistemic consistency norms is one thing. The *commitment* to a hard core metaphysics or to the ethical desirability of the policy recommendations is another. The two are different. Moreover, economists functioning within a given paradigm can put forward economic policy recommendations in the form of disinterested statements without necessarily being personally committed to that paradigm's specific conjectural worldview or the policy objective. There is an important difference between the commitment to a paradigm (meaning accepting its hard core) and the operation within the parameters of a paradigm. The commitment of an important number of influential members of the epistemic community to it is crucial. And in the case of the state of economics in Soviet Eastern Europe, this aspect may actually be extremely important for the understanding of the dynamics of the paradigm change.

Two possible directions are opened up by the Glass and Johnson interpretation. The first is related to the very functioning of the Eastern European epistemic communities within the Marxist paradigm. The second is broader and bolder and uses the notion of commitment to expand the analysis projecting it at an entire different level.

The first direction is one in which the mechanics of the rise and fall of Marxism in the economics epistemic community and, even more important, of its daily functioning during the peak of the regime, may be treated in a nuanced way by separating the personal commitment aspect from the actions taken under the routine and in conformity to social and political pressure. In the East European case, the rise of Marxism was related to the political influence of a small number of committed people. It was in the end the story of an 'external' political and social factor at work. The economists were forced to function within the institutional and conceptual constraints imposed from above by those people and their political allies. Therefore, in many cases the theory building and economic analysis produced by the Marxist community was not an expression of a personal commitment. In a similar way, in many cases the policy recommendations coming out of the economics community in socialism were not a symptom of a personal commitment. It may seem paradoxical but that was a common reality during the communist regime.

In the light of the above analysis, the lack of personal commitment of the members of the East European epistemic community to the hard core of the Marxist program may emerge as a significant clue for one of the puzzles related to the paradigm shift process. The mere number of texts and policy recommendations produced at a given moment in time as well as the statistics of 'Marxist economists' may not be entirely reliable indicators of the real state of the paradigm. The system operated as long as the external power, pressure and incentives to keep it producing the Marxist analysis were there. The evidence gathered in the previous chapters seems to confirm that in the 1980s it was already functioning in a sort of institutional inertia through reasons and incentives poles apart from the motivation given by a commitment. When the neoclassical alternative became available, people from the epistemic community migrated en masse to it. In what measure that was the result of genuine commitment to the newcomer and in what measure the result of more enticing incentives and a better institutional basis is a different issue. The fact is that this transition, irrespective of reasons, was facilitated by the massive lack of personal commitment to the Marxist hard core. And thus separating the commitment element from the policy and theoretical elements offers a useful insight into the change of ideas process.

COMMITMENT AND SECULAR RELIGION

The second direction of analysis illuminated by Glass and Johnson's discussion of the fundamental issue of the *commitment* to a hard core metaphysics and the worldview, values and conjectures embedded into it is ampler and bolder. It takes as a starting point the fact that the 'core' paradigm consists of statements that are not empirical, i.e. it consists of the worldview, values and conjectures that cannot be falsified by experimental trial. Furthermore, in the case of the political economy schools of thought core statements are even more the expression of an imperative belief in 'what ought to be' than in the case of the natural sciences. That pushes the discussion on the political economic belief systems in a very interesting direction. With it the entire set of problems regarding the non-scientific and non-rational factors determining the paradigm choice outlined by Kuhn regain a new life. The issue of commitment to a metaphysical worldview raises profound issues regarding the deeper psycho-sociological anchors of belief systems.

Traditionally, the literature on belief systems stresses the fact that the necessary condition for such systems to survive and expand is to continuously be able to solve two key problems that they are forced to face in practice: the problem of commitment and the problem of validation. First, belief systems persist because they are directly (or through the social vehicles that convey them) able to generate and maintain commitment. But in order to maintain the commitment, a belief system must also, independently, appear to be valid. In their *Sociology of Belief*, Borhek and Curtis (1975) stress the fact that the two conditions are independent:

> Commitment and validation are two separate (though mutually relevant) phenomena, in spite of the near universal myth that we are committed because our beliefs are valid. Beliefs must not only seem external and valid, but also worth whatever discomforts believing entails. We often take the trouble to validate our beliefs because we are committed to them. (Borhek and Curtis, 1975, p. 85)

The problem of validation has largely been covered by the discussions regarding the relationship between beliefs and the reality with all its epistemological and philosophy of science extensions. On the other hand, the issue of commitment may be considered either as a psychological or a sociological problem. Although the psychological problems such as the mental construction that permits social actors to devote themselves to ideas or the personality dynamics of commitment are fascinating, they are beyond the limits of the present study. In a similar way, sociological problems such as which social processes regularly produce commitment in humans, although closer to the focus, will not be the object of the present section. Instead, the very interesting problem of commitment is to be approached from a comparative perspective able to approach through analogy and similitude some of the processes associated with the rise and demise of political economy paradigms in Eastern Europe.

The starting point of the argument is that the closest parallel of the political economy paradigms with other belief systems seems to be religion. Indeed an increasingly sophisticated literature has been accumulating over the years illuminating and investigating the parallel between the traditional religious and theological belief systems and the political economic ones. This literature explores both the functional similarities between traditional theologies and the modern political economy paradigms and at the same time tries to highlight the relevance of the traditional, and better understood, religious mechanisms of conversion and commitment for our understanding of the modern political economic ideologies. From this perspective, the paradigm shift in economic ideas in Eastern Europe may be seen as part of a broader historical and cultural context. The major economic themes as they developed in the past 300 years are accordingly seen in the context of the broad movement of philosophical and religious ideas. The literature develops that perspective in two directions. First, it points out the functional equivalent of theology that economics tends to substitute today in the modern world and second it traces the major schools existent in economics directly to religious and theological doctrines (Nelson, 1991; Thrower and Leniston, 1992). Common to all authors contributing to this literature is the notion that political economy emerged during the past three centuries as one of the most powerful intellectual factors in history and that 'political economy is the theology of modernity' (Dunn, 1989).

Robert Nelson has documented the rise of political economy to public life pre-eminence and has synthesized the secular functionalist theology view in a series of books on the relationship economics and theology in the twentieth century, books that have very relevant implications for the study of paradigm change in Eastern Europe. Nelson starts by pointing out that belief systems have always been anchored in religion. Traditionally, theology, as the propositional expression of religion, 'gave the meaning of human existence and the context in which events should be interpreted' and thus theology established 'the legitimacy of social institutions, and of the people whose task was to develop and frame these institutions'. The modern period is in no way different. If economics 'offers a way of thinking about the modem world', and if economics 'gives legitimacy to many modern institutions', the question arises 'whether in some real sense economics might offer a modern theology' (Nelson, 1991, pp. xx–xxvii).

The point is not that political economy reflects numerous value assumptions and that sometimes those values are religious or that economics has often been misused and distorted for unscientific purposes. The point is that political economy as a worldview has similar functions with the traditional theology: to frame the perception of social action and of the basic parameters of human existence. A view of economics reduced to a mere hypothesis creating and testing is missing the central role economists and the economic way of thinking have played in the modern age. Therefore, in describing economics as a 'theology', the term is used in a functionalist way: economic theology offers 'a set of principles and understandings that give meaning to, define a purpose for, and significantly frame the perception of human existence' (Nelson, 1991, p. xxv).

Following Nelson one could build on the functionalist definition of religion and outline the substance of this modern, secular theology. Two basic assumptions lay at the basis of this secular theology. The first is that material scarcity is the source of evil. The second is that applied rationality in the form of economics could deliver humankind out of material constraints (and implicitly from evil). As regarding the scarcity thesis, Nelson claims that an historical overview of the modern period reveals a 'widely held belief' that economic progress is able to solve both the material and spiritual problems of humankind. For those having this belief, 'to solve the economic problem would be, therefore, to solve in large part the problem of evil' (Nelson, 1991, p. 3–8). The more the secular theology got its grip on the minds of the people, the more material scarcity and the ensuing struggle for limited resources have been seen as the original sources of human misery.

The central role played by economists is a direct result of the normative dimensions of political economy. If the priests usually asked 'whether an action was consistent with God's design for the world', in the message of contemporary economics the 'laws of economic efficiency and of economic growth have replaced the divine plan'.[3] For many people of today, 'the power to eliminate evil in the world is no longer a divine prerogative, but is instead primarily a matter of eliminating economic scarcity' (Nelson, 1991, pp. 5–9).[4] The second key idea of economic theology is related to the instrument that could save humankind from its scarcity predicament. This instrument is reason or better said rationality. The discord, social conflicts and social problems ensuing from scarcity are in the last analysis due to a failure of rational understanding. If the world becomes more rational, then all these problems are diminished. The role of economists is to expose and disseminate the fundamental rationality upon which is and should be built the social order. Be it a spontaneous order created by rational individuals or a great social system to be centrally planned by scientific knowledge, the idea is the same. There is a rational order, the economist sees it, understands its working and then guides the people towards it.[5]

This view seems to be shared by the majority of economists, not only by those of Marxist or socialist persuasion. Karl Marx was one among the many thinkers to advocate that when the problem of the material necessities of life is solved, humanity will be able to achieve a better social and psychological state. Marx connected that view with a specific social theory centered on the proletariat and made the political triumph of a specific class the condition of success but the class-based social messianism is not a necessary ingredient. Vincent Ostrom, while noting the messianic element of Marxism, points out that on the one hand it explicitly rejects religious presuppositions but on the other hand in the *Communist Manifesto* it promises to free the oppressed of the world in final 'class warfare' of epic and historical proportions. 'According to the Manifesto, the revolutionary struggle led by Communists would be the penultimate war to end all civil wars and would achieve the Liberation of Mankind. This was a new form of secular religion that was being expounded while explicitly repudiating religion' (Ostrom, 1997, pp. 190–1). On the other hand, John Maynard Keynes, in no way a revolutionary, was a standard bearer of the economic theology credo, too. For Keynes, the economic order of his time was a 'transitional phase' after which 'much else' will also 'suffer a sea-change' and the history will enter a new era with renewed mentality and attitudes (Keynes, *Essays in Persuasion*, quoted in Nelson, 1991, p. 3). But in his case, the emergence of the new era was more the result of the work of an enlightened economists elite. In spite of the differences the fundamental vision is similar.

If we accept this perspective, then both the differences and similarities between the two competing economic worldviews in Eastern Europe are significantly distinct from those emerging from a mere comparison of their conceptual and theoretical content. Both of them share the same basic message pivoting around the idea of improving humanity's condition in a rational and scientific way. This deep religious dimension is in a sense paradoxical since Marxism is notoriously antagonistic to religion and neoclassical economics is at best religion-neutral. Yet, in retrospect, the clash between the political economies may well be seen as a clash between two secular theologies.[6] Vincent Ostrom offers a clue to that paradox while discussing the 'anomaly' that strong religious elements 'occur as an essential feature among those who deny or repudiate the idea of religion'. He stresses the fact that religious presuppositions are ontological necessities and necessary epistemological conditions in the constitution of systems of knowledge. Consequently, we would expect 'those presuppositions to manifest themselves among those who explicitly reject a belief in religious presuppositions. We would expect of new Secular religions.' (Ostrom, 1999, p. 190).

The Ostrom conjecture is undoubtedly true regarding Marxism. A large number of authors have established that below its economic analysis and statements on the economic laws of history lies a simple biblical eschatology with alienation, the laws of history and proletarians playing a major role (Thrower, 1983; Thrower and Leniston, 1992; Feuer, 1975; Popper, 1966; Nelson, 1991; Tismaneanu, 1998; MacIntyre, 1984). Typical for this approach is Thrower and Leniston's *Marxism–Leninism as the Civil Religion of Soviet Society* (1992). Thrower and Leniston note that the discussions regarding the reasons of the speed with which Marxism–Leninism has collapsed focus too much of their attention on its economic failure, while the failure of Marxism was more than the failure of an economic system: it was, in fact, 'the failure of a total world view'. The focus on the inefficiency of the system 'ignores the failure of Marxism–Leninism to capture the minds, hearts, and more significantly, the imaginations of those who were compelled to live under its jurisdiction'. Thrower and Leniston echo an entire literature that emphasizes the fact that in order to appreciate the conditions of the collapse of Marxism–Leninism it is necessary to know something about 'what might be called its phenomenology – that is, about its own self-image and about how it was understood and practiced by its adherents'. Only when Marxism–Leninism is approached 'from a perspective derived from the history of religions that the full implications of its failure to become the historical successor to the religions that it sought to supplant become apparent' (Thrower and Leniston, 1992, p. viii).

On the other hand, the scientific aspirations and the effort to meet scientific methodology standards in the case of neoclassical economics is significant indeed. Therefore, we might expect some reluctance to embrace the idea that modern Western economics has anything to do with secular theology. Although Nelson (2001) gathered all the evidence available and demonstrated convincingly that that was precisely the case, the analysis of the paradigm change could proceed even based on the weaker assumption. If we bracket the problem of the theological nature of the neoclassical paradigm and we consider only Marxism in isolation, then the story of the paradigm change is the story of the fall of a secular religion faced by the assault of the science and by its own excesses. Alternatively, if we concede the strong 'theological' normative content of the neoclassical paradigm we can return to the clash of secular theologies interpretation.

Consequently, there are two possible readings of the East European political economy paradigm change developments. The first is to simply interpret the replacement of Marxism in secular ideologies terms. In this view both paradigms are major players. Their tension is similar with the one between Christianity and Paganism, Protestantism and Catholicism, Islam and Christianity, etc. and should be explored, explained and interpreted as such. The second is to set neoclassical economics aside and to simply focus on Marxism as the major player. Its rise and fall is more than anything the result of its own internal structure and dynamics. As a belief system it failed to sustain the necessary conditions for survival. In the long run, the inability to validate undermined the commitment to the hard core of the paradigm. The result was its inability to satisfy the validation and commitment criteria. In the end the two belief systems are of a different nature and their dynamics is explained by different concepts and theories. In what measure the void created by the demise of the Marxist belief system has been occupied by a scientific paradigm is a story to be told from a different conceptual background.

Read from this perspective, the narrative of the rise and fall of the Marxist paradigm is rather straightforward. Marx was one of the most influential 'theologians' who ever lived (Tillich and Braaten, 1967, p. 476). The Marxist gospel in the twentieth century spread over Russia and China, and from there many other nations were converted, most of the time by force. What gave it its strength besides the strong power apparatus behind it was that the religious element was combined with and obscured by a large body of apparently 'scientific' arguments. Jules Monnerot, one of the first experts in the socio-psychology of communism, argued that Marxism's strength came not only because it satisfied a religious or ethically inspired demand for the establishment of a just society, but because it was also 'scientific'. It combined science with morality. During the modern era, science achieved such a credibility and status that a modern belief system had 'to pass itself off as science before it can be safely established'. In Monnerot's view, if Marxism is reduced to its intellectual terms and the scientific message, its essence is missed. Yet usually the intellectual or scientific message has been over-valued at the expense of all the rest. Marxist theory has been a conceptual vehicle of a secular religion resulting from a compromise between two opposing tendencies: 'namely collective passion on the one hand and the tendency to scientific objectivity on the other' (Monnerot, 1960, p. 136).

In that combination of scientism and religiosity lies both the strength and the weakness of Marxism. The success of Marxism in Russia was pivotal for the twentieth-century life of this doctrine. That success was facilitated by the fact that it fell back on a traditional 'religious conception of the czar's authority and a deep belief that land belonged to God'. The religious faith of the Russian people was converted into the new secular religion. Russians 'could very readily pass from one integrated faith to another'. Indeed, as perceived by many Russians, 'the world mission of the Communist Party Third International echoed Orthodox Christian messianism, which saw Moscow as the Third Rome' (Nelson, 2001, p. 25).

But that mixture of science and faith was a self-undermining blend. The very idea of a scientific system, irrespective of how mutilated it was, had nevertheless imported some standards of rationality and the expectations of rationality into Marxism. The very existence of those standards and expectations, even if not applied to dogma, were enough to slowly under-mine the commitment to the paradigm. Creating expectations and then brutally neglecting them destroyed the validation basis of the paradigm. With validation gone, the commitment vanished too. Second, Marxism had made very concrete promises. Science was an instrument and guarantor of the fact that the system will deliver the promised progressive social state. The more reality diverged from ideals, the less was the perceived validity. Again the commitment to the entire belief system had to suffer.

Finally, there is the disillusionment that undermines any secular religion irrespective of whether it generates expectations related to science or not. The reason is lucidly explained by Jules Monnerot:

> They have placed all their hopes in this world, and yet every time they stretch out a hand to grasp what ought to be sufficient, its insufficiency is glaringly revealed. So the secular religions decline into a materialistic cynicism and begin to appear horrible. There is no longer any justification for the human sacrifices they call for and make. Lapsing into final absurdity, they make men suffer and inflict tortures upon them in order that mankind be rescued from suffering and torture. (Monnerot, 1960, p. 154).

If this is the case, then the clues regarding the paradigm change in Eastern Europe should be looked for outside the epistemic community and among the public and population at large. The basic approach would be to trace the change in the climate of public opinion about Marxism and to ease the degree of commitment to the Marxist public religion over the years. Given the fact that the idea of public religion is interpretable the simplest thing is just to determine the attachment to Marxist ideology and objectives leaving aside as a presupposition the correct interpretation of the meaning of that ideology. Thus, the dynamics of public opinion regarding key elements of the Marxist worldview remain a mere empirical question. Unfortunately, following this analytical direction is not possible as opinion polls were not encouraged and even forbidden in the Soviet states for long periods. Also, the early study of public opinion in the Soviet space was hindered not only by the official restrictions but also by the Western belief that 'opinion research in socialist systems is biased and unreliable, that opinion is largely manipulated and not "spontaneously" formed, and that public opinion has little, if any, influence on decision and policy making in Communist countries' (Gitelman, 1977, p. 1; quoted in Miller et al. 1993, p. 5).

Despite these restrictions, indirect methods of study were employed, sometimes with some success. Besides the analysis of critical events such as the 1956 Hungarian and 1968 Czechoslovak uprisings, the analysis of mass media and other publications, the émigré studies and the letters to the editor from soviet magazines were a valuable resource (Miller et al. 1993). Only at the end of the 1980s did the studies start to offer a reliable view of the situation. All these studies provide evidence of steady mounting dissatisfaction with the performance of the economy. Moreover, they documented the inability of the regime to offer a credible agenda as the public discouragement about the economic future at both the national and personal levels was marked by negativism, pessimism, and cynicism. By that time its results were accumulating and it was possible to make longitudinal comparisons for short periods of time (1985–1989). Their conclusions revealed a mounting popular disenchantment with the Soviet regime and its economic policies. These studies also suggested that regime legitimacy declined as citizens came to believe that the regime had been instrumental in undermining their welfare.

That disenchantment needs no further documentation since starting in 1989 its direct political consequences were obvious even for skeptics. The Marxist system collapsed and with it collapsed the Marxist political economy paradigm that was supposed to give it a meaning and a direction. In this respect, it is hard to presume that the political economy epistemic community was in any way different from the rest of the population. Even if economists were still employing in their discourses and analyses residues pertaining to the official Marxism, as demonstrated by Glass and Johnson in the study discussed earlier in this chapter, that was not to be taken as a sign of their commitment to the hard core of the paradigm. With extremely rare exceptions, that was just a routine procedure or an expression of the still feared power of the party and its ideological police. The reality was that their commitment had vanished long before even the political changes started to take shape.

To conclude: this detour in the area of factors alien to scientific rationality and the domain of approaches based on various interpretations of the issue of commitment undoubtedly offers a fresh and challenging perspective on the problem of economic ideas change in Eastern Europe. By separating commitment from the daily routine and procedures of an epistemic community one gets a plausible account of how it was possible for economists to continue to produce Marxist discourse without necessarily being personally committed to the Marxist world picture. Also, it provides an explanation of the fall of Marxism in the East European economics epistemic community where economists were forced to function within the institutional and conceptual constraints imposed from above. When the neoclassical alternative became available, most people, although they had no dedication to it, also had no genuine commitment to bind them to Marxism. Thus, most of them were able to discount commitment on both sides and switch to the alternative that offered more enticing incentives and a better institutional basis. In the end, it is important to note that this approach, although stressing commitment, is actually clearly referring back to the factors of choice and rationality.

The religion-like approach to paradigm change in political economy although more difficult to break down to the 'epistemic choice' element still depends on it. The failure of Marxism was not a mere failure of an economic system: it was, in fact, 'the failure of a total world view', the failure to capture 'the minds, hearts, and more significantly, the imaginations of those who were compelled to live under its jurisdiction'. This approach takes on the issue of commitment to a metaphysical worldview and raises profound issues regarding the deeper psycho-sociological anchors of belief systems. Conversion is not a rational matter. However the disillusion created by the clash between the reality of 'workers' paradise' and the expectations created by the belief system implies a role for rationality. And thus the notion that one can understand the dynamics of economic ideas in Eastern Europe without making explicit reference to epistemic rationality and rational choice principles seems counterintuitive. As formulated by Vincent Ostrom in his pioneering work on what he called the problem of 'epistemic choice': 'The principles of choice applicable to the warrantability of knowledge are different than the principles of choice applicable to the choice of goods in market and public economies.' Yet although 'the modes and criteria of choice vary among different types of objects of choice' the element of choice and the implicit rationality is there even with the approaches shunning the sphere of rationality (Ostrom, 1999, p. 91).

THE CHALLENGE OF RATIONAL CHOICE

The interpretation of the spread and change of economic ideas in terms of factors diverging from critical rationality is able to inspire a challenging vision. Yet it is difficult to make a fully compelling argument basing it on the theoretical assumption that the neoliberal revolution in economic ideas is a process to be explained mainly outside the scope of rationality. Even when the non-rational factors (such as commitment and conversion) are emphasized, the role of rational choice and functional rationality is unavoidable (Adams, 1989). The question is, how could an approach centered on rationality avoid the trap of remaining focused only internally, that is, only on the endogenous epistemic processes in the pure sphere of ideas? To be operational, the analysis of the spread and change of ideas should be more than a mere replication on the old literature on the 'logic of scientific discovery'. Similarly, such an exercise should be able to link in a functional way the sphere of ideas with the rest of the social system. The challenge is to start with the endogenous dynamics and then go in the direction of the 'external approach' anchoring in the broader environment the ideas studied, without relaxing the rationality approach and without reducing the entire dynamics to a mere play of accidents and path-dependent processes. The rest of this chapter will try to face this challenge.

The framing of the rise of neoliberalism from a rational choice theory perspective deserves special attention not only because of its promise but also because of the pre-eminence this theory has in social sciences these days. Moreover, besides promise and salience, rational choice type theories are among the most likely candidates implicitly applied to the case, as the discussion of the marketplace of ideas model or of diffusion theory have already demonstrated. Rational choice theories are based on the assumption that social actors have a clear set of preferences and pursue them in a way that is consistent with formal definitions of rationality (Calvert, 1995). From this perspective the analysis of the consequences of the social actors' attempts to achieve their most-preferred outcome in the least costly manner is the key to understanding social order and change. That applies to the study of ideas too. Once the premises are formulated this way, the question is: given the initial rational choice assumption, what are the most plausible explanations of the various paths leading to the neoliberal preeminence? (Campbell and Pederson, 2001; Knight, 2002, p. 40). As one may expect, there are numerous ways of approaching the problem within the rational choice theory parameters. To simplify things, one may group them at three levels: First is the individual or micro-level, the level of social actors and their individual decision making together with the immediate environment affecting those decisions. Second is an intermediate, what one may call 'meso'-level, the level of institutional structures defining the phenomenon of concern – in this case the institution of production and diffusion of social scientific ideas. Finally is the societal or macro-level, the level of social institutions, structures and broad political and economic parameters.

The elementary notion of cost–benefit and its application to the analysis of selection of economic ideas illustrates the first level. Indeed, cost–benefit or cost-effectiveness concerns continuously affect selection of ideas: 'For inquiry – in science and elsewhere – is a human activity which, like any other, requires the expenditures of effort and energy in a way that endows the enterprise with an unavoidable economic dimension' (Rescher 1978, p. 29; Wible, 1998, p. 154). Conceiving the process of production and dissemination of science as an economic process leads to a perspective on the dynamics of economic ideas that is based not only on the internal, epistemic processes but also external elements. This approach, writes Wible (1998, p. 80), 'correctly calls attention to the notion of opportunity cost' in the selection of research projects. Most philosophy of science and studies of the spread of scientific ideas 'are conceived without reference to constraints, incentives, and markets. But the economic dimensions are crucial'. This type of analysis, explains Radnitzky, pivots around 'the logic of the situation facing an individual scientist in evaluating his professional research commitment'. The scientist's calculus is a complex one and is not reduced to just a pure scientific assessment. Simply put, a research program is abandoned for another if an alternative delivers more of what a scientist values: a research program facing increasing costs and diminishing benefits would be replaced by a rival with decreasing costs and increasing returns (Radnitzky in Wible, 1994, pp. 92–3). Assuming that one has the freedom to do that, the researcher chooses one paradigm over another (for instance neoclassical economics over Marxism) based on the individual's appraisal of the relative net benefits of each of the competing alternatives and the balance of assets and liabilities. Among the benefits are explanatory value, novelty, simplicity, accuracy of detail, comprehensiveness, robustness, relevance, descriptiveness, congruence with theory, generality, rigor, scope, precision, parsimony, intuitive appeal, and to this list it should be added social and material potential benefits. Among the liabilities are time, effort, energy, and money (Wible, 1994; Rescher 1978, p. 69; Radnitzky and Bernholz, 1988). This way of thinking of the choice of economic ideas in terms of a cost–benefit model may be a restatement of previously discussed themes such as the perceived attributes issue, already introduced by diffusion theory, or just a reformulation of the basic logic of choice implied in most other frameworks. Yet the restatement is offering a fresh look at the problem.

As a brief reference to the problem of commitment to a paradigm reminds us, there are indeed difficulties of operationalizing the cost–benefit model in the case of paradigms or of belief systems that have a high normative content. If the secular religion thesis is right, the spread of Marxist and neoclassical ideas may have additional, difficult to fathom dimensions. Accepting that thesis or not, it may not be easy anyway to define the opportunity costs of a researcher and there will always be a temptation to *post hoc* arguments, i.e. to derive a benefit balance out of the evolution of the paradigm and not the other way round. However, despite its limitations, the concept offers very important insights.

These insights could be further elaborated at the second level, the institutional level. The most effective way to do it is to follow Wible's (1998) work, probably the boldest attempt to integrate various rational choice (economic) approaches to ideas selection and paradigm change. In a world characterized by uncertainty and thus epistemic scarcity, the continuous creation, destruction and annihilation of knowledge is one of the key functions of social order (Wible, 1998, p. 173). That function is fulfilled by social institutions. Following the traditional Hayekian line, markets are first in line as they are social mechanisms of dealing with dispersed and complex information and of generating social and economic order. But

Wible is keen to add that 'markets are not adequate in all cases to reduce the inherent chaos in human affairs to a functional level' (Wible, 1998, p. 173). As a consequence, the limits of the market leave room for other ways to cope with the epistemic scarcity. Non-market institutional structures and hierarchical arrangements may be in certain circumstances very effective in reducing epistemic scarcity. The point made by Wible is that science is among those non-market institutional structures. 'Science as an organizational process is engaged in the production of abstract theories about the fundamental properties of our world rather than prices. While these properties are often quantifiable, they cannot be mass produced in standard units and commodified'. Markets and science 'both produce abstractions, but they are different types of abstractions'. The economic role of science is 'to produce these theoretical abstractions and any specialized instrumentation otherwise unattainable through the marketplace or the firms' (Wible, 1998, p. 176).[7] Science is a *sui generis* phenomenon. The functional separation doesn't mean that science is totally separated from markets or the rest of the institutional and social order. In reality, both market and non-market organizational structures have a crucial role to play in science. But from Wible's perspective what makes science really interesting are the non-market structures that are 'different than those found in any other set of arrangements in society' (Wible, 1998, pp. 176, 181).

In order to elaborate this point, he introduces the concept of 'dual economy', a concept originating in economics and designating those economic systems in which market and non-market structures coexist. The dual economy of science has two sectors. A primary sector that consists of non-market, non-commercial institutions and processes, and a secondary sector that consists of commercial structures relying on markets. Wible (1998, p. 179) calls the first 'primary science' and the other 'secondary science'. Seen from this perspective, Kuhn's normal science is defined mostly in terms of primary science as it includes not only the paradigm but also an entire array of educational and organizational structures, textbooks, the journals, the academic departments and research facilities, promotion and tenure rules, peer review, professional associations, foundations and government agencies providing financial support. The Kuhnian normal science is thus based on an entire set of non-commercial, non-market institutional arrangements. On the other hand, there is another set of institutions which 'serve the more conventional economic demands of science' providing labor, resources, equipment and technology and economize on time and effort, allowing the scientist to focus greater attention on the primary science research. The commercial economy part of the science is the one that establishes the relative wage structure that may play an important part in the individual decisions to become a scientist or to the decision to specialize in one science or another. Finally, secondary science is also that part of science 'which has gone commercial once the basic research has occurred and fundamental discoveries have been made' (Wible, 1998, pp. 176–7). The unique organizational arrangements and processes called primary science combined with the commercial arrangements of the secondary science are the total environment within which the scientific and paradigmatic change should be understood.

One of the most interesting aspects of this argument is that the dualism aspect of science may be seen not only as a key explanatory framework for the scientific process but also for economic performance of a society in general. 'The institutional structure of science is a dual economy which is just as essential for efficiency and growth as any other set of institutions in society'. Given the fact that the product created by science could not be created by other sectors of the economy, 'science is a complement to the other fundamental organizational structures of the economy'. That is to say that science is part and parcel of the economic system: 'Rather than conceiving of science as an exception to economic processes, an alternative would be to expand our vision of economics. To the major markets and sectors of the economy we could add science'. That is to say that in addition to the usual sectors of goods, money, bonds (financial markets), and labor, 'science could be added as another fundamental economic process' (Wible, 1998, p. 155).

The implications of this vision are not at all irrelevant. For instance, a direct consequence of significance for the study of the political economy developments in Eastern Europe deserves to be noted immediately. If Wible is right, then the economics epistemic community in Eastern Europe should not be seen and studied other than in conjunction with and as a part of the rest of the socialist economic system. The linkages between the 'social sciences sector' and the rest of the economic sectors as well as its productive input for the economy become crucial elements of a study of the dynamics of ideas produced or supported by economists.

Seen through these theoretical lenses, a decision to sustain a line of research (i.e. a paradigm) is an investment decision. To make such decisions, one needs good information and thus one stumbles again on the old Hayekian problem of the uses of knowledge in society. The problem is that for investment decisions in the private sector, the calculation is determined based on the signals. In the public sector, the basis is the bureaucratic process. That gives a new clue about the problems of the epistemic communities in socialism. In a modern society science as an economic sector needs to be integrated, linked to the entire economy. A plug into the system of prices and information given by the rest of the economy is needed. The less the epistemic community is connected to the economy the less viable and adaptive will be the paradigm upheld by it. While market processes force corrections on the private sector's mistakes, when a government agency or a government-sponsored program fails, it may survive in spite of all its errors. The same model may apply to scientific paradigms. Normally, a research project which no longer has scientific merit would be eliminated on purely scientific reasons. But if science's institutional structure is entirely state-based, then the problem of surviving failures might loom large. In other words, a paradigm or research program that has failed in fact a long time ago might seem viable just because it is subsidized. And that is pre-cisely the case of Marxist political economy in Eastern Europe. In a rigid and dysfunctional economy it is no surprise that the institutional structure of economics as a science was similarly designed and that it functioned the way it did.

Thus focusing more precisely on the mechanisms at work, the notion of a dual economy of science seems to be of some help. In the case of Western economics it was clear that there was on the one hand a primary sector con-sisting of non-market, non-commercial institutions and processes and a secondary sector consisting of commercial arrangements related to markets. These secondary sector institutions, that 'serve the more conven-tional economic demands of science' providing labor, resources, equipment and technology and that establish the relative wage and the specialization structure, managed to connect the epistemic community to the rest of the economic system. Through it, the normal science with its non-commercial, non-market arrangements was fuelled and depended on the dynamics of the market-oriented structures and their success.

The utility or relevance of research done in the secondary sector (or the applied research) seems thus to be crucial for the success of the competing paradigms. And in this respect it is clear that Marxism had no such 'second sector' agenda: Marxist ideas had no meaningful managerial, operational or administrative implications. On the other hand, the applicability of the market research or economic research done by neoclassical economists to firms resulted in demand for economics by businesses. Western economics could be expanded and made relevant not only for academia and govern-ment but also for the private sector. While neoclassical economics extended to the firms, financial markets and even social problems and expanded through business schools at the heart of the business community, Marxism had basically no secondary sector. Socialist governments indeed had a specific demand for Marxist products. But that was largely rhetorical and in no way asked for dynamism and creativity. In the case of the East one con-sumer (government) dominated while other consumers, firms, etc. were not relevant because the product was not relevant for them. That monopsony suffocated the epistemic community. It is true that neoclassical economists worked for the government too. But their work was balanced by two factors: The first was that the governments they worked for were democratic and liberal (i.e. relatively more open to policy diversity and limited experiments) and the second was that the work stood in solid connections with the market. Even when removed from the direct interface with it, the epistemic communities in the West were still not as artificial and shaky in their structure and output as the heavily subsidized Eastern European Marxist contemporaries. In the East, the cost–benefit structure of the researchers was not only distorted by propaganda and pure pressure from the state but also by the subsistence system. The result was an epistemic community apparently viable but in fact a shell kept alive by sheer power and subsidies.

To conclude, science in general, and social sciences in particular are more often than not remote from the influence of the market. Western economics was a little closer or at least relatively closer than its socialist competitor. And that explains quite a lot. The existence of various interlocked markets for secondary products of social science made sure that prices reflected more the needs and interests of the society and the output of economics was more in tune with the social needs. And indeed it also got better funded. Thus, in the end when at the beginning of the 1990s the collapse of the Soviet system happened, the neoclassical synthesis had not only the intellectual credentials but also a solid institutional and financial basis out of which it was able to take almost overnight control of the Eastern Europe epistemic communities.

Interesting as it may be, this rational choice explanation still leaves out too much of what most of the people interested in the problem of neoliberalism find fascinating: the big, macro picture and the relationship between ideas and the large macro-level structures and processes. For that one has to turn to another facet of rational choice theory.

Jack Knight's explanation of the rise of neoliberalism in Latin America illustrates the third level of rational choice theory and at the same time opens up a way to develop a better understanding of the linkage between the 'ideas sector' and the rest of society. A rational choice approach used to understand the spread of neoliberalism should look, writes Knight, at transaction costs and should focus on 'the preferences of the relevant social actors', the efficiency effects of 'the resulting economic and political institutions' and 'the pressure of competition'. Looking at the overall social system of a country, the key questions are: 'did the new neoliberal arrangements enhance the efficiency of economic and political activity?' Were there 'other institutional possibilities that would have had even greater efficiency effects if they had been established'? Were the new neoliberal institutions 'the ones that were most preferred by all of the relevant economic and political decision makers'? In other words, the choice of neoliberal ideas is in fact a choice of institutions. The interest of social actors is concentrated not on worldviews but on the pragmatic, efficient polices and institutions implied by those views. One may say that the selection is in reality one between models or images of institutions and policies. So in the end, one still may say it is a choice of ideas but it is one in which interests and efficiency are crucial. Moreover it is a matter in which the focus is not on the core 'theoretical' ideas but on the 'policy' periphery. And so the choice of neoliberalism is in fact a rational corollary of a calculus cost. Out of the explanations of neoliberalism that have been proposed, the 'shock therapy', writes Knight, 'comes closest to approaching the voluntary contract version of the transaction costs theory. From this perspective the argument is that political and economic decision-makers preferred those institutions that minimized transaction costs and thus maximized aggregate economic benefits' (Knight, 2002, p. 41). Yet Knight himself ends up by questioning the viability of the transaction cost explanation of neoliberalism in Latin America. The existing evidence of 'the significant institutional variation across countries' and of 'the substantial political conflict throughout Latin America over the nature of the institutional reforms' as well as 'the subsequent responses to political pressure after the initial period of reform' lead to the conclusion 'that the competitive selection mechanism will not adequately account for the nature of neoliberal institutional change' (Knight, 2002, p. 42). If that is the case for Latin America, the conclusion applies even more to Eastern Europe.

Looking for a substitute within the rational choice frame, Knight identifies as a candidate the process of bargaining over the alternative distributional arrangements. Here the social context enters the analysis in the form of the asymmetries of resources that exist in a society. The nature and results of the bargaining are determined by the distribution of resource ownership in a society – more precisely by the power generated by the initial asymmetries. In the bargaining explanation of the rise of neoliberalism the keys are: the interests of the relevant social actors, 'the existence of asymmetries in bargaining power that translate into advantages in the political and economic competition over institutional creation and change' and 'the distributional consequences of the resulting economic and political institutions'. As Knight put it, in this case the primary questions are referring to the 'asymmetries in the distribution of the benefits of political and economic interactions', the conflicting preferences of the relevant social actors 'over the possible institutional alternatives', the conflict associated to the process of institutional change and whether the 'resulting neoliberal institutions favor those political actors who had an ex ante advantage in the relevant measure of bargaining power' (Knight, 2002, p. 42).

The bargaining approach offers indeed a rational choice alternative to the transaction costs account. Yet bargaining theory leaves little room for a real role or even a real interest in ideas. A framing function is still left for them but that function is secondary. The approach is more of an explanation of institutional change and less interesting as a frame for discussing ideas change processes. In fact one may see it as an extension of the traditional Public Choice theory that typically analyzes social change using interest group theory and as such, as part of the battery of interest-based explanations of social change (Olson, 1965; Becker, 1983). Olson (1982) offers a grand narrative of the ebb and flow of societal prosperity, underpinned by the encroachment of interests and a subsequent collapse. If such a collapse is foreseen, then policymakers may escape via renegotiation – all parties might benefit from constitutional change (Buchanan and Tullock, 1962). Alternatively a dominant group may have an all-encompassing interest in negotiated reforms since they'd capture the consequences as private returns (Olson, 1993). In some cases a regulated industry may engage in non-price competition to such an extent that they only make normal profits, and would therefore benefit from deregulation (see Stigler 1971 for the underlying model, and Douglas and Miller 1974 for an application). And finally, the advent of unforeseen technology could erode the power of incumbent interest groups and therefore facilitate negotiations leading to social change (Foldvary and Klein, 2003). However this is not to say that such avenues will always be possible. In most cases, these 'interest' explanations are a necessary but not a sufficient condition for a theory of political change. They require an ideas explanation to underpin them. Even Olson, one of the fathers of the interests based (rational choice) theory, acknowledges that whenever the circumstances 'leave an opening for new ideas' such as 'when the different organized powers or interests more or less offset one another, ideas may make a big difference' (Olson, 1989, p. 46).

Consequently the problem is that the standard rational choice theory ultimately entails an explanation based on 'power', i.e. an approach in which 'resources' dictate the direction of ideas, yet at the same time, behind it looms an approach based on the impact of ideas. However this crucial nuance usually escapes rational choice analysis. As in classical Marxism, ideas follow the power/resources dyad as a superstructure. Some ideas get selected by powerful groups because they are rationalizations of the groups' interests. Thus, those that happen to have power, impose the ideas convenient to them on the rest of the society. The (scientific) truth of ideas, or the intrinsic features of their normative dimensions are deemed almost irrelevant.

But even assuming the correctness of this emphasis on resources, interest and power, important questions still remain: where are those rationalizing ideas coming from? Why are those specific ideas and not others, with similar features, selected to play the rationalizing function? For instance, why was neoliberalism and not a revamped 'socialism with human face' called to rationalize interests and resource asymmetries in Eastern Europe? After all, it is known that socialism is far better than capitalism in preserving and creating asymmetries of power and resource control. Why has a specific way (the neoliberal one) of framing the interests of resource holders evolved the way it has? In the end, the rational choice approach on the lines illustrated by Knight does not touch on these questions and as such is not fully operational regarding the very problem of the spread of economic ideas. To postulate a general relation between 'material forces' and ideas may be a good starting point but it is not enough. When we study specific cases we want to know what is the more precise relationship between them? What is the precise mapping algorithm between the structure of resources and the emerging superstructure of ideas? For instance in Eastern Europe what is the relationship between powerful groups such as *nomenklatura* and powerful ideas such as neoliberalism? Does it make any sense to talk about a unitary *nomenklatura* group or class with homogenous interests and ideas?

Furthermore: Assuming that the correlation between resource holding groups or structures and ideas change is somehow established as a universal constant, the East European situation is then confronting us with a paradox. In the Latin American case, one may say that there were structures in place able to coordinate or enable such a sophisticated process of coordination between ideas and institutional change that led to the adoption of neoliberalism. But in the Eastern European case the uncertainties and profound transformations of the transition preclude such scenarios. To say that the demise of Marxism and the rise of neoliberalism as dominating paradigms are the result of a bargaining process in which the resource holders imposed their interests is a difficult thesis to sustain. To claim that the switch to neoclassical economics across Eastern Europe could be traced to a plot of *nomenklatura* (who had the 'asymmetric resources' and wanted to justify their privatization) is a very bold conjecture. In order to make a plausible argument about the Eastern European dynamics one has sooner or later to introduce into the picture ideas as autonomous or at least powerful forces able to shape and guide the perceptions and actions of social actors. The point of this exercise of questioning the rational choice theories is not to foundationally challenge the possibility of an approach based on interests. The point is that such an approach, in order to be more than a speculative heuristics, needs to become more precise and empirically grounded. And that means to take seriously into account the role of ideas.

PUTTING THINGS IN PERSPECTIVE: CRITICAL JUNCTURES AND INTERPRETIVE CIRCLES

Our investigation would be incomplete without discussing even briefly the framework in which ideas are seen not just as dependent or intervening variables but as the pivot of change, forces able to lead large-scale institutional transformations and to shape the reconfiguration of social structures. But that means nothing else than to place the entire discussion in the broadest feasible conceptual setting. And although the key role played by economic ideas in the process of transition is not the main object of the study, the more one advances in exploring the neoliberal revolution in Eastern Europe, the more one understands that the issue of spread and change of these ideas could not be fully separated from the issue of their functions and role. A discussion of the functional role they assume in 'critical junctures' emerges as a necessary element of the battery of possible approaches and probably as one of the best ways to articulate a meta-level framework for the study of spread and change of ideas.

As we have seen, rational choice theories tend to treat moments of radical institutional change in

> the same way that they treat the shift from one equilibrium to another; as a relatively unproblematic switching of statics where the 'reasons' for the collapse of the old order lead to new institutions that are 'designed' to overcome pathologies that are self-apparent to the agents involved. (Blyth, 2001, pp. 2–5)

The problem with this approach is that it neglects the key factor in such situations: uncertainty over the likely states of the world that such crises engender (Denzau and North, 1994; Roy et al. 2007). In such circumstances ideas become one of the few functional ways of coping with that uncertainty. Seen in this light, the entire Eastern European transition reveals itself as one of those cases in which ideas had to play such a functional role commensurate with the magnitude of uncertainty induced by the crisis and transformation of the old socialist regime. Such a reading of the case is intrinsically connected to the notion of 'critical junctures' seen as 'critical periods of politics', moments of 'special sensitivity of the system when the uncertainty is high and the possible directions of change are many' (Blyth, 2001, p. 76). Blyth, one of the leading authors advancing this approach, draws attention to two elements of the so-called critical junctures: the uncertainty faced by agents in such moments, and 'the set of ideas or mental models available to them for diagnosing what has gone wrong in the first place'. If that is the case, he suggests, one is required to go beyond the standard models of institutional change that 'dictate that institutional supply follows from the "need" for agents to realize their "given" interests' and in which the causal account 'tends to dissolve into a functionalist just-so story' (Elster, 2000 in Blyth, 2001).

Following this line of argumentation, one could explore the functional link ideas have with the issue of uncertainty. Moreover one could do that by using the very notion of 'interest'. In situations of institutional stability, writes Blyth, agents' interests are relatively unproblematic because under stabile institutional and social circumstances, those interests are stable or change in relatively predictable ways. In situations of institutional instability, the definition and conceptualization of one's interests becomes a problem. Because the situation is 'in a high degree unique', agents are unable to anticipate the outcomes of the evolutions, and hence the definition of their interests vis-à-vis the evolving circumstances. Thus the parameters of agents' interests in such an environment 'cannot be given by either assumption or structural location and can be decided only in terms of the ideas that agents themselves have about the causes of uncertainty'. Without reference to such ideas, 'neither interests nor strategies would have meaning under conditions of uncertainty'. As Beckert quoted by Blyth cautions, 'it becomes important to look at those *cognitive*, structural and cultural *mechanisms* that agents rely upon when determining their actions'. That is to say that 'cognitive mechanisms, *pace* ideas, are important because without having ideas as to how the world is put together, it would be cognitively impossible for agents to act in that world in any meaningful sense, particularly in situations of uncertainty' (Blyth, 2001, pp. 2–5).

To sum up: there are special circumstances and moments when ideas meet a pressing social function and become extremely potent. That function is not one of filling a predetermined role. Their impact is not predefined but open-ended, being the outcome of the very content of the ideas in point. The content of the available ideas that come to be used both as interpretive frameworks for the changing environment and to mobilize collective action becomes crucially important in determining the form of new institutions. Understanding that helps any effort aimed at analyzing social change process in which ideas are pivotal. This functionalist interpretation of the role of ideas works in other circumstances too. For instance, when interests are in deadlock, a policy window opens, a niche is created in which ideas can, if not dictate, at least shape policy. When a new institution is created, it can embody the beliefs of those who were involved in its creation, meaning that the ideas of original decision-makers become part of institutions and law (Goldstein, 1988). This is Goldstein's 'dual role' of ideas: firstly they influence actors, and secondly they become embedded in institutions that survive after the original actors depart. Therefore 'ideas do not influence behavior simply at one moment in time. Once a set of beliefs has become encased in institutions, these ideas can influence policy even after the interest of their creators have changed'. And 'once a strategy or "policy idea" is selected by politicians, for whatever reason, it has long-term ramifications' (Goldstein, 1993, p. 3). The bottom line is that ideas have a far deeper and more substantial function in social change, since in the end they may even be not only those that define and shape what interests are but also frame the very construction of social reality. The 'critical junctures' are those instances when this function is most visible and consequential.

Returning to the neoliberal revolution in Eastern Europe, it is obvious that one has to deal with one of those 'critical junctures' – i.e. one of those 'moments of special sensitivity of the system when the uncertainty is high and the possible directions of change are many' (Blyth, 2002a, p. 76). It was the typical situation in which social actors need ideas able to 'provide both an interpretation of the environment and a prescription as to how that environment *should be* structured' (Denzau and North, 1994, p. 4). The last years of the communist regime in Eastern Europe were indeed marked by a crisis of large proportions. It started not so much as a generalized collapse of social order but as a situation in which those in power become 'too feeble to govern but strong enough to block reform' (Skidelsky, 1995). That created a stage for change – enabling circumstances for a clash of ideas inducing a new configuration of institutions and interests. When the crisis deepened, one could recognize even clearer the contours of one of those moments that alters the direction of the ordinary interest-driven politics. Later in the process, a common theme throughout the Eastern Europe was the appreciation that time mattered – no two days were the same. A state of deep uncertainty became the norm. At the same time, there was a feeling that a unique window had opened and reformers had to 'seize the moment'. This time dependency leads to the 'procedural irregularities' that characterize genuine critical junctures. There was a genuine sense of now or never – when circumstances align and when the existence of a 'set of ideas or mental models for diagnosing what has gone wrong' and suggesting what should be done becomes vital. In a situation like the Eastern European one when the crisis manifested itself with salient intensity in the economic sector of society, the need for economic ideas becomes paramount. In other words, because the crisis was felt primarily as an economic crisis, an interest in (and a corresponding salience of) ideas able to give an economic diagnostic and prescription was absolutely normal. People were in search of solutions and it was just natural to look in the direction of economics for help. Indeed, as Blyth put it:

> Complex sets of ideas, such as ideas about the workings of the economy, allow agents to order and intervene in the world by aligning agents' beliefs, desires, and

goals. Only then can agents diagnose the crisis they are facing. In such circumstances ideas about social and economic order do not simply identify a given causal relationship in the economy for agents. Such ideas also serve to restructure those causal relationships by altering the agents' own beliefs about the interests of others, upon which the realization of the agents' own ideationally derived interests depend. (Blyth, 2002b, pp. 39–41).

To identify the social circumstances of the moment as creating a functional need for ideas and at the same time to recognize the neoclassical mainstream economics as a potential source able to meet that need is a good first step. To add that in Eastern Europe Marxism wasn't able to fill that function anymore is a second important component of the analytical narrative. Marxism was rendered impotent by the events: a theory about the crisis and collapse of capitalism has nothing to say about the crisis and collapse of socialism. This is the point where the problem of neoliberalism and neoclassical economics fully enters the picture. While the temptation to simply reduce the approach to the empirical observation of the succession of two families of ideas is powerful, simply stating the obvious historical fact that neoliberal ideas were there to fill the need may not be sufficient. Once this temptation discarded, the specific questions of what kind of ideas and how and why those very ideas were coming forth to meet the need become salient. And there is no doubt that precisely these questions are the important ones if one believes that ideas do really matter.

CONCLUSIONS

The excursion through a number of theoretical frameworks reconfirmed that the case of the spread of Western economic ideas and of the demise of Marxism in Eastern Europe is more complicated than simple and intuitive theses such as the 'triumph of the marketplace of ideas' may suggest. The dynamics and circumstances of the post-communist changes are complex and difficult to capture using just one model or theoretical perspective. A sample of approaches, from diffusion theory to secular religions, and from rational choice to institutionalism etc. was able to illustrate how the danger of being trapped in the search of a framework able to explain everything, and therefore explain nothing, could be avoided. The excursion showed how, in conjunction, these frameworks are able to offer a multifaceted perspective, combining the most relevant angles from different intellectual traditions and academic literatures. One has learned that the notion of 'marketplace of ideas' is more functional as a metaphor than as a model. Yet, one has also learned that key components implied in the notion are crucial for the analysis of the case. Scarcity is a vital factor in epistemic endeavors and the notion of choice is central for the situational logic facing an individual evaluating ideas and one's commitment to them. Diffusion theory demonstrated its descriptive and heuristic virtues – after all, any analytical narrative of the case relies implicitly on it – but also its explanatory limits. The 'growth of knowledge' perspective produced a series of interesting insights about the role of commitment and a very challenging speculative account of the entire process in terms of 'secular religions'. The focus on 'critical junctures' demonstrated how one could combine a contextual analysis with a broader conceptual perspective and showed thus a possible way of elaborating the kind of balanced approach required for an analysis that is both empirically and theoretically informed. In the end, one has learned that the difficulty is not in demonstrating that ideas matter or in finding interesting ways of looking at their spread and change, but in showing how one could fit the various possible approaches and theories in complementary and constructive ways.

The end result emerging out of this effort is instructive in multiple ways. In terms of methodological relevance, two such insights deserve a special note. The first is the recognition of the fact that in order to understand the dynamics of economic ideas, one is bound to return again and again to the very substance of those ideas, to their content: to what those ideas say about the world. That may seem a trivial observation but it is worth restating it as a conclusion because its methodological and analytical implications are so significant. The second is the recognition of a certain circularity of analysis involving the various theoretical frameworks apt to be mobilized and applied to such cases. While dealing with ideas, one deals with issues of understanding. And understanding calls in these circumstances for a sort of 'hermeneutic circle': The limits of one framework call for the mobilization of the strengths of another and so on until the circle is closed. This successive application of theories – sometimes perfectly complementing each other, sometimes challenging each other – may not be able to bring to light the ultimate and unique 'theory of neoliberalism' or the ultimate master explanation of the diffusion and change of ideas in Eastern Europe. However it is certain that it could lead to a more complex and nuanced understanding of the phenomena of interest.

NOTES

1. Kuhn has put a great importance on education. But in his view the educational process means training. Training does not require critical thought from the student. It is a process that inculcates or even indoctrinates the student into the current paradigm. Kuhn sees training as a routine, a manipulative activity that focuses on attaining through repetitive practice certain skills. The teacher's role is to guide the student dogmatically with text-

books as the central tool in the process. They are designed to enable the student to master the techniques of the paradigm while discouraging questioning and critical thinking (Kuhn, 1962, p. 150).

2. First there always will be a commensurability problem. In general a research program contains some, but not all, of the empirically confirmed explanatory content of its rival. Also, it contains an additional amount of explanatory content not contained in its competitor. Second is the timing. The moment the evaluation is made is of crucial importance. It is very difficult to appraise precisely a research program at a given point in time because in fact 'such an appraisal necessarily involves not just the appraisal of tested theories but also the appraisal of untested (though testable) and untestable theories'. In other words, it is very difficult to estimate precisely the heuristic power of a research program at a given point in time (Glass and Johnson, 1989, p. 112). Consequently, the comparison of research programs becomes a very complicated endeavor indeed.

3. This view is also articulated from a slightly different perspective by Cole, Cameron and Edwards: 'In the past judgments of valuation and worth were not the prerogative of people called economists but belonged to other people often calling themselves bishops and kings. Theology has always concerned itself with value and worth as has the study and exercise of law. For economists to gain predominance required a change in society which came with the development of exchange through relatively autonomous markets. The market grants the experience of not being directly governed by representatives of either gods or kings. The extension of markets into more and more areas of life was thus a revolutionary and in many ways liberating experience for the mass of people and a threat to vested interest. The expression of this experience in the realm of ideas was a shift towards justifying the valuation of the activities produced by markets in the form of prices' (Cole et al., 1991, p. 6).

4. The belief in economic progress as a universal solution is not a disciplinary obsession of economists. On the contrary, it is widespread outside the economics profession. Nelson even conjectures that precisely because this belief has been so widely held, economists have had such a central role in modern society. But this belief would not have pushed economists to pre-eminence if it were not associated with a clear and rational notion about the instruments of its implementation (Nelson, 1991, p. 3).

5. Nelson notes that the term 'rational', as employed by economists, has multiple meanings but one of them remains constant for all: 'Rationality' is a term of moral approval. Equipped with both the understanding of the basic human problem and the moral and instrumental principle that offers the solution to it, the modern economist becomes a major social figure of high authority: 'As the priest of this economic theology, economists today properly sit at the centers of power. They have no personal wealth, lands, empire or military supporters to give them influence. Their influence is rather a moral authority – the power to dispense legitimacy in the contemporary welfare state. Government acts that advance the economic progress and the rationality of society receive the blessings of economists; those that impede progress are deemed illegitimate. (. . .) Those modern leaders who have genuinely contributed to the economic progress of mankind will receive a favorable verdict in history. Those condemned will instead have obstructed the laws of growth and economic development, thereby serving to perpetuate economic scarcity – which is the fundamental cause of humanity's current condition of strife and misbehavior' (Nelson, 1991, p. 9).

6. *The Encyclopedia of the World's Religions* includes a chapter on Marxism, on the account that it meets all the essential requirements of a religion.

7. In Wible's view the failure of the commercial market to organize most scientific research is clearly reflected in the very emergence of the notion of a 'marketplace of ideas'. His point is that this notion emerged precisely because the standard market model was not able to capture what was really happening in the reality of science: 'The mere existence of the concept of a "marketplace of ideas" shows that we are beyond the realm of the commercial marketplace and firms' (Wible, 1998, p. 176).

PART III

Facets, themes and cases: diversity and change in the neoliberal revolution of ideas

This section of the book continues to explore the spread of economic ideas in Eastern Europe by focusing on a series of cases that illuminate and exemplify very concrete facets and themes of the process. Out of the cases available (as a result of several field-based research projects run between 2001 and 2006), we have chosen four: The case of 'Austrian economics' – the school of thought always identified as the bearer of the most radical pro-market vision, and whose very presence makes clear the contrast between the mode and magnitude of the spread of the truly radical pro-market ideas, as opposed to merely neoclassical mainstream economics; The case of local intellectual responses to Western economics – an in-depth look at the local reactions to neoclassical economics and at the resourceful modes in which Western ideas were received and adapted in ways that go beyond the pre-defined Western expectations; The spread of the flat tax in Eastern Europe – a case of endogenous initiative in policy ideas that by showing Easterners taking the lead in a key economic policy area, challenges the standard image of the Easterner subservient to the Western economic orthodoxies; And finally an in-depth look at how the limits of policies and strategies inspired by neoclassical economics invited a challenge that led to the subsequent rise to salience of the so called 'institutionalist' perspective. The assumption behind the section is straightforward: Once the broad, macro-level perspective is replaced by fine-grained approaches focused on particular examples of the Eastern European transition in the realm of economic ideas, two things happen: first some of the basic myths or misconstructions regarding the nature and dimensions of this transition are exposed and second, new facets and processes are revealed.

The cases illustrate many themes identified in the previous sections as deserving special attention: the specific processes and channels of diffusion, the interplay between ideas and interests, the need of a more rigorous comparative analysis, the internal dynamics of epistemic communities, the impact of the creativity and versatility of adopters, the role of accidents and circumstances as well as the elements of rational calculation involved in ideas selection, etc. Each case illustrates more than a single such theme and many themes illuminated by one case overlap with some of the themes exemplified by another. Yet, despite this diversity, there is something that connects and unites all of them. Separated and in conjunction they challenge several notions that, sometimes openly and sometimes at a subliminal level, are plaguing the way many people perceive the Eastern European transformation of economic ideas: the notion of the standardization and 'regimentation' of economic thinking as a result of the spread of Western ways of doing economics, the belief that the Eastern Europeans have been passively embracing this uniformity and standardization and, last but not least, the myth that extreme forms of pro-market views (so-called 'market fundamentalism') have been dominating the region. Yet, without denying that the standardization tendency and the straitjacket put by mainstream economics on economic thinking have been real and in many ways stultifying, a closer look at the reality on the ground shows that the truth is more nuanced than that.

To be more precise, the spread of the Western way of conceptualizing economic order has been increasingly seen as part of the larger 'globalization' phenomenon – i.e. as a regional manifestation of a global trend. That way of defining it brought with it an entire baggage of criticisms framed as variations on the general themes used by the critics of globalization. For instance, it has been argued that it leads to uniformity in economic thinking and encourages formulaic analysis; that it introduces a standardized approach (same methodology) that expunges the role of values; that it stifles the local, cultural and national perspective on economic issues, in a word, that it obliterates and undermines alternative models and interpretations, thus generating a lack of diversity in thinking about the market. As one could easily see, all these are projected as an avatar in the specific area of economic ideas of a so-called 'logic of globalization', a logic assumed to be at work in everything 'globalization' touches. That sets up a stage for two theses. The first is indeed the above mentioned 'uniform logic of globalization' conjecture. The second is the opposite: In the cultural and intellectual arena one expects that markets and open competition will be introducing more diversity, choice and creativity (Cowen, 1998). The challenge is clear: Is the field of 'ideas about the market' different? Are ideas about markets and capitalism converging into a single, monopolistic doctrine? Is this trend consequently stifling diversity? Or can one actually find elements of originality and diversity?

The cases presented in this section are each in their own way a contribution to this discussion. A closer look at the specific aspects and processes exemplified by them demonstrates that neither did the realignment of the epistemic communities lead to an absolute regimentation nor did the substance of the Western ideas go unchallenged. What happens when market ideas penetrate an epistemic community that is not just imitating and absorbing some model but is filtering it through a very powerful normative vision? What happens with the actors involved? Is there something that might be defined in terms of a specific, local, national culture reaction? What happens when those adopting specific economic ideas go further in the application of those ideas than those diffusing them? What are the comparative conditions shaping the international diffusion of such pioneering ideas? This section provides inciting evidence relevant to these questions. The emerging evidence tells a story in which the locals and their epistemic communities were not simply brainwashed in the gray uniformity of the 'neoclassical synthesis' of the Western economics. The more the process of spread of ideas and paradigm shift advanced, the more one could see not only uniformity and regimentation but reactions, resistance, ideas evolving and new bolder developments. One could see how the bold policy idea of a flat tax took off and gained a new life in Eastern Europe, how Austrian economics ideas were given a new and very interesting twist and how new institutionalist views received a boost due to the transition and reform trials and failures of neoclassical recommendations. In a word, a careful observer is confronted with a very dynamic field not only in terms of replacing the old with the new, not only of spreading the Western mainstream economics but also in challenging and changing it. Looking from this angle at the cases selected, one discovers a more nuanced and realistic perspective while the 'neoliberal revolution' in economic ideas in Eastern Europe gains new dimensions that make it appear to us an even more fascinating and momentous historical event.

6.   A test of market fundamentalism: Austrian economics

The notion that the transition process following the collapse of communism in Eastern Europe represents a triumph of 'market fundamentalism' has become commonplace in many quarters (Kuttner, 1997; Soros, 1998; Stiglitz, 2002). One would imagine that such strong claims regarding the spread of the so-called 'market fundamentalism' would be based at least on a modicum of research and evidence. Yet the dearth of such investigations in a context of a broader dearth of studies of centre-right politics in Eastern Europe (Hanley, 2006b, p. 9) and the relative scarcity of non-biased histories of libertarian and radical pro-market movements is an acknowledged reality. And so, prima facie, most claims of 'market fundamentalism' simply seem to rest more on rhetoric and speculation than on analysis. This chapter tries to confront this issue. Its thrust is that the claims made about the hegemony of 'market fundamentalist' ideas could be probed by looking at one specific school of thought that typifies the radical pro-market approach. By looking at the prevalence of the 'Austrian Economics' epistemic community in the region, one could test some of the claims made about the sway of radical pro-market ideas in that part of the world.

There are several reasons why a focus on Austrian ideas in Eastern Europe is an appropriate vehicle for such an enterprise. First, Austrian economics is such a suitable proxy for radical free market ideas because no other school of thought places as much emphasis on the primacy of markets. This means that it is an 'extreme case': we are not only looking at a general pro-market position, but also at the most radical, free-market subset of economics. One could claim that intended or otherwise, Austrians as ideal-type pro-market libertarians seem to be the exemplary target of those who criticize neoliberalism.[1] Second, Austrian economics is viewed by many as a heterodox school of thought that is distinct from neoclassical economics (Snowdon et al., 1994). This ensures that their boundaries are clear enough to be effectively documented. When discussing the ideational distinction between Austrian and neoclassical economics, it is important to defend the notion that it is only the former, not the latter, and not both, that approaches 'market fundamentalism'. It is true that economists hold a set of beliefs that systematically differ from the general public (Caplan, 2001) and wide consensus exists over the efficiency of market interaction under a set of basic assumptions. However, most economists routinely feel that these assumptions fail to hold, and that this necessitates an intervening role for government (Klein and Stern, 2007). As Bryan Caplan points out,

> The charge of 'market fundamentalism' is silly, failing even as a caricature. If you ask the typical economist to name areas where markets work poorly, he gives you a list on the spot . . . *Market failure* is not a concept that has been forced upon a reluctant economics profession from the outside. It is an internal out-growth of economists' self-criticism . . . True market fundamentalists in the eco-nomics profession are few and far between. [emphasis in original] (Caplan 2007, p. 184)

Even one of the godfathers of 'shock therapy', Jeffrey Sachs, was clear that 'the role model [for post-Soviet Europe] is the West European economy', that successful reforms would require some form of Marshall Plan from the West, and he explicitly extolled an empirical agenda with a role for the state: 'I am not myself a free market economist in all its glory, in the sense that I believe in a significant role of government in many areas'.[2] And even Milton Friedman, 'has no quasi-religious need to defend the impeccability of the free market . . . [Despite being] a legendary liber-tarian, [he] makes numerous exceptions on everything from money to welfare to antitrust' (Caplan, 2007, pp. 184–5). One could thus echo Caplan's view that that the only group of economists that 'categorically reject the notion of suboptimal market performance' are Austrian – the 'followers of Ludwig von Mises and especially his student Murray Rothbard'.[3] But as Caplan notes, 'The closest thing to market fundamen-talists are not merely outside the mainstream of the economics profession. They are way outside' (Caplan, 2007, p. 185). Indeed, neoclassical eco-nomics are 'middle of the road' in comparison,

> The monetarism that Friedman and his followers were preaching was not quite as conservative as advertised. In fact, the University of Chicago professor was treading not far from the middle of the economic road, flanked on the left by the likes of Galbraith and Leontief and on the right by Hayek . . . Hans Sennholz . . . and Ludwig von Mises. (Malabre, 1994, p. 144; cited in Boettke, 1995, p. 35)

To sum up, mainstream economics, the 'neoclassical synthesis' in any of its avatars, distances itself consciously from a radical pro-market position. It is impossible to maintain that the typical economist is a 'market funda-mentalist' (Klein and Stern, 2007). Aside from the semantic incongruity of accusing an entire scientific discipline of being 'dogmatic' and 'extremist', most economists do not believe in the universal superiority of markets over government. The typical economist is moderate center-left. Indeed, the Austrians are the only ones that come close. And therefore they are a suitable focal point for the study of free market idea dissemination in Eastern Europe.

Finally, it is noteworthy that Austrian economics has foundational relevance to the economics of transition. Not only is it the school of thought that restlessly predicted that socialism would fail (Mises, 1981) but also its history is indelibly tied to Eastern Europe. The two most important founders of the Austrian school – Carl Menger and Ludwig von Mises – were both born in the Galicia, which at the time was part of the Austro-Hungarian Empire. Menger was actually born in the city of Nowy Sacz, which is now in southern Poland. In addition to this he received his doctorate in Law from the University of Cracow, making him an 'Austrian economist' to be sure, although in fact he was Polish. And the city of Mises's birth was Lemberg, now known as Lviv, part of western Ukraine (Kirzner, 2001, p. 2). This is why one may consider that for some the spread of Austrian economics to Central and Eastern Europe has a deep significance as it returns the ideas to the homeland of the early protagonists. As the Czech economist Josef Sima (2006) emphatically declares, 'We used to be part of it, and we are part of it again'.[4]

'AUSTRIAN ECONOMICS': AN INTELLECTUAL TRADITION

'Austrian economics' is a heterodox school of thought and despite the formation occurring in Vienna, the topographic title has no real contemporary relevance. The genesis of Austrian economics as a distinct intellectual framework can be traced to 1871, and the publication of Carl Menger's *Principles of Economics* (Grundsatze der Volkswirtschaftslehre). Menger was one of three economists together with William Stanley Jevons and Leon Walras to concurrently (and independently) assert that economic behavior is determined by marginal utility, where 'marginal' refers to one extra unit of the good or service being consumed. The 'Austrian' prefix came to prominence when Menger's student, Eugen Bohm-Bawerk, wrote an account of Austrian economics for the Annals of the American Academy of Political and Social Science (Bohm-Bawerk, 1891). It's important to note that the label 'Austrian' was a pejorative term invented by critics: during this time the Methodenstreit (strife over methods) was pitting Austrian economists on one side, and members of the German Historical School on the other.

From the very first moments of an Austrian identity, the school was characterized by its method of 'abstract generalizations', and although it had common roots with what became known as neoclassicism, it evolved as a separate tradition. A significant moment in the exposure of the Austrian school occurred in 1974 when Friedrich Hayek was awarded the Nobel Prize in Economics, but perhaps a more important event had occurred one year previously, with the death of Ludwig von Mises in 1973. This precipitated a sequence of conferences organized by the Institute for Humane Studies, which deliberately united the somewhat isolated scholars working in the Austrian tradition.[5] These conferences also pioneered a lingering attention to self-contemplation and although debates on scholarly 'purity' can curtail the professional advancement of the school, such tight conceptual boundaries actually help to map out the revival process. The easiest way to ascertain whether someone is an 'Austrian economist' may be to simply say, 'if you call yourself an Austrian you're an Austrian'.[6] However, the errors of commission and omission necessitate a dual approach; self-definition as an aid to identify possible Austrians, but in addition to an effort to subject their ideas to some objective criteria – to deem whether this label fits. This requires an overview of the key characteristics of the school.

Lachmann provides three clear tenets that unite Austrian theorizing: individualism, subjectivism and time (Lachmann, 1978, pp. 1–2). Attention to individualism means that all economics events must be reducible to the actions and plans that exist within the minds of economic actors. This leads to an aversion to formalism and aggregation within econometric techniques and macroeconomics (Vaughn, 1994, p. 105). Subjectivism applies not only to individual preferences but also to expectations, and since these will differ between people knowledge will be imperfect, and information asymmetries. The fact that action takes place over time, and underlying economic conditions are constantly changing, means that accurate forecasting is misguided and that all decisions take place under conditions of uncertainty. We end up with a stable of economic premises synonymous with Austrian economics, the role of a-priori theorizing, the importance of applying such theory to interpret and explain economic history, the subjectivism of utility and costs, conditions of market coordination (as opposed to equilibrium) in light of imperfect information and uncertainty, the generation and function of knowledge, the function of entrepreneurship, the role of both profit and loss, attention to processes over time rather than static end states, the structural effects of relative price changes, the role of private property in economic calculation, and causal theoretic frames that explain spontaneous orders (and institutions more generally) in light of human action (Boettke, 1994).

The Austrian school also takes much of its heart and soul from the socialist calculation debate, and although one needs not recap the main arguments there are several implications worth noting (Lavoie, 1985; Boettke, 1993; Boettke and Leeson, 2005). First, the Austrians demonstrated that the notion of a socialist economy – given the stated intermediate objective of advanced material progress – was logically impossible. This is because rational allocation requires economic exchange, exchange requires prices, and prices require private property. The idea that private property is a prerequisite for rational economic calculation – and thus for a functioning economy – is an obvious intellectual justification for privatization. However it would be wrong to infer that Austrian ideas are consistent with typical privatization policy. While neoclassical theory recommends the strategic auctioning off of some elements of state property to the private sector, Austrians would advocate the elimination of state ownership, period. The key point to note is that Mises's argument was a technical one, and was not based on whether the central planners were able to provide the incentives that would motivate the workforce. Although the incentive problem of socialism is widely accepted, the calculation problem is distinctly Austrian. The idea that public bodies are unable to replicate the information content of prices that emerge from a free market generates a basic dualism between markets and states that is a further area of Austrian relevance (Hayek, 1945). Many Western economies operate a hybrid model that combines principles associated with both social democracy and laissez-faire capitalism, and this mixed model has been presented as 'a third way'. Austrians would reject the coherence and plausibility of such a system arguing that 'the issue is always the same: the government or the market. There is no third solution' (Mises, 1981b, p. 28).

Further illustrations of how Austrian policy ideas differ from neoclassical orthodoxy can he found in the monetary system and public finances. Although a consensus of economists favor a stable monetary framework, this is manifested within the mainstream either through a currency board (often used for developing countries), or, for more developed nations, an independent central bank. By contrast, the Austrian position would 'privatize' financial instruments, and completely de-politicize the money supply. This might be achieved through a gold standard, and the aim of zero growth of the money supply (White, 1989). The main reason for zero money supply growth is to prevent politicians from being able to inflate their way out of debt, and this has direct relevance on public finances. Whereas the ambition of most economists might be some form of balanced budget provision (to reduce budget deficits), a fully privatized 'Austrian' economy would seek to reduce government spending for its own sake. Their aim is not to balance the books, but to drastically slash them.

To sum up, in the context of transition economics the Austrian school is distinguishable from similar positions on account of the fact that (i) the information problem that makes socialism impossible necessitates complete private ownership of property; (ii) a third way is incoherent; (iii) the money supply should be free from political interference; (iv) the size of government should fall drastically; and (v) when seen in the context of Eastern Europe it's not merely anti-communist, it's pro-market. These issues are magnified by the uneasy tension between the power of Austrian economic policy implications on the one hand, and on the other, the lack of faith that Austrians have over policy solutions. After all, politics is about compromise and therefore fundamentally incompatible with such extreme, 'fundamentalist' positions. As a parenthesis, one may note that at some primary level, the claim that Eastern European transition is an example of 'market fundamentalism' is challenged by the fact that by definition 'market fundamentalists' are so uneasy about any conventional public policy effort. As Mises said about this perennial conflict, 'a liberal government is a contradicto in adjecto' (Mises, 1996). Since then, the mark of true market fundamentalists was that they have rarely been at ease or functional in the policy arena. However, this simple point is not sufficient to fully assess the truth claims of the position, and a more detailed overview of the regional situation is required.

AUSTRIAN ECONOMICS IN EASTERN EUROPE

Although it is impossible to present a comprehensive overview of Austrian groups and thinkers across the whole of Eastern Europe, a brief overview of several major countries – Poland, the Czech Republic, Slovakia, Hungary, Estonia, Latvia, Lithuania, Bulgaria and Romania – as well as due attention to influential events in the USSR/Russia could offer a clearer picture of the measure in which the Austrian 'market fundamentalism' is present or not in the landscape.

If somebody takes seriously the thesis that 'market fundamentalism' has played an important role in the collapse of communism and the subsequent transition process, there are many reasons why the Czech Republic would be the first place to look for evidence. The emblematic nature of figures like Vaclav Klaus is one reason. Another reason is that translations of Austrian and radical pro-market texts into Czech have a longstanding tradition. Some of those translations have been written by those who went on to become ministers. For example the works of Bastiat have been available in Czech since 1923 and the 1990–1992 minister of privatization, Tomas Jezek, has transcribed Hayek's *The Road to Serfdom and Law, Legislation and Liberty*.

Sean Hanley traces the advent of 'neoliberal economics' in Czechoslovakia to the late 1960s and the 1970s which 'not only came to reject reform communist notions of socialist market' but gravitated from the Keynesian 'neo-classical synthesis towards neoliberalism of the Austrian and Chicago schools' (Hanley et al., 2007). This was facilitated by a period when Czechoslovakia enjoyed a brief moment of liberalization and economic literature by the likes of Milton Friedman, George Stigler, James Buchanan and specifically Austrian works became available to students, including Vaclav Klaus. Klaus has been indelibly tied to the post-communist history of the Czech Republic: in December 1989 he became the Minister of Finance in the first non-communist government, and went on to lead the civic Democratic Party to elected victory in 1992 to become Prime Minister. Like many early reformers Klaus was able to leave Czechoslovakia and spent time studying in the United States (Sima and Stastny, 2000, p. 157), and his role sheds most light on both the dissemination and influence of pro-market ideas. Klaus has said, 'Hayek as an economist, ideologist, philosopher and methodologist was a source of thinking of all those who refuse in today's Czechoslovakia not only socialism, but also constructivism based on the ambitions of technocrats and left intellectuals and leading toward a new dictatorship of state over the individual' (cited in Sima, unpublished). And he also credits Austrian ideas with the statement, 'Hayek had a great influence on me. However, I think that I learned the most from Mises' *Human Action*, and that has been true up to now' (Junglich et al., 1998, p. 133, cited in Sima and Stastny, 2000, p. 163).

In addition to these proclamations, his free-market credentials are impressive: Klaus was the first East European to join the Mont Pelerin Society and Murray Rothbard no less proclaimed that 'feisty free-market economist and Prime Minister Vaclav Klaus was able to drive through rapid change to a genuine free market' (Rothbard, 1996, p. 396). Klaus made his own contribution to the literature on transition (Klaus, 1997) and these works echo one of the most important Austrian points. First, that radical, thorough and speedy reforms are necessary. 'The only practical and realistic way to the improvement of the living standard will be to abolish totally the institutions of central planning to dismantle control over prices, wages, the exchange rate, and foreign trade and to radically transform the existing system of property rights' (Klaus, 1991, p. 4, cited in Sima, unpublished). And second that there is no logical third way – it is a dualism between markets and states, and 'market socialism' is incoherent. 'Thanks to these [Austrian-school] insights we in the Czech Republic have never toyed with hybrid systems and "Third Ways" of various designs' (Klaus, 1996, p. 256, cited in Sima, unpublished).

Despite all of the above, many consider Klaus's rhetoric as often conflicting with his actions and pro-market radicals and Austrians have been critical of his inconsistency (Sima and Stastny, 2000). This is a recurring theme in East European politics, as former dissidents and idealists became confronted with the practical constraints on policy-making. Klaus's record shows that he adopted rent control, slammed 'predatory pricing' and was even involved, in 1990, in the selection of Paul Samuelson's *Economics* as the first non-Marxist textbook (Sima and Stastny, 2000, p. 170). Indeed, Klaus's economics can be said to be fairly modern mainstream and his affection for Austrian economics to be more of a consequence of his conservative political leanings. But in the end even giving him full credentials of being a 'market fundamentalist' could do nothing more than to point out how few such figures of his stature and convictions have been even more stringent and are present in the public life of Eastern Europe.

The first Czech free market think-tank was the Liberalni Institut, formed in 1990 as an offshoot of the F.A. Hayek Club that was founded one year previously, during the 'Velvet Resolution', by Jiri Schwarz and Mirosla Sevcik. Some of the notable translations provided in the early 1990s included Paul Hayne's textbook, *The Economic Way of Thinking*, which has subsequently become co-authored by Austrian economists Peter Boettke and David Prychitko (Heyne et al., 2005) not to mention the works of F.A. Hayek, Ludwig von Mises, Israel Kirzner and Murray Rothbard. One of the chief pioneers of Austrian economics in Prague (and indeed to wider Central Europe) was Josef Sima (Sima and Stastny, 2000, p. 174). As Sima pointed out, in the comments made to the Austrian Scholars Conference, in 2006 at Auburn, Alabama, it is only recently that students of liberalism have no longer been confined to private study, but could receive a systematic training. The Liberalni Institute facilitated an influx of Austrian literature, and produced its own contributions to the field. One of its founders, Jiri Schwarz, has become Dean of the Economics faculty at the University of Economics, Prague, being one of the few Austrians in Eastern Europe able to provide an imbedded institutional method of influence. Although Prague would appear to be the first place to expect radical ideas to emerge, it is only relatively recently that we see genuine idea-carriers exert influence and form networks. And even then, the predominant diffusion channel has been through wider education to students rather than policy reform. And given the notorious limited presence Austrians have in academia, that speaks a lot about the magnitude of the presence of Austrian school market fundamentalists in the country.

The Slovakian epistemic community has been heavily shaped by the influence of the neighboring Liheralni Institute, and it is their translations and public events that are responsible for the first glimpse of Austrian ideas for many Slovaks. Currently the main organization that disseminates Austrian ideas is The F.A. Hayek Foundation Bratislava (FAHF). It is an independent NGO founded in 1990/91 to offer market solutions during the reform process including pension reform and the flat tax. The FAHF also sought to educate young students through 'Liberal Weekends' which were affiliated to the Liberalni Institute. The President is Dr Jan Oravec and it contains a number of economists engaged in the works of Hayek. For example Matus Posvanc works for both the FAHF and the spin-off Hayek Consulting Ltd, and runs an Austrian course at the Economics University Bratislava. However it's important to note the chronology: Posvanc himself only became aware of Hayek in 1999, and the FAHF only published *The Road to Serfdom* in 2001. Another organization that deals in Austrian ideas is the Institute of Economic and Social Studies (INESS). It was formed in 2006 and is a traditional think-tank operating in the space between academic ideas and policy implementation. As their web page boasts, in its first year, INESS members have published '73 articles in the major Slovak newspapers and magazines, given 58 interviews for 3 most popular Slovak TV stations and 12 interviews for the 2 major Slovak radio stations'.

The general impression one gets about the Slovak pro-market economics is that a wider strain of Conservative ideas is prevalent. Typical is the 'Conservative Institute of M.R. Stefanik', chaired by Peter Zajac, which began publishing materials in 2001. Through this institute Peter Gonda and Pavel Chalupnicek published *In Defense of the Free Market* (Gonda and Chalupnicek, 2007), a collection of lectures stemming from the 'Conservative Economic Quarterly Lecture Series' (CEQLS) in Bratislava. Other conservative organizations include the Institute for Free Society and the Right Spectrum, plus Eunie, a Euro-skeptic portal. One of the crowning glories of the Slovakian development of liberal economic ideas was when Bratislava hosted the 2001 Mont Pelerin Society meeting, but notice this occurred a decade after the fall of the Berlin Wall. Indeed the current scene looks more like it is neo-conservatism, rather than neo-liberalism, that has found marginal policy relevance.

In the Poland case the impact of the radical pro-market Austrianism seem to be easy to trace. The leader of Polish shock therapy, Leszek Balcerowicz has always demonstrated his knowledge of the distinction between mainstream neoclassical economics and the work of Mises and Hayek:

I was struck by the level of absurdities as propagated by top-level Western economists, even in the 1950s and in the '60s, because they constructed models which were very elegant. But they have only one weakness. They have assumed away all the complications of the real world and with this simplified model, they have declared a victory of socialism over capitalism. So since I studied the socialist economic system and knew that it was basically flawed because it deprived people of economic freedom, which is one of the other fundamental freedoms, private property, and the right to set up enterprise. I was really very, very surprised that in the West most of the economists, who were technically very good, could propagate such absurdities for such a long time. And against this background people like Hayek or von Mises or then Friedman but especially Hayek and von Mises, came to me as people who were not mistaken, who could recognize problems early on before they really emerged. . . So there were economists and economists, and much of the economics profession was wrong in the West. (Leszek Balcerowicz, personal communication)[7]

Balcerowicz received an MBA from St Johns University, New York in 1974 before returning to Warsaw to become an economics expert for Solidarity. He recognized the distinctly Austrian position that socialism is fundamentally unworkable, and reforms had to be more than superficial movements towards a 'Western' economic model. He credits Jeffrey Sachs who 'played a very important role in Poland in persuading those who needed as well as advisers with Polish roots such as the LSE's Stanislaw Gomulka, and Jacek Rostowski'. His views on the required economic changes are telling: 'you have to have private ownership, stable money, sound public finance and unbureaucratic regulation of businesses, etc'.[8] But according to the Austrian criteria previously set forth, and despite Balcerowicz's rhetoric, his premises would have more in common with neoclassical orthodoxy than Austrian economics. Indeed his criticisms of 'Western economists' were contextual and by the early 1990s he was working more with Sachs than with any members of the Western Austrian economics epistemic community. And thus Balcerowicz illustrates very well the ambiguity emerging at the boundary between neoclassical economics and more radically pro-market perspectives.

The presence of scholars such as the Polish philosopher Milowit Kuninski who became familiar with classical liberal thought, published in 1999 *Knowledge. Ethics and Politics in F.A. von Hayek's Thought* and the first Polish translation of *The Fatal Conceit* do not change the fact that the Austrians are in no way major players in Polish economics. Such examples are telling. One could see how far from the top table of policy the scholars that disseminate Austrian ideas are, in fact, and also how far such ideas could be from being policy. Despite Poland appearing as a locus of 'neoliberal' reforms on account of the shock therapy employed, a search for a 'market fundamentalism' hegemony is found lacking.

The same limited impact of Austrians could be seen in Hungary. Janos Kornai established a global reputation as an inside critic of central planning. His salience at home and abroad dwarfed a possible Austrian alternative in his country. In 1957 he published his dissertation that criticized the command economy and when it was published in English in 1959 he became the first Hungarian economist living in Hungary to have a book published in the West (Wagener, 1998, p. 370). In 1963 he was able to travel outside of Hungary and joined the faculty of Harvard in 1986 to cement his reputation as one of Eastern Europe's foremost economists. *Anti-Equilibrium* (1971) was a critique of Walrasian general equilibrium analysis, *Economies of Shortage* (1980) attempted to explain the nature of shortages, *The Road to a Free Economy* (1990) offered a proposal for transition, and *The Socialist System* (1992) is a definitive firstblood assessment of the failings of the planned economy – all books that could be interpreted in the Austrian tradition. In *The System Paradigm* (2000) Kornai demonstrates his awareness of Austrian thought, praising the fact that unlike Oscar Lange, Mises and Hayek 'do not sidestep the fundamentally important fact that politics and the economy are tightly connected'. But although Kornai adopts the Austrian position on the socialist calculation debate – accepting that there's no such thing as a third way – there remains a clear intellectual chasm. According to John Cassidy, Kornai mentions Hayek's work in passing, but he doesn't say that Hayek 'made precisely the same points more than 50 years ago in *The Road to Serfdom*, and amplified them in a series of books during the ensuing 45 years' (Cassidy, 2000). Indeed, even socialist John Roemer acknowledges that Kornai followed in the path of Hayek:

> (. . .) to the extent the planners would require anything (other than profit maximization) of the firm managers, the managers could not then be held responsible for losses the firms incurred: thus, any interference with the market by the CPB [Central Planning Board] would let the managers off the hook and, in effect, place all responsibility on the planners for the outcome. This point [of Hayek] brilliantly foreshadows the political sociology of the soft budget constraint as developed by Janos Kornai . . . some thirty years later. (Roemer 1994, 31–2, cited in Gordon, 1995)

To sum up, the Hungarian case is encapsulated in Kornai. His brand of criticism of Socialism left limited room for the Austrian tradition. Far from being a carrier of 'market fundamentalism' Kornai, although not the 'average Hungarian economist', probably typifies best the attitude to economics prevalent in Hungary in the 1980s and 1990s.

Moving to the Baltic states, one of the most vocal, visible and radical reformist politicians from the entire Eastern block was Estonian Prime Minister Mail Laar, an idealistic leader who was instrumental in the adoption of a flat tax (Evans, 2005). Laar was influenced by libertarianism, but the fact that Milton Friedman's *Free to Choose* was the only economics book that he had read demonstrates his initial unawareness of Austrian ideas. Indeed the fact that so many internal advisers advised against adopting a flat tax shows how rare such sentiment was inside Estonia at the time. It is telling that Hardo Pajula served as economic adviser to Laar for a brief period in 1996 after the flat tax had been adopted. Pajula spent the early 1990s studying at the University of Cambridge, England, and is now a Professor at the Estonian Business School. According to Estonian economist Kaire Poder, Pajula was recommending *The Road to Serfdom* to students in 1994. But it wasn't until 2001 that he translated it into Estonian (in a project financed by the Friedrich Naumann Foundation, Hayek's *The Fatal Conceit* had already been translated in 1996) and the fact is that overall the availability of Austrian ideas has been sparse and recent.

An informal Estonian Hayek Society ran during the mid-1990s and together with Hardo Pajula contained Peter Lohmus (former Deputy Governor of the Bank of Estonia), Anvar Samost (head of business news of the Baltic News Service (BNS) and Meelis Kitsing (a former Tallinn city councilor, and now an academic). Kitsing wrote a bachelor's thesis on Hayek's approach to history demonstrating a familiarity with ideas developed during internships in the USA (in 1993 under the Open Studies Foundation, and in 1994 under a Charles Koch Fellowship). He was also President of the Res Publica society (a community of young conservatives) from 1992–1995 – and it subsequently became a political party in 2001. He also helped to form The Estonian Free Society Institute in 2007, with Paul Vahur. The Institute's advisory board members include Taavi Veskimagi (former Minister of Finance), and Heikki Kranich (former MP, Minister of the Environment) and the patron is Sum Kallas, (Estonian Prime Minister 2002–2003 and current vice-president of the EU Commission). In terms of academic influence, the Estonian Business School has facilitated and financed a number of projects since the turn of this century but focusing on methodology rather than policy applications. Overall Estonia seems to be the Eastern European country where pro-market community fares best in the political and public sphere.

The Lithuanian Free Market Institute, founded in 1990 has been marginally involved in the reform process and provided analysis that has informed and influenced Lithuanian policy. For example it has been involved in most legislation that has liberalized the banking sector, moved toward a flatter and lower taxation regime and campaigned for deregulation of private enterprise. But despite the 'free market' label of the institute, the specific Austrian credentials aren't obvious. Plus their real policy involvement has all been since the mid-1990s, implying that the institute has responded to the post-Soviet institutional environment, rather than created it.

In Bulgaria immediately after the Second World War, the economics of Hayek was analyzed by the likes of Hristoforov (1946) and relative to other pails of the region Austrian economics has received some more consistent academic attention. In his book Avramov (2007) 'deals occasionally with the spread of Austrian economics and different types of capitalist theories in Bulgaria. This is an important, but mostly implicit line in the text.' Of particular significance is Nikolay Nenovsky. He has written a biography on Simeon Demonstenov, the early twentieth-century economist he labels as a 'Bulgarian Austrian', and Cantillon (whom he sees very much as belonging within the tradition of an 'Austrian' monetary school) (Nenovsky, 2002) demonstrating an attention both to history of economic thought and Austrian biography. He has also utilized Austrian analysis of interwar monetary policy (Nenovsky, 2006) and macro-stabilizations (Nenovsky et al., 2007). It is his capacity as a Member of the Bulgarian National Bank Governing Council that makes his familiarity with Hayek (Nenovsky, 1999) all the more important. He explicitly refers to it with regard to the implementation of Bulgaria's currency board in 1997 that successfully combated inflation:

> Under a smoothly operating currency board, we could undoubtedly claim that Hayek's recommendations have been followed in the closest possible way in Bulgaria. Monetary policy has been removed, central bank functions limited, and money supply fluctuations smoothed. The role of government is limited and rules dominate over discretion (Nenovsky, 1999, p. 20).[9]

However it is important to put this in context with the far larger pressure for a currency board from the International Monetary Fund. Seen in this light, the claims of Austrian influence gain different proportions.

More recently, The Bulgarian Hayek Society was founded in 2002 by students from the University of National and World Economy, and economists of the Bulgarian National Bank led by Nikolay Nenovsky.[10] Again this demonstrates the freshness of organizational development, and the lack of evidence to claim that Bulgarian reforms were based on epistemic communities extolling radical, Austrian ideas. On the contrary, not even a subset of the relevant population was aware of these ideas. Overall the Austrian economics in Bulgaria continues to be not only far from a dominating presence but also far from being sufficiently known outside a limited circle, a situation that is in the end pretty much similar to that of the other countries in the region.

Romania stands apart from the countries overviewed so far on account of the degree to which it was closed off from other countries, even within the Eastern block. However an interesting example of dissemination arose when Mihail Radu Solcan of the Philosophy Department of the University of Bucharest looked through a shop window and discovered Milton Friedman's *Capitalism and Freedom* on the front cover of *The New Industrialist Review*. Solcan was typical of many Romanian academics of this period in that he engaged in encyclopedic research to maximize his exposure to foreign ideas. Although he had influence over students passing through the Philosophy program, few would contend that this generated significant influence over Romanian economics or the political class. Also, this disciplinary distinction is important because it provides an explanation for why the boundary between libertarianism and Austrian economics can become so blurred – the exposure to Austrian ideas is primarily though the perspective of political philosophy rather than strict economic theory. Indeed it was only after the collapse of communism that seminars dedicated to the subject of economics began to appear; and even then, focusing more on the normative implications of Austrian ideas rather than technical economics arguments. The Mises Seminar was founded in 1994 as a private meeting to discuss the libertarian and anarcho-capitalist interpretation of von Mises. The group specializes in the translation of texts into the Romanian language as opposed to influencing public policy debates (Glavan, 2004, 2005).

The Center for Institutional Analysis and Development (CADI), run by Horia Terpe, is another avenue for Austrian ideas but that is a relatively recent organization and its influence is a matter of the future. The original policy-relevant think tank in Romania is the Romanian Academic Society (SAR), founded by a group coordinated by Alma Mungiu-Pippidi in 1995. SAR has had a close influence with broadly pro-market (specifically anti-corruption and pro-flat tax) reforms via journals, working papers, and policy proposals. However there is no Austrian economist associated to it. Sorin Cucerai (Cucerai, 2003) and Cosmin Rogojanu have found outlets for libertarian journalism but it is telling that one of the most radical policy reforms (such as the flat tax) was being led by frontline politicians such as Theodor Stolojan, as opposed to professional academic economists. Outside of Bucharest the strands are thin and more consigned to academic circles rather than genuine public influence, although Radu Nechita runs a Hayek seminar for students in Cluj-Napoca. The Romanian Mises Institute is one of the most developed organizations that actively cultivate Austrian ideas, but it is also one of the least influential. Despite being an incubator for a number of committed and knowledgeable young scholars, their impact over politicians or wider society is intentionally small. This encapsulates a telling lesson of the history of economic thought in Eastern Europe: the most passionate are also the most marginalized.

Finally, Russia deserves a special note because so much was made of the 'radicalism' of its pro-market reforms. It is interesting to consider the Austrian content of some of the more 'radical' reformers of the period. In the late 1980s outside of St Petersburg, a group of Russian academics met in a seminar including Yegor Gaidar, Anatoly Chubais, Sergei Vasilie, Pyotr Aven and Sergei Ignatiev. However once again, the familiarity with Austrian ideas did not necessarily translate into adherence. It's important to note that the similarities with Austrian reforms are true only inasmuch as there is fairly wide economics consensus on the importance of trade liberalization, monetary stability and privatization. As already mentioned, Sachs, a visible reform adviser in the region was no 'market fundamentalist', seeing a large role for the government. Sachs went on to Moscow in November 1991. But although Gaidar recognized the role of Jeffrey Sachs and Richard Eyre (in dealing with creditors for example) he maintained 'the role of Western advisors in the Russian transformation was extremely exaggerated'. In a PBS interview, Gaidar recognized that Western intellectuals had no real experience dealing with transition (this was a new discipline), and no real accountability for the advice being given. He is also somewhat dismissive of the Austrian economic ideas behind the reforms: 'Yes, I read Friedman's books with interest, and also Hayek. They were very authoritative for us, but all the same far away from our domestic realities'. For more practical measures of implementing reforms Gaidar claims that their 'bible' was by Janos Kornai.

It is also worth directly looking into the zenith of supposed 'neoliberalism', the infamous loans-for-shares 'scandal'. The scheme was proposed in 1995, however an election was scheduled for 1996 and there was a real chance that the Communists would return to power. It is important to recognize that Yeltsin was an anti-Communist, plain and simple, and this policy has little to do with a positive pro-market agenda and more to do with a current political battle. Anatoly Chubais, a member of the St Petersberg group who became one of the chief impulses behind the 1990s privatizations and a main target for criticisms of the reforms reveals two things. Firstly, he is bullish about the reforms despite their obvious failure to create a capitalist, free market society, 'Tomorrow I would do the same, if only for winning the battle with the Communists, which it was at the time'. But secondly, he saw the main reason for the collapse of communism being the 'diversification of people's demand', and therefore a problem of scale rather than scope. In other words, he didn't possess the Austrian position of the structural incoherency due to the calculation problem. But the bottom line is the fact that he wasn't trying to promote markets as a goal in itself but was interested in using them as a means to beat the communists.

A reformer who has been critical of the superficiality of Russian transition is Grigory Yavlinsky. In 1982 he published a book arguing that the Russian economy needed serious reforms but this too stressed incentives rather than information. He joined the Soviet government in the late 1980s and visited Warsaw in 1990 to see their reforms first hand and meet Balcerowicz. Later that year he left the government of the Soviet Union to join the government of Boris Yeltsin and in early fall visited the Brookings Institute and the World Bank and IMF. He made an attempt to get Yeltsin to accept a 500-day plan for transition. The main difference between Yavlinsky's plan and the path that Yeltsin took was the ordering of price liberalization and privatization: Yavlinsky felt that prices could only be liberalized after private property rights were assured, and by liberalizing prices first, simply shifted state monopolies into private hands (Boettke, 1993). Indeed a number of economists within Russia criticized Yeltsin's reforms on free-market grounds such as Larisa Piyasheva, Nikolai Petrakov and Mikhail Leontyev (Boettke, 1993). One of Gaidar's protégés was Andrei Ilarionov who worked his way through academic channels to the halls of power. Ilarionov founded the free market think tank 'Institute for Economic Analysis' in 1994, and his work at the 'Center for Strategic Planning' secured a position with the Kremlin in 2000. Yet, it is imperative to realize that when assessing the Russian economic reforms those economists most sympathetic with the Austrian position were marginalized, and outside the policy debate.

All of the above are not meant to deny that radical ideas have played a role in post-Soviet Europe. However, these ideas – as championed by the likes of Balcerowicz, Laar, Miklos and Ilarionov – were too many times more salient as rhetoric than they were employed in practice. When one speaks about 'market fundamentalism' and Austrian economics in Eastern Europe the spotlight should go naturally to Western organizations that sought to inject free-market ideas into the region. For instance, one may look at experience of IHS and the Auburn-based Mises Institute that provided a role in disseminating free market ideas. As the Mises Institute President Lew Rockwell reports, 'I was especially impressed with the leaders of the Republican and Liberal parties in Poland, the right wing of Lech Walesa's Centrum Party, the Sajudis independence movement in Lithuania, the Latvian National Committee, the Estonian National Independence Party and the Estonian Christian Democratic Party, and I was able to distribute free-market books to them'. Tom Palmer was the Director of Eastern European Outreach Programs, at the Institute for Humane Studies, George Mason University during the transition period, and 'was responsible for disseminating classical liberal ideas in Communist and post-Communist European countries'. This was done through four primary channels: translations, funding, curricula and organizations. Numerous Austrian texts by the likes of Mises, Hayek and Kirzner were translated into local languages as were Austrian-sympathetic, free-market textbooks such as Paul Heyne's *The Economics Way of Thinking* (into

Albanian, Czech, Hungarian, Romanian and Russian), and Donald McCloskey's *The Applied Theory of Price* (into Czech). According to Brian Doherty, '[Hayek's *The Road to*] *Serfdom* has . . . been translated into more than twenty foreign languages – and that's just the authorized versions. Underground translations in Russian, Czech and Polish circulated behind the Iron Curtain before it fell. Though the Russian occupying authorities in postwar Berlin tried to ban its import into Germany, tenacious admirers of Western liberty smuggled copies in [to Germany] that were reproduced and spread'.[11] The John M. Olin Foundation provided financial support for 'promising students' that were 'likely to contribute to the establishment of free societies'. Conferences were held to reform university curricula in Hungary and Czechoslovakia, and organizations were established such as the Liberalni Institut of Prague, CADI of Bucharest and Catallaxy Publishing of Moscow.

Impressive as it may sound, one has to keep in mind that ultimately these are contributions to a dissident culture, promoting radical ideas that retained their radical edge both before and after 1989. Although many members of that underground did go on into government positions it's naive to think that they simply lapped up and then implemented free-market ideas. The main point is that while Western agencies such as the World Bank and IMF were training Eastern leaders in the prevailing ortho-doxy of neoclassical economics, Austrian economics remained samizdat and more or less smuggled to students. To sum up, embracing the market economy because one has no other choice is one thing. Having an epistemic community that is genuinely understanding and advancing the cause of the market economy is something else. And having an epistemic community, a climate of opinion and a policy agenda dominated by market fundamen-talism is something totally different.

TOWARDS STYLIZED FACTS AND GENERAL CONCLUSIONS

This survey of Austrian and near-Austrian ideas across such a large amount of space (Eastern Europe) and time should be regarded in no way to be a comprehensive account. Such a story would require an entire book. Ultimately what one could hope is to open up some avenues on which such future research might proceed. However, the fact that one could cover so much of the territory, and overview so many of the main protagonists, is telling. In short, it suggests in yet another way that the Austrian School of Economics in Eastern Europe is far from being a major force either in terms of impact or sheer numbers. It is several years after the fall of the Berlin

Wall that one begins to see isolated scholars forming networks, and begin to resemble the soil of epistemic community that would he required to exert real social and political influence. Although there is biographical evidence that reformist politicians expressed an interest in Austrian ideas, closer scrutiny reveals that most of the time they skipped them in practice in favor of the prevailing mainstream.

In summary, even a superficial overview of the radical pro-market economic ideas in Eastern Europe confirms that although there are multiple instances in which such ideas were present the conclusion has to be that they were far from being dominant. In a word, the claim that post-Soviet transition is the moment of unfettered hegemony of fundamentalist pro-market ideas needs to be nuanced if not reconsidered. As we have seen, one may rightly expect the Austrian epistemic community to be at the fore. But in fact the spread of Austrian economics behind the Iron Curtain significantly lagged behind the spread of mainstream economic ideas, and despite some highly visible political rhetoric, the empirical evidence contradicts the claim of a rampant 'market fundamentalism' of the Austrian variety, or for that matter, of any other variety. Radical free-market economics has been growing but from a non-existent base. It remains outside of orthodox economic discussion or mainstream policy debate, and despite moments of visibility is only rarely prevalent. Thus the emerging evidence is that for better or for worse, market fundamentalism has not enjoyed any hegemony in the region. For some this statement may be a matter of semantics. One may decide to call the mainstream economics 'fundamentalist' and thus to protect the comfort of long-established prejudices, but the difference between it and the real pro-markets radicalism such as the Austrian ideas is too obvious to be neglected.

NOTES

1. Although Austrian economics possesses a sociological concurrence with libertarianism, it's important to stress that the two are analytically distinct. See Rothbard (1976) and Rizzo (1992) for the Austrian position that economic science is neutral with regard to ultimate ends. Also, for an answer to 'Why are there no Austrian socialists?' see Boettke (1995).
2. Interview with PBS 'Commanding Heights'.
3. 'Caplan on the Myth of the Rational Voter', an interview with Russ Roberts, 25 June 2006.
4. Sima's comments made to Austrian Scholars Conference, 16–18 March 2006. Auburn, AL.
5. They took place in South Royalton in 1974, University of Hartford, Connecticut in 1975 and Windsor Castle, England in 1976 (Dolan, 1976; Garrison, 2004; Sparado, 1978) – and were concerted attempts to solidify and define the Austrian school, addressing the following questions 'What is the distinctive Austrian contribution to economic theory?'

and 'What are the important problems and new directions in Austrian economics today?' (Dolan, 1976, p. vii). Vaughn (1994) highlights the South Royalton conference in particular as being the 'revival' of the school.

6. Apparently William Hutt wondered why Ludwig Lachmann was at the South Royalton conference, since Lachmann was 'a Keynesian'. According to Peter Boettke, in 1984 a George Mason University student asked Lachmann whether he though Hutt was 'an Austrian', Lachmann's response was 'If Hutt believes himself to be an Austrian economist then he must be an Austrian economist'.

7. Interview with PBS 'Commanding Heights'.

8. Interview with PBS 'Commanding Heights'.

9. Nonovsky also cites the influence of Albert Aftalion. It is little known that the great French inter-war economist Albert Aftalion (1874–1956) was born in Ruschuk (today Ruse) in Bulgaria. His 'psychological theory of money and exchange rates' has a symbolic significance in today's Bulgaria which in 1997 chose stabilization based on a currency board. In many ways this is similar to stabilization devices adopted elsewhere after the war. At the time, Aftalion was exceptionally popular in Bulgaria, perhaps owing to the fact that numerous Bulgarian economists had studied or obtained postgraduate degrees in France (Nenovsky, 2006).

10. The founders of the Bulgarian Hayek Society also include, Georgi Kirov, Georgi Angelov, Dimitar Chobanov, Svetlin Alexandrov, Petya Lozanova, Darina Koleva, Kalina Dimitrova, Janeta Nikolova, Boris Petrov, Kahn Hristov.

11. 'From Socialism to Social Democracy'. Commentary by Lew Rockwell. Reprinted from The FREE MARKET Auburn AL: Ludwig von Mises Institute, July 1991. www.lewrockwell.com. Accessed 27 August 2007.

7. Western economics and local responses: a closer look

The story of the spread of free-market economics has always been rife with speculation regarding the motivations and intentions of the individuals and epistemic communities adopting and diffusing pro-market ideas. In many cases the rhetoric has came close to questioning either the moral integrity or the intellectual acumen of those adopting free-market views. Therefore it is no surprise that the 'neoliberal revolution' taking place in the world in the 1980s and 1990s has received a similar treatment. And understandably, the remarkable Eastern European episode of radical switch from socialist to Western economics was not at all immune in this respect. But the natural impulse to discredit what one finds objectionable should not be a substitute for facts and analysis. That is the reason why probably the best way to take a step further beyond the speculative stage of the discussion (in which facts and arguments make room too easily for broad strokes and blurred images in which social actors and their motivation and beliefs are lost in the mist) is to simply get down and talk to the economists of the region themselves. Instead of speculating about their reasons, one may simply listen to them. Giving them voice and letting them speak their mind is the most straight-forward way to deal with the questions surrounding their beliefs, reactions, opinions and motivations in adopting Western views. It is true that one may still have doubts about the face-value of their responses or one may try to depict them as bearers of a 'false consciousness'. Yet, addressing and questioning the perceptions and motivations at play, not in abstract terms but directly through interviews with Eastern Europeans themselves, is undoubtedly a step forward.

This chapter is a reflection of precisely such an exercise: the dynamics of the East–West encounters in the realm of economic ideas is given voice through interviews with Eastern European economists, public intellectuals and other opinion leaders involved in the production and dissemination of economic ideas. More exactly, this exploratory discussion is focused on the case of one country, and even more exactly on one group: the Romanian epistemic community of economists. This exploration is based on a set of interviews produced under a series of European Union funded projects (Dioscuri-Access) between 2001 and 2006 in several countries in Europe, including Romania. The Romanian economists interviewed had diverse and complementary backgrounds and experiences. The panel contained top researchers, professors, leaders of the national professional organizations, public commentators, top economic decision-makers with academic backgrounds in economics, a series of students with Western experience as well as economists engaged in the private sector. Besides the recorded interviews (partially published and abstracted in the Dioscuri-Access project archive) a large number of informal interviews was conducted. However, despite that diversity, one may still suspect that the panel reflects a selection bias. The sole response is to simply point out that it is hard to dispute at least a heuristic representativeness for such a group that ranges from a former president of the Society of Romanian Economists, to professors at the prestigious universities, and from influential economic affairs editorialists, to young researchers.

REALISM, METHOD, EXPERIENCE AND LOCAL KNOWLEDGE

Taking a bird's eye view on the entire set of interviews, one of the most notable observations is how the interview discussions tend to gravitate in a very persistent and relatively critical way around the nature of the Western way of thinking and doing economics. When asked to address the issue of Western economics, sooner or later those interviewed seem to have surprisingly convergent opinions about the Western approach and method. The pro-market vs. anti-market or the pro-capitalism vs. anti-capitalism dichotomies that are so salient for those commenting from outside the region on the fate of Eastern European economists, did not show up in conversation as an issue of major concern. That doesn't mean that they were neglected. Yet, when speaking as professionals about their profession, those interviewed seem to place that specific dichotomy and associated issues lower on their list. In all cases, the 'market fundamentalism' theme was not salient on the agenda. Instead, when asked to discuss their discipline, the interviewees were more eager to talk about their reservations regarding the conceptual and methodological dimensions of the Western approach to economics than to talk about anything else.

When asked about their first encounters with the Western ideas, the reaction reported by most of the economists interviewed was one of surprise in the face of the complexity and advancement of Western economics but also of relative unhappiness at the revelation of their own information and professional limits. Those interviewed remembered their initial thoughts with no obvious ideological baggage or connotations. Most of their reactions were on the pure professional or epistemic level.

I was surprised by a lot of things: by the way the economic research evolved, and, especially, by [the evolution of] of economic research that was unknown for us. I was surprised, and I remember, back in the 1990s, we effectively didn't know who the Nobel laureate in 1990 was. (Dioscuri-Access Interview 2)

For some that provincialism brought a sense of embarrassment:

In our literature and media appeared information regarding Galbraith, the notion of 'transition cost', instead of 'transaction cost', or the 'lonely rider' as a blemished translation of 'free rider'. (Dioscuri-Access Interview 3)

At the same time, the Romanian economists who have lived under an information blockade for so long expressed surprise at the singular trajectory that economics as a scientific discourse has taken in the West:

They seem to me very different from the rest of the social scientists, and very, already, very alienated from the rest of the social sciences. I don't think the Western economists have neither the interest nor the means to integrate researches from outside economics. (Dioscuri-Access Interview 10)

Yet, others decried the confusion created by the rapidity of change at the interface between Western and Eastern ideas, a change that in their views has generated 'a chaos':

I was surprised by the chaos in economic thinking . . . I was not expecting that the interface between the western and Romanian economic thinking, this meeting point to create such a chaos, misunderstanding and to be so destructured and disorganized. (Dioscuri-Access Interview 4)

However once the impact of the first encounters dissipated, for those interviewed the most important issue seemed to become the very substance of the Western approach to economics. Their critical stance is palpable in this respect. They start by noting that Western economics is grounded in Western institutions and history and that Western economists don't seem to be aware of that:

Western Economics, as I perceived it is very insensitive to other types of economy than the ones that are indeed very developed, the ones that managed to develop somewhere after 1800 and that are already very structural and institutional different from the rest of the world. (Dioscuri-Access Interview 10)

The fact that the comments of those interviewed are not so much driven by resentment or misunderstanding is demonstrated by the fact that they see a distinction between the Western approaches that are more sensitive to their concerns and the mainstream hard core, the object of their criticism:

Development economics, seems to me that made an effort of approaching and conceptually understand, of applying some abstract concepts to the case of the developing countries or to non Western cases of economies, well, very different to the Western ones. It seems to me that with minor exceptions Western neo-classical economists over-sophisticated themselves in some schemes that by now do not have any necessary relevance neither for economic policies, nor – I would say – for a structural concrete analysis of a specific situation. (Dioscuri-Access Interview 10)

And thus, interview after interview, the theme of 'realism' and concrete empirical and institutional knowledge emerges as central:

Some of those Western economists lost the links with reality . . . So, what does this mean? It means they take a subject, a problem, and they run it through a model, apply for instance an aggregated demand model (. . .). The higher you are and the more elaborated and fine you are in your thinking, [the more] you begin to lose the sight of regular business. They begin to wander from the problem. In contrast I see those that tried to stay anchored on the ground realities and reach very concrete things. (Dioscuri-Access Interview 8)

What surprised me was the more or less limited understanding of some realities from these countries. Whether this understanding could be better, if the mass-media was more professional it is another problem . . . (Dioscuri-Access Interview 10)

One may speculate regarding the reasons why those interviewed assigned such an importance to the issue of connection to real life problems and empirical realities. But setting speculations aside, the fact is that the theme of 'realism' seems to be the pivotal criterion in their assessment of a professional economist. There is no doubt that the perceived lack of 'realism' of Western economists has already become a part of a stereotype among their Eastern counterparts:

The large part of the economists from the West and not only from there, and more and more from the academic institutes here, are not connected to the challenges of the real world and they live in a certain detachment from the economic realities and, I would say, even in a certain contempt to the real economy. (Dioscuri-Access Interview 5)

The theme is amply illustrated with examples. Some of them may reveal some resentment and the local economists' frustration with the emerging professional status differences:

When a foreign consultant comes, he is differently perceived, so, he is perceived as somebody who brings information, knowledge . . . above all doubts, he is 'somebody'. When the Romanian consultant comes, he lived here, so it is assumed that he cannot have anything relevant to say. So, it is all about

> perception ... The American consultant came and the people from the
> Chambers of Commerce looked at him as 'Sir, he is God, he knows everything'.
> And, it is true, that man knows, he read specialty studies, economic studies,
> maybe he was in a few transition countries before and found out some common
> things. But, according to my opinion, if you didn't live [here in the country], if
> you didn't live, maybe you don't know the relevance of certain aspects you are
> discussing or giving advice about ... (Dioscuri-Access Interview 8)

Whether some resentment or envy is involved or not, the bottom line is
that, as perceived by the local economists, the major issue is one of local
knowledge and experience vs. the lack of 'realism' of the outsider and not
one of pro-market, pro-neoliberalism vs. statist alternatives. What seems to
preoccupy the Eastern economists is the very profile of the discipline. For
instance, related to that is a criticism of excessive formalism and econometrics. Western economics is seen by many as deficient precisely because
of its excesses on those lines. Implicit in that is a concern shared by many.
While the Westerners have the privilege of being 'high theorists' the locals
are increasingly pressed into a very restrictive role:

> The excess of econometrics is exported through those programmers and this is
> not something to make you happy, you know, 'scientific is only what can be mea-
> sured'. Well, this dogma that is exported through these programs is the obses-
> sion to measure. Research process becomes mainly a measurement chain.
> Financing of this type [of research] induces, determines a certain specialization.
> Romanians are the measurement guys at the end of the chain. And this is some-
> thing not that benefic on long term. (Dioscuri-Access Interview 7)

As one may expect, there are degrees of discontent with this situation.
Some of those interviewed went even further and openly deplored the
potential negative influence of the western mainstream economics on the
new generation of Romanian economists:

> Very many young men, extremely capable, brilliant minds, do not see further
> than the fascinating, beautifully resonated, theoretic constructions, further than
> the abstract reasoning of the today's western dominant thinking. But [what they
> miss is] that are not relevant to the concrete realities of a country that is only in
> process of constructing a market economy. (Dioscuri-Access Interview 1)

It is important to note that the qualms and criticisms are not radical. Not
only do they seem to be motivated only in a small measure by ideological
bias, pure resentment and frustration but also they are pretty reasonable in
tone and general attitude. All those interviewed have a moderated stance.
Or at least they manage to project without any visible effort the image of a
thoughtful understanding of the problem:

No matter what hesitation we have regarding a certain way of researching economics in the Western world, I think it is useful to understand their conceptual and theoretical developments and to see in what degree their formal and econometric methods are applicable to the study of some phenomena from within the Eastern Europe and transition economies. Of course, the problem that seems important to me is up to what point this type of approach can be applied to some economic structures, that were not meant to be initially explained by this type of approach. (Dioscuri-Access Interview 4)

The degree to which these perceptions are shared by the Romanian economists interviewed is demonstrated by the fact that even those studying abroad entertain them. Thus one could not argue that having a systematic and inside exposure to the Western thought automatically leads to a change of opinions in the direction of embracing without reservations the Western attitude towards economics:

The economic science, as perceived by me in the context of an American university, is very insensitive to other type of economies than the ones that are really developed. So, probably – if you would ask me, whether I should choose another department – I would say that I would like to do development economics, which seems to me that as a subfield made an effort in its approach and in its conceptual understanding, of applying some abstract concepts to the cases of the developing countries or to non-orthodox economies, that are, anyway, very different from the Western ones. (Dioscuri-Access Interview 10)

In this respect it is important to emphasize that the interviewees did not limit themselves to broad comments but also revealed very precise and concrete concerns with the distorting consequences of a wholesale embracing of the Western framework. The argument is pretty straightforward. The Western concepts are distorting the analysis of the Romanian situation and by implication the national policies:

Definitions from the West hide the Romanian painful realities instead of revealing them. For example, let's take the unemployment rate. In Romania, at one point the official unemployment rate was of 8–10%, depending also on the good will of the Institute for Statistics and on the Government objectives. According to the Western definitions, an unemployed is a person who manifests his desire to work, who goes certain bureaucratic procedures, like submitting a request for unemployment aid and who renews this request permanently. In Romania, because of this definition, the official unemployment rate, as called by the county level officials, was about 8–9%. In fact, in Romania, almost half of the active labor force was at that time unemployed, meaning that it didn't have jobs, it was not protected by social insurances, couldn't buy on credit, couldn't have rights like motherhood vacation . . . It was practically out of the market, and, saying that the unemployment rate in Romania was of 8% was totally unrealistic. (Dioscuri-Access Interview 5)

In the end, the asymmetry between, on one side, the Romanian economists and, on the other side, the Western is undeniable. But does that preclude a functional relationship between them? Is this a win–lose situation?
The Romanians interviewed didn't seem to think in terms of zero sum
games. Many accepted the asymmetry but wanted to downplay it and put
it into context:

> Yes. I think there is an asymmetry, maybe not so unnatural, taking into consid-
> eration that we are the ones that have to catch up and to understand some fun-
> damental principles, towards which we are heading or we wish to head.
> (Dioscuri-Access Interview 10)

And thus, it looks like that neither this asymmetry nor the 'neoliberal'
pro-market ethos but what was perceived as a disconnection from 'reality'
of the Westerners is the most sensitive issue. It may be a matter of debate
what 'reality' means to the Eastern economists but irrespective of the
semantics involved, it seems that this issue is indeed one to which they
attach importance. Thus even when asked the simple question of what
could the Western economists learn from the Romanians, those interviewed
came back to their basic point:

> [The western economists should] learn this adequacy to reality from the
> Romanian economists or Eastern Europe economists or the economists from
> developing countries, and to connect themselves much better to the realities and
> specific dynamic. (Dioscuri-Access Interview 1)

> I don't know if they [the Western economists] would have anything to learn at
> the conceptual level. Definitely nothing. Maybe an attention to the empiric,
> towards – maybe empiric is not the best way to put it – towards recognizing prob-
> lems; so, maybe this seems to me – again, I'm speaking from outside the problem
> of the economists or the economy in the western countries, maybe in the USA
> . . . It seems to me they don't look to problems in the real economy with open
> eyes and when they do they try to answer them purely conceptually. It seems to
> me they over-sophisticated themselves in some schemes that already are not nec-
> essarily relevant neither for economic policies, nor for a concrete structural
> analysis of a situation. What in Romania and in any other developing country
> is this stringent problem of the immediate, of responding to some real pressures
> of some problems that are felt, and, well, that request a solution in terms of a
> very clear policy, put a pressure on us that lacks in the West. I think there is
> implicitly a much-dedicated approach toward economic policies in the develop-
> ing countries that imposes a certain pressure, versus a strict conceptual analysis,
> I don't know, in abstract terms. (Dioscuri Access Interview 8)[1]

To sum up, open interviews with Eastern European economists indicate
that at least at the level of such 'conversations' their first preoccupation
seems to be not at all the 'market fundamentalist' hegemony but with issues
that define their craft, and the relevance of their discipline is thus related to

their professional identity and their standing as professionals. The concern with the 'realism' and practical aspects of the discipline overshadows the pro-market vs. anti-market cleavage. In the measure in which the cleavage is discussed, that happens mostly as a corrollary of this concern. A major theme emerging out of the interviews is the uneasiness with the ways Western mainstream economics has been anchored in local realities; an uneasiness not so much with its theoretical and policy implications but with its general orientation. For those reading the interviews expecting to find them suffused with the 'market' vs. 'state' dichotomy it may be a surprise. The fact that Romanian economists, when asked to discuss the experience of their encounter with Western economists and economics, see their interaction with the West primarily in the light of their craft and the essence of their discipline and less in terms of economic policy debates of the day should be even more surprising for those who want to see the change of economic ideas in Eastern Europe more or less as an ideological, pro-market indoctrination operation.

GLOBALIZATION AND THE HOMOGENIZATION OF ECONOMIC THOUGHT

The interviews also challenge or at least introduce some nuance into the discussion about the local responses to the impact of the process of globalization of Western market economics. The conventional wisdom suggests that the spread of Western economics market ideas and of the ways of seeing through the lenses of market neoclassical economics leads to uniformity of economic thinking and stifles local perspective. From this standpoint, one may see the intellectual landscape in the wake of the 'neoliberal revolution' as more or less an explicit application of the more general 'leveling logic of globalization' to the specific area of economic ideas. Globalization is the great homogenizer and that applies to ideas too. There is no doubt that such a process is at work in the world of economic ideas. But the interviews revealed that a sort of counter-reaction is also taking place. And this dialectic generates an internal tension and a very interesting question. Is the Western model the inescapable future or is there a place for a 'national school'? This tension is genuine; the discussions with the Romanian economists revealed that for them it was far from a mere speculative issue.

The majority of those interviewed seemed to agree that reproducing Western economics without any originality should not be the way to go: 'There are some valuable things in the Romanian economics profession. The tragedy is that all those obsessed with success will try to just imitate

Western-style mainstream economics, with no contribution of their own' (Dioscuri-Access Interview A). The question is what this 'contribution of their own' should look like? Should it be on the lines of advancing the neo-classical mainstream agenda or on the lines of adding a local or national flavor to what is already out there? Is it possible to adapt all this into a 'National School'? Apparently in some quarters there is some guarded opti-mism regarding the emergence of such a School. If one insists, one could discover that those willing to contemplate these prospects have relatively well-formed views on the matter:

> As for the prospects for a future Romanian School of Economics, I think that the times are very favorable. As we have just ended a, by and large, disastrous communist era, economic matters have come to the forefront of the public debate, and knowledge of economics is both relevant in daily affairs and gener-ally sought by the people. But the chances of this Romanian school depend, I think, on the thoroughness with which young Romanian economists assimilate the teachings of the Western schools and integrate them as a natural part of their knowledge. As a rule, the first and surest strategy to rise to a high level is to climb on the shoulders of giants. (Dioscuri-Access Interview B)

> In my opinion the possibility of a sound 'Romanian School of Economics' is conditioned by the power of its members to self-sacrifice or to the willingness of the community, of the private businesses to support such an enterprise. A school of sound economics can in no way be subsidized by any Government on the long term. (Dioscuri-Access Interview E).

Thus, the march of Western, neoclassical economics seems able not only to homogenize the field but also to generate new tensions and dynamics. One discovers a continuous vacillation between guarded hopes of the pos-sibility of a specific 'national school' steeped in local conditions, and the rejection of the idea of a 'national school' in the sense of a national culture and tradition-driven enterprise. To further illustrate the tensions and com-plexities of the situation one has to look at the 'national' vs. 'universal' in economics, from the perspective of traditions of thought other than neo-classical economics. By doing that one could discover reasons against a national school that transcend the usual concerns with the 'neoliberal rhetoric' and its 'global hegemony'. The argument against the emphasis on the 'national' element comes from multiple perspectives. For instance, a follower of the Austrian school argues:

> A national school of economics may be looking more like a joint State-Academia job, adding another point on the list of 'must have'-s that brings pres-tige to a nation and keeps masses bound together in their national pride. But sincerely, I feel like not trusting too much in government's tastes! (Dioscuri-Access Interview D)

And thus we discover a motivation to reject localism based not on mechanical or strategic adaptation to the reigning, 'mainstream' paradigm but because of well thought out, and clearly expressed reasons. While rejecting the 'mainstream', another economist also makes clear that the recourse to a 'national tradition' sounds dubious or even downright dangerous:

> The Romanians do not have such a great legacy in the study of economics. Arguably, the only worldwide read Romanian economist was Mihail Manoilescu, who had fascist sympathies and who wrote a treaty in which he tried to 'scientifically prove the necessity for protectionism' and to give a scientific method for the determination of the tariffs to be applied at a certain moment. But there was no significant classical liberal counterpart. (. . .) Romania has, unfortunately, never known any genuine effort to argue for (let alone apply) the classical liberal program. This basically means that, should a young Romanian strive to become an economist in the true sense of the word, he would have no chance to succeed if he limited himself only to the materials and teachings provided by Romanian forerunners. (Dioscuri-Access Interview B)

These quotes are a testimony of the multiple facets of the domain of economic ideas in the wake of the 'neoliberal revolution'. They are a living challenge to the widely circulated thesis that postulates an uncritical embrace of 'Western neoliberalism'. Local economists seem in most cases well aware of the complex dimensions of the intellectual history moment they are going through. What is the significance of this fact is a different issue. For now, it is important just to register its existence and the evidence brought by it.

NOTES ON INTELLECTUAL TRADITIONS AND 'THE LEGACY OF THE PAST'

The discussion of 'national tradition' touching the issue of 'national' and 'universal' in economics invites a brief elaboration using as a vehicle the Romanian case. In order to understand the context of the attitudes revealed by the Romanian economists interviewed, one has to look not only at the Western academic centers, their influence and the reactions to them but also at the intellectual history of economic thought in the country during the past six or seven decades. Some recurrent attitudes and nuances in the discourse of the Romanian economists may thus be put in a better light and better understood as part of a historical tradition. From this perspective, the Romanian public economic discourse was characterized by a strong discontinuity, as it went through several major stages that were determined, on the one side, by the institutional-political factors, and, on the other side, by the conceptual evolutions from within the discipline. There were at least four stages: 1920–1944 was an eclectic period, dominated by the influence of the German Historical School, and a trend toward nationalizing the economic discourse (this trend was in a large part the result of the double influence of endogenous nationalism and the anti-universalism and historicism of the German school); 1944–1948 was a short moment of revival of the liberal discourse, inspired by the classical and neoclassical French and British schools, always in a tensioned coexistence with an ingrained nationalism and indeed the rising Marxism; 1947–1975 saw total domination of the Marxist discourse, with moments of resurgent nationalism and vague Keynesian influences after the second half of the seventh decade; and 1975–1990 saw outright attempts to 'localize' and 'nationalize' Marxism by appealing to inter-war authors doubled by an embrace of a Third World-type ideological discourse of the New International Economic Order.

This highly fragmented evolution has generated a lack of conceptual unity in the post-1990 period, as well as the lack of a solid institutional infrastructure to provide stability to the Romanian epistemic community. However at the same time there is a unifying theme: the 'national' perspective anchored in a reverence for the intellectual world of the 1920–1940 period. The fragmentation and institutional deficit represent the first key legacy of the past. Yet, out of all the episodes of the past, compared with the situation experienced by most Romanian economists during their lifetime, the inter-war period represents a golden age. As such it still provides for many the major background on which the current developments are projected. Even if, from a theoretical or conceptual point of view, a large part of the inter-war discourses seems today far from the modern standards, the inter-war authors had a force and professionalism that still fascinate. This salience of the period was noticed by many researchers of the Romanian intellectual history. Joseph Love (1996) noted how robust the economic discourses and the epistemic communities were in Romania of that time. Thus even if in its substance, the inter-war economic discourse diverged from the current models, it still represents in the eyes of most Romanian economists a standard that the current economic discourse hasn't yet reached. Its shadow was cast for too long not to deserve a serious consideration of its effects on the Romanian economists' minds.

But this is not the sole background influence of the past on economic culture in Romania. The second and the biggest influence of the inter-war economic discourse on the postwar developments was the continuous concern with 'nationalizing' economics, i.e. with indigenizing it and making it if not normatively at least conceptually nation-specific. 'Specificity' and 'national-specificity' have always been a major concern for the Romanian epistemic community. Thus it may be the case that there is a direct connection between the roots of the Romanian inter-war economic thought and the current reactions of the Romanian economists confronted with Western ideas. That may illuminate why that type of discourse concentrating on local 'realities' and the national perspective as opposed to Western 'abstract universalism' seem to be so popular with the Romanian economics epistemic community. Intellectual history is not indifferent for the way in which we understand the nature and resorts of the contemporary Romanian economic discourse.

In other words, the intellectual archeology of epistemic communities and the background information brought by it matter. There should be no surprise at all if today we notice that a significant number of the economists are still concerned, after years of transition and exposure to the universalism of Western economics, with the 'local' or 'national' nuances. Besides the spontaneous strategy of local economists to ascertain their primacy over Westerners, when it comes to Romanian issues, that may also be interpreted as an echo of the dominant tradition of the Romanian inter-war economic thinking and the partial revival of that tradition during the communist regime. The 'legacies of the past' of the Romanian academic economic culture might offer a clue why there was such astounding convergence in the ways the local economists have chosen to identify and describe the key issue-areas defining their encounter with Western economics and economists and also might explain their broad agreement in interpreting the nature and the impact of the Western paradigm in the post communist period. Why so much focus on 'realism' and local knowledge and context? Why do these preoccupations shadow the preoccupation with the issue of the 'hegemony of neoliberalism' or the 'shock therapy vs. gradualism' debate? One has some clues and the beginning of an explanation by looking at the epistemic community's history of vacillating between the universalism of Western economics and the local and national sentiment.

To sum up, a closer look at the Romanian case reveals that the encounter between Eastern and Western economics is not as smooth as one might believe from reading the statistics of exchange students or the European Union grants, but not as bad as the adepts of the thesis of a 'neoliberal hegemony' imposed from the region from outside implies. So, at minimum we know that the case is not closed either way. Whether the Romanians' reaction to (and their shared assessment over) their encounter with Western economics is unique to Romanians, or on the contrary, if it is widespread in the region is an important question. If it is specific to them, then one needs to explore in a comparative framework the sources of that uniqueness and the above comments on the legacies of the intellectual past might be a possible direction to go. If the reaction is shared with other countries in the region but not with all, one needs to see why that is so, and what the sources of those similarities and differences are. In other words, an entire research agenda may emerge. What are the differences of perception regarding the relationship between local knowledge and universal knowledge between Western and Eastern economists? Are there significant intra-regional differences? Is there a pattern of antagonism in Eastern Europe towards the mainstream economics approach? If yes, what is its nature? What is the role of national traditions and intellectual histories in this respect? Is there a difference of perception regarding economic policies deriving from the differences of attitude towards Western economics? These and similar questions open up the possibility of a real engagement with the process of ideas diffusion and change in the region and helps us to avoid the analytical and interpretative dead-ends so prevalent today in the discussions about the East European evolutions.

EXPLORING THE ORIGINS OF PRO-MARKET EPISTEMIC COMMUNITIES: IDEAS AND INTERESTS

The study of the origins of pro-market epistemic communities has been shaped by several parameters. First, any such study comes sooner or later to a discussion of the motivation behind their existence: are they inspired and fuelled by ideas or by interests? Second, and somehow paradoxically, the implicit reference point in such discussions are the epistemic communities related to the environmentalist movement. The interesting point is that when it comes to the origins and incentives of environmentalist epistemic communities, the literature finds them almost exclusively in scientific ideas and values (Haas, 1992). In the ideas vs. interests dichotomy, they are seen as being overwhelmingly on the ideas side. For some reason, despite the model set up by the study of the environmentalist epistemic communities, there has been a reluctance to engage in the study of pro-market epistemic communities with the same tools, assumptions and thoroughness. Many discussions simply imply that their origins are in incentives given by the capitalist system, corporate money, propaganda, greed, irrationalism and 'fundamentalism'. In the ideas vs. interests dichotomy, they are seen as being overwhelmingly on the interests side. From that a challenge: to explore more profoundly the processes surrounding the emergence of pro-market epistemic communities. Could one trace them back in clearer ways to ideas or to 'interests'? Refining the question: What are the conditions leading to the processes by which pro-market epistemic communities are constituted in developing and transition countries? Refining the question

further: What are the motivations and incentives by which 'market fundamentalist' epistemic communities are constituted in developing and transition countries at the interface with Western economic ideas? We assume
that the originating mechanism will be a combination of 'ideas' and 'interests' but what is the ratio between them? Such questions could be dealt with
only through an in-depth look at relevant cases.

The example of the case of a group of young scholars from a top
Romanian university may be used to demonstrate how such cases could
advance our understanding of the phenomenon in question. The in-depth
interviews with its members may be able to put in a clearer light some of
the intrinsic reasons, motivations and processes surrounding the emergence
of radical pro-market epistemic communities. But one could go further.
The formation of the 'Austrian Economics Group' at a major Romanian
university can be used as a vehicle to explore not only the question 'What
are the local responses to globalized, Western market economics?' but also
'What are the motivational factors underling their creation?' and, 'What are
the specific intellectual innovations that are created during the process of
cultural adoption?'

From the very beginning one of the most striking things when reading
the interviews of the five assistant-level faculty that decided to create an
'Austrian Economics Group' amidst the apathetic intellectual environment
of a major Romanian academic institution, is the depth of the convictions
of the young scholars interviewed. In a place where one would expect a
standard professional discourse embedded in career pragmatism, one is
surprised to discover a totally different rhetoric. 'In fact, I see teaching and
research in economics as one of the ways of pursuing and disseminating
truth; it is more about calling than career', says one of them (Dioscuri-
Access Interview A). The concept of 'calling' is taken seriously as are the
concepts of 'truth' and 'liberty'. In some cases they sound pretty dramatic:
'In 1992, I came to Bucharest . . . and my foremost desire was indeed to
understand how the economy works. But, in fact, I came here with love for
liberty' (Dioscuri-Access Interview A). Not only 'liberty' but also 'truth'
comes again and again as a recurring theme:

> Then comes the problem of truth. For most present schools of thought (in eco-
> nomics and in everything else), this problem is somewhat embarrassing. In the
> age of postmodernism and relativisms of all sorts, when – as Chesterton might
> say – everybody is guided by the 'fallacy of success', and when having a strong
> theoretical position is deemed obsolete, Austrians point to the common sense fact
> that some questions have answers: definite ones. (Dioscuri-Access Interview B)

The very notion of a common search for 'truth' (as pretentious as it may
sound) seems to be the major force defining their identity and reinforcing

the unity of the group. Their accounts have a very interesting consistency in this respect. In none of the other interviews done with other Romanian economists was the issue of the 'search for truth' stated in such categorical and unabashed forms. If one is to follow their narrative, the history of their group is not at all a history on institutional incentives at work and only in a limited measure a history of a theoretical or methodological eye-opener as a result of the encounter with a Western concept followed by a change of vision and attitude. Instead, it is a series of personal engagements in the search for truth:

> How did relations with the Austrian Group colleagues developed? Purely and simply from my admiration to see persons interested in finding the truth. I want science to offer one truth not many. I want to share that with them. I considered them friends whom I can count on. (Dioscuri-Access Interview C)

> Genuine interest in fundamental research is very scarce in the Romanian acade-mic environment. A mad race with time in order to make the steps required to become a full professor or to be up to date with the latest, most fashionable the-ories, and a sense of purpose which strives almost entirely for success, fame etc and almost at all for genuine knowledge seems to be the order of the day. Therefore, the Austrian Group was a strange (when not ignored) animal within our Department. (Dioscuri-Access Interview B)

The perseverance with which this vision is maintained and elaborated is remarkable, as is the way in which the issues of science and epistemology are wedded to the notion of liberty and the implied libertarian principles:

> Even if good discernment and uncorrupted search for truth are the greatest enemies of 'science abuse', endemic lately within the corpus of social sciences, I must admit that I'm profoundly indebted to my friends from the Austrian Group for not wandering years after years among myriads of misconceptions or half-truths. Furthermore, the embracement of the Austrian School of Economics cannot be separated by the fully recovery of the Classic Liberal teachings, made by the Libertarian School, which both gave me an epistemological and ethical perspective of economics and political philosophy, in the absence of which, it feels to me now, I would never had the chance to hope becoming, one day, a decent and relevant scholar. (Dioscuri-Access Interview D)

Step by step one could see how this in-depth look at the Austrian Group allows one to go beyond the elusiveness of the standard accounts and reveal the potential diversity of the specific ways, conditions and contexts in which the spread of Western ideas takes place. When confronted with such cases or with attitudes like those displayed by the Romanian interviewees, one is undoubtedly forced to reconsider the 'one size fits all' theories about the nature and spread of neoliberalism. Such cases illuminate the very role of principles, values and ideas as major drivers in ways in which no general theory of 'diffusion of ideas' could. Only through such an in-depth focus could one see that the main thrust of the process is not necessarily taking place at a general level through abstract patterns and forces. On the contrary, one could see it at work through particular venues, some of them quite surprising:

> It was the monopoly theory that triggered my attention to the Austrian Economics. The specific issue was whether or not Microsoft was a monopoly. I was then no fan of Microsoft but I realized in the end that even if their products were not high quality ones, they were indeed serving the market very well. Even if we would talk of monopoly in the Microsoft case it is not the result of free market anyway but the result of the involvement of governments which are the only ones in fact which can support a monopoly. (Dioscuri-Access Interview E)

These particular venues betray a pattern. But probably the best thing for the 'neoliberalism' literature would be to spend more time at the micro-level, at the level of the variety of particular paths and individual and group dynamics, before returning to the broader levels of generalization invited by these patterns. For now the temptation of exposing them should be resisted. Only so one could break the hold of conventional wisdom. That leads to an observation-driven understanding of the facts on the ground. One could see for instance how the already mentioned theme of 'truth' is additionally supported by a certain understanding of professional standards and scholarly life. In the specific case of the Austrian group, those interviewed have very high scholarly standards derived from a specific universal model of scholarship. The creation and the attachment to the group seem to be strongly related to a commitment to those standards:

> I come to join the Austrian Group due to the fact that one of the members impressed me by logical coherence and strong ability to sustain argumentation. I perceived something 'deeper' and I tried to dig more. He offered me *Human Action* by Mises and *Man, Economy and State* by Rothbard and that was, at least for me, sufficient to convince me definitively. (Dioscuri-Access Interview C)

The references to explicit or implicit standards and the high scholarship expectations are abounding in all interviews. One may say that the young Romanians following the Austrian economics credo are misguided. But the fact is that, misguided or not, this is what is on the minds of these East European economists and no variation on the themes of ideological 'hegemony' or 'rational choice' theories could do justice to it. Taking note of it as an empirical reality is a must. It is interesting that these expectations or standards seem to have pre-existed the contact with the Western, Austrian ideas and pre-existed even the initial contacts with other members of the group:

> I came to join the Austrian Group trough Mr. S. As a fourth year student in international business and economics I chose the Comparative Economic Systems course he was teaching. As I thought of myself of being a fairly well read person (generally, and in economics) it came as a surprise to me to find out during the lectures of Mr. S. that almost everything I knew (remember, I was a final year student) was either incomplete or simply wrong. I was stunned by the fact that, in four years of learning, nobody pointed me to relevant episodes in the history of economic thought – like the Methodenstreit or the impossibility of economic calculation in a socialist commonwealth debate. For somebody who was, in a small but relevant proportion, an offspring of communism, these things mattered. (Dioscuri-Access Interview B)

Such insights into the minds and personal histories of the members of the East European epistemic communities challenge the inclination to use facile theoretical generalizations to 'explain' and sometimes even to describe the reality of the transformation of ideas taking place there. For instance, getting to know the members of the group one could recognize their genuine commitment to ideas. They have constructed their group driven by serious intellectual aspirations and the Austrian economics satisfied those aspirations.[2] They are an almost ideal case of an ideas-driven community:

> I choose Austrian Group as a way to further my intellectual study and to have capable people to discuss with. Austrian Group is not institutionalized. It is more like a partnership. How did relations with the Austrian Group colleagues developed? Purely and simply is my admiration to see persons interested in finding the truth. I want science to offer one truth, not many. I want to share with them that. I considered them friends whom I can count on. (Dioscuri-Access Interview C)

This is the context in which one could further ask, at this concrete level, questions illuminating the issue and new facets of the phenomenon. In this case, one may ask, how important was the direct contact with the West? How decisive were the 'encounters'? The case of the Austrian group shows how such simple questions could challenge some pre-conceived notions. It seems that such direct, face-to-face, personal encounters were not at all as instrumental as one may expect in the light of the conventional wisdom:

> I made contact with Western ideas and economists especially through reading the 'Austrian' literature on economics. The Internet was the main vehicle of information as Romanian libraries – mainly state owned – are quite poorly provided with books. Paramount was the on-line presence of thousand of pages on

the site of The Ludwig von Mises Institute (USA). As for contacts with western economists I have not met many. I benefit in a way from the connections of the others (especially the president of Mises Institute Romania) have. Although I have traveled abroad (Russia, Bulgaria, USA, Austria) I cannot say I have some strong connections. (Dioscuri-Access Interview B)

Again, it seems that there is substantial consistency in interviews regarding this issue. No personal interactions, no institutional incentives, no financial or material gains in play. The direct encounters leave the center stage for books, libraries and the Internet as the main modes of ideas transmission:

> I discovered the Humanitas [major Romanian publisher] books and found most interesting the 'Civil Society' series. They published at the time important books like Popper's *The Open Society and Its Enemies*, Hayek's *The Road to Serfdom* or Hannah Arendt's *The Origins of Totalitarianism*. It was the interest that the books of Hayek and Popper aroused in me which prompted me to search for other books of theirs within the French, British and American Libraries in Bucharest. (Dioscuri-Access Interview A)

The theme is unmistakably recurrent and the lack of even minimal contacts with Western counterparts during the conversion to the new ideas is noteworthy:

> Being in the early period of my formation, books are for the moment my best friends. I made contact with pieces of the works of the most famous exponents of the Austrian School such as Carl Menger, Ludwig von Mises, Friedrich von Hayek, Murray Rothbard, Israel Kirzner, Walter Block, Jorg Guido Hulsmann. Of course, I would be honored to establish links with the representatives of the Austrian School, as we share more than one common language. (Dioscuri-Access Interview D)

In summary, the conventional wisdom regarding the adoption of Western market ideas is if not challenged at least amended by the evidence emerging from such micro-level detailed case studies. 'Calling', 'truth' and other values and beliefs that usually are paid lip service in the literature but in fact are considered secondary when it comes to explanations and analysis, seem to be major triggers. And, indeed, this is reconfirmed if one looks at the specifics of the institutional context. For the 'career advancement interest' theory of the spread of Western economics in Eastern Europe, cases like the Austrian group should provide food for thought.[3] Careerism doesn't seem to be a strong force in the worldview of the group, as the notion of benefiting materially or career-wise from the Western contacts is only remotely present into the picture.[4] That doesn't mean that self-interested, material gain driven conversions did not take place in the East. Yet the evidence shows that such conversions should be considered typical so easily. To sum up, the case of the 'Austrian group' offers a challenge to conventional wisdom, an example of how illuminating could be small case studies for the large research agenda of the East Europe transformation of economic ideas.

HYBRIDS AND INNOVATION: RELIGION AND ECONOMICS

The researcher that leaves the office and goes into the field is confronted by a wealth of challenges and interesting observations. That is undoubtedly true for any line of research. But in the case of the issue of the spread of Western economic ideas in the East, the researchers should be prepared for more than the standard share of surprises. For instance, the contact with the members of the 'Austrian Group' reveals not only the pivotal role normative and personal commitments had in the adoption of a specific set of Western economic ideas but, even more interesting, that this group has engaged in a process of articulating an intriguing intellectual synthesis: an attempt to combine traditional Austrian economics perspectives with local orthodox religious ones. The result is an original and unique discourse. This intellectual effort is fascinating not only as a case in itself but also because it offers a contribution to the increasingly sophisticated literature that has been accumulating over the years illuminating and investigating the parallel between the traditional religious and theological belief systems and the political and economic ones. In section two of this book we discussed how Robert Nelson has documented the rise of political economy to public life preeminence as a sort of 'theology of modernity' (Dunn, 1989). The point is that political economy as a worldview has similar functions with the traditional theology: both frame the perception of social action and form the basic parameters of human existence (Nelson, 1991, p. xxv). They meet a special social and anthropological function. This is precisely why the explorations of the Austrian group are so fascinating. These young scholars are certainly not shy in engaging in a unique intellectual effort in an area that the mainstream avoids touching openly and explicitly. The direct engagement with religion and the particular ways they combined religious ideas with economics deserves thus some attention.

The case illustrates the complexity and diversity of the dynamics of ideas in Eastern Europe in the wake of the 'neoliberal revolution' and although one could not generalize based on it, the bottom line is that once one becomes familiar with such cases the tendency to subscribe to the conventional wisdom generalizations loses some of its appeal. How else could one react to the discovery that for a group newly converted to Western economic ideas, economics is 'not only science but also the detailed description of God's harmonious making of the universe, of the benefits of human freedom and human interaction.' That may immediately trigger the notion of 'fundamentalism'. And that is indeed a legitimate reaction. Yet one has to keep in mind a more nuanced interpretation. What these young Romanian economists have in mind is an issue of limits and boundaries. Both science and religion have limits. In fact, in their view one of the distinctive marks of their Austrian School-inspired credo should consist 'precisely in understanding the limits of science and education in societal transformation'.

> The fight for good needs much more than mere teaching. In fact, economics does not in any way explain how to establish a free community or makes clear which beliefs are compatible and which are not with freedom. It is only religion which, in a thoroughly consistent manner, makes clear that virtue is possible only with 'outside help' and is intellectually coherent solely with a Good God and eternal life. Traditional liberalism effectively destroyed the foundations of freedom by trying to substitute a worldly religion for Christianity and by arguing that a little evil (the minimal state) is necessary for the preservation of social cooperation. (Dioscuri-Access Interview A)

For those interested in the 'leveling logic of globalization' and the local reactions to it, the way a young Romanian sees the basic attributes of a possible Romanian reaction to the Westernization of economics may be very instructive. The other side of the story is one of new combinations made possible by the presence and impact of Western ideas:

> One field in which Romanians could come up with valuable contributions is the compatibility of liberalism with Orthodoxy: that is Eastern Orthodoxy. This tradition is somewhat behind with the explicit social teaching because of its focusing more on the spiritual endeavors of the individual to get closer to God by means of participation in the liturgical life of the Church, prayer, fasting and charity. Yet taking seriously the social teachings implied in the writings of the Holy Fathers, one task of a presumptive Romanian School of Economics would be to scrutinize both the writings of the economists and those of the Fathers of the – mainly Eastern – Church and to bring to surface relevant arguments in support (or against) of the liberalism–Orthodoxy affinities. (Dioscuri-Access Interview B)

In the view of these young intellectuals a synthesis of ideas in innovative directions becomes possible. The argument is based on a comparative analysis informed by the newly gained access to Western literature. In other words, the arguments seem to be well grounded in an analytical effort and not just the result of whim or intellectual confusion. But even allowing for the inherent confusions that usually emerge at the interface of changing cultures, traditions and schools of thought does not diminish the intrinsic relevance of the perspective put forward by the members of the Austrian group.

> Like many others that passed even sporadically through Max Weber's work, I always tented to believe that Protestantism was the most 'business-friendly' branch of Christianity. Later on, I found, through the prolific discussions with my fellow Austrians from our group, that only Orthodoxy, as revealed through the writs of Holy Fathers of the Church, contains the proof that individual liberty and private property are perfectly consistent with the Christian dogma, in the sense that the idea of virtue assumes with necessity, on its first, laic, layer, the unadulterated respect for justice seen as the respect for every human being's person and legitimate property. (Dioscuri-Access Interview D)

The impression of a well-grounded and documented approach is reinforced by all interviewees. Indeed the members of the group seem to have striven to get a solid grasp of the historical and conceptual issues involved:

> What is interesting however is an historical study of how religious ideas have influenced state and public policies through the agency of law. Religion promotes a certain ethics that obviously influences the scales of values and the means that individuals choose in action. However, as a wertfrei science, praxeology and economics has nothing to do with religion. Economic laws have nothing to do with God. What is interesting however, is the influence of religion on state and public law. This is the point of connection between economics and religion: see taxation, usury laws, Prohibition in America, criminalization of prostitution, etc. I would be interested in furthering the research in such areas. I already criticized in a brief article (inspired in fact by Rothbard's critique done in his 'History of Economic Thought') the Max Weber argument that capitalism was promoted by Protestantism. . . . I would be very interested in furthering the analysis of the influence of Islamism (no taxation) on public policies (see 'modern' Islamic states like Saudi Arabia). (Dioscuri-Access Interview C)

Quite unsurprisingly, the foundational relations between religion and economics are a key subject of meditation and analysis. This without a doubt affects the way one understands the very nature of social sciences. The first question that arises is: How original is all this? An encapsulation of social science in a religious worldview has the familiar echoes of the Western (Catholic and Protestant) efforts in the same direction. But the point for now is not so much one about originality. The point is to simply take note of an interesting presence in the intellectual landscape of post communist Eastern Europe, a presence made possible by the diffusion of Western radical pro-market ideas.

> For me, the relation between Religion and Economics was that Economics led me to Religion. Even if when being a child my grandparents took me to the

church, later I stopped asking myself questions about the existence of God. The Austrian economics and especially the Libertarian ideas made me realize that orthodox teachings are very consonant with the free market and the respect for the person. I was once more convinced that one can find the final truths in Religion because Economics and Ethics did not offer by themselves to each individual the incentives for doing systematically right instead of wrong. As long as people that don't believe in God choose to be good people only because they are conservative or fear some retaliation from others this can be no solid foundation of a free society. (Dioscuri-Access Interview E)

To sum up, the Austrian group offers a striking example of the intellectual experiments emerging at the interface between Western economic ideas and Eastern traditions. The nature and potential applications of such hybrid innovations are difficult to predict and their evolution even more so. They may be transient phenomena, a momentary deviation from a 'leveling and standardization' trend or they may be having a more resilient nature. The fact is that they are noteworthy cases. Even if transient, a closer look at them offers new windows and deeper insights into the larger phenomenon of ideas diffusion and change. And even assuming that the insights may not be sometimes generalizable, the example used in this chapter showing a 'hybrid' emerging out of the combination between Western economics perspectives and different intellectual traditions could be fascinating in itself. General theories of diffusion or models based on ideological biases may easily miss some of the most remarkable facets of these phenomena. As one of the members of the Austrian group put it:

The idea is that, in the words of Saint Maximus 'The Confessor', man has two wings: grace and liberty. As grace is (always) a gift from God, man's job is to realize his modicum of freedom (as Mises said) and put it to good use. Because this is what God wants from men. At once – alongside the wing of freedom – affinities with liberalism become apparent. Because, in the end, the Eastern theologian cannot not to answer questions like 'does payment of taxes beget salvation?' 'Is welfare by means of the welfare state really welfare and genuine charity?' And if the orthodox cherishes the great gift of liberty which in his eyes in necessary, as virtue is truly virtue only if freely chosen, the welfare state must not be to his liking. Neither the payment of taxes. Starting the other way around, liberalism – holding liberty as the 'highest political end', as Lord Acton said – is very much open to the endeavor of freely chosen virtue, especially if this endeavor maintains the general possibility of freedom for all, concomitantly. And the true Christian spirit certainly passes this test. (Dioscuri-Access Interview B).

A CHALLENGING AGENDA

What are all these interviews telling us? Two types of dynamics seem to be at work in Eastern Europe: The first is indeed the 'leveling wind' of neo-classical economics. From this perspective, one could tell a story of standardization and uniformization on the lines of the typical 'forces of globalization' account. Yet, there is no doubt that this trend although not rejected by local economists is not always embraced without reservations. Their most important mode of voicing the reservations is to point out to the empirical deficiencies and the 'superficiality' of Western economics and to the important role local knowledge and experience have for understanding the 'real' economy. With that comes an effort to downplay the theoretical and methodological sophistication of the Westerners. However, outside academia and even in some pockets within academia, innovative ways of thinking about the economy and about economic theory may be emerging. Once can find instances of rejection of standard economics, and real strides toward heterodox Western economics and new combinations of local and Western ideas. Furthermore, one could discover people that are very passionate about ideas and values, willing to sacrifice material and financial gains to follow what they see as a 'calling'. While it is usually implied that the origins of pro-market groups are in incentives given by the 'capitalist system', the evidence emerging from this chapter points to a different direction. By any standard, the Romanian Austrian economics group discussed in this chapter is something driven mainly by ideas and values. By its very nature, it contradicts a basic tenet of conventional wisdom in a deeply ironic way: in choosing their economic ideas these young scholars display a striking lack of interest in 'interests'. This demonstrates that even in the case of one of the most standardized intellectual items diffused from West (market economics) it is possible to have diversity and resourcefulness. The challenge is: in what measure is the situation discussed by the Romanian case an accident? What is its validity and relevance? What are the real intellectual merits of the conclusions we derive from the Romanian study? Is this an eccentric case? It may be. But it is from these cases that we build our understanding of the range of the phenomenonon of interest. And as long as we don't look carefully at the concrete empirical reality we do not know if and how many such cases that form the point of view of the conventional wisdom mired in eccentricity are out there.

We should definitely be wary of arguing that the Romanian findings are generalizable and thus speak for the entire region. It may be the case that once focused at this level of micro-level detail, the specific reactions in other countries prove to be different and the Romanian case to be an outlier. That is the reason this chapter considered it necessary to elaborate the theme of the specifics of Romania and the Romanian tradition of economic think-ing. Yet, even if the insights may not be generalizable, by focusing on very specific instances and specific issues in the Romanian case, we were able to apply a minimal test to some theses voiced regarding the dynamics of Western ideas in Eastern Europe. What such explorations based on direct contact with the relevant epistemic communities show is how surprisingly intricate the real dynamics of economic ideas is. Such cases are a signal that draws attention to the danger of discussing the 'neoliberal revolution' basing our judgements more on stereotypes, projections and imagination than on facts, and of explaining it by calling its various aspects 'nothing but' expressions of biases, interests and ignorance.

NOTES

1. In terms of what should Western economists do to improve their relationship with the Eastern economists, the following answer is most telling: 'I think that we could be part-ners with them and that we have inventive capacity, and a capacity of adaptation and a capacity of seeing beneath the appearances, which could prove fruitful in a partnership with them. So what I recommend them is to treat us as partners' (Dioscuri-Access Interview 5). When asked the question what the Romanians could learn from the Western economists, one of the most telling answers was to stress the diversity of Western tradi-tions and schools of thought: 'Let us look at the western economic thinking in its whole diversity. It is an essential condition for being able to learn something, because they can always learn not from the analysis of a collection of ideas, but from the confrontations of ideas' (Dioscuri-Access Interview I).
2. The dedication of the members of the group is put in a brighter light by a side comment that deserves to be quoted in this context: 'As far as my colleagues are concerned, I feel some of them interested, others intrigued, and the rest indifferent. Even if pacifist by its nature, the "anyway it doesn't matter" attitude is criminal for human intellect, as it allows no rational dispute and no claim for truth' (Dioscuri-Access Interview D).
3. That doesn't mean that people are not aware of the career advancement dimensions of things. The incentives and reasons that are setting into motion this embracement of the local economists of the Western paradigm are always a key issue: 'Never be against the wind, they say, but why? – Because it costs you. Either in a very more or less sophisticated manner people want to have success and they give up the exact expression of their own thoughts or they give up the effort of investigating when they feel something is not all right, they give up making the analysis in order not to be in countersense with the dominating trend of that period, not to lose materially or socially' (Dioscuri-Access Interview 1).
4. In this context it is appropriate to note two comments: 'The first thing to keep in mind regarding the Romanian economics environment is that we do not have (yet) a real main-stream, providing in a direct way services to the top bureaucracy and having a stake in its ideology. After the fall of communism, the academic attitude toward non-interventionists has been tolerant. I really believe we enjoy a greater degree of academic freedom than our colleagues in the United States. Besides, many members of the department are very young and not ideologically active. The management staff (older professors) are not in the least disturbed by our meetings and pronouncements. They consider us, perhaps, part of the mainstream and consumed teachers. We greatly benefit from the fact that we know what they have to say but the reverse is not true, so we come all the time with "new" ideas and viewpoints. It is my personal belief that my Austrian colleagues' success in the classroom won the respect of the rest of the department' (Dioscuri-Access Interview B).

8. The flat tax in Eastern Europe: a comparative perspective

The flat tax has a special position among a broad package of neoliberal ideas. Unlike many other economic policy ideas (for example privatization or monetary reform) it is not just a response to the past, an attempt to turn around previous errors or an echo to policies already implemented in the advanced industrial democracies. On the contrary, it goes beyond the current definition of what the standard package of feasible economic reform policy ideas is supposed to contain. It is not an attempt to 'catch-up' with the richer Western economies, but actually a means to 'get ahead' using cutting-edge free-market ideas. In this respect it could be truly called 'neoliberal': it seems to be a natural extension or even the beginning of a new phase of the 'neoliberal revolution'. It looks like a signal that Eastern Europe, after absorbing the neoliberal worldview, is now able to experiment by itself, moving on independently of the advice and concerns of the Western countries. And therefore, the flat tax is swathed in an irony: it is former communist countries that seem to be leading the way in liberal, free-market economic reforms. We see Western academics travelling to Eastern Europe not to teach, but to learn, and the lesson is that the implementation of radical economic policy is more feasible than one has been used to thinking.

The remarkable thing about the spread of the flat tax is that in less than 15 years it has gone from being deemed 'impossible' to being almost 'inevitable', as more and more Central and Eastern European countries follow suit. Today, despite increased attention from Western European countries and the US, the contagion has been somewhat contained to former Soviet economies. That makes it an even more challenging and interesting case for a study of how such economic ideas have spread thus far, in order to understand how they may spread further. By doing that, one may get a glimpse of a not very well-known and even less studied facet of the neoliberal revolution in Eastern Europe. One could see how specific economic ideas, inspired by Western economics, grow and take off in a dynamic that is relatively independent of the original Marxism vs. neoclassical economics episode. By focusing on the 'flat tax', one makes a step outside the theoretical core of economic belief systems towards their policy belt. But the study of the spread of the tax gives the researcher not only the feeling that one could get a glimpse of an already new stage in the evolution of the Eastern European landscape of economic ideas but also an insight of the intricate relationship between that theoretical core of neoliberalism and its social and intellectual context.

An exploration of this radical policy idea in Eastern Europe is interesting in yet another way: by going beyond the aggregated level and concentrating on a specific issue of taxation and public finance it concentrates at a level that allows a better focused and more systematic comparative analysis. As sections one and two of this book demonstrated, one could go only so far when the research topic is an intellectual phenomenon as broad as the neoclassical economics and its spread over half of a continent. Such an approach illustrates how bits and pieces of deeper understanding could be created by centering the analysis on specific facets and stages of the phenomenon in question and how those pieces could contribute to our general understanding of the dynamics of economic ideas in Eastern Europe. Finally, the case of the flat tax is at the same time a challenge for those that claim that Eastern Europe had a passive (and even victim) role in the face of the Western, neoliberal invasion. The flat tax is, if not a refutation, at least a serious challenge. Far from being paralyzed and lost in the rapid developments as many have suggested, Eastern Europeans seem to have been proactive enough that at one point they looked even able to take the initiative. What are the factors and conditions that may explain this remarkable development? What are the most plausible possible explanations for the spread of the flat tax in Eastern Europe? This chapter will try to explore this issue by engaging in a comparative study.

THE IDEA OF FLAT TAX

The flat tax itself (or 'proportional tax') is neither new nor radical – it has been used throughout history and remains a common form of taxation (most sales taxes are single-rate). The radicalism stems from the specific policy of a flat tax on income, which replaces sliding tax scales with a single fixed rate (alongside a tax-free personal allowance).[1] Although Hong Kong has had a flat tax for more than half a century (see Reynolds, 1999) and two of the Channel Islands (Jersey and Guernsey) have had a flat tax on personal income for many years, none of these cases are independent or autonomous nations. Similarly there are flat-rate state income taxes in Illinois, Indiana, Massachusetts, Michigan and Pennsylvania. These examples suggest that a flat tax is not totally alien to the current economic policy practice, without detracting from the transformative nature of the Eastern Europe instances that *are* under investigation. The Eastern European flat-tax phenomenon is in this respect *sui generis* and deserves to be treated as such.

Before analyzing the channels through which the flat tax has spread, it's important to establish a clear chronology of who has adopted a flat tax, and when.[2] The first movers were Estonia, where a flat rate of 26 per cent on personal income and corporate profits was introduced in 1994. Their Baltic neighbours soon followed suit – also in 1994 Lithuania flattened their tax system (with a 33 per cent rate on personal income),[3] and in 1995 Latvia launched a flat tax at 25 per cent. In January 2001 Russia established a flat rate of 13 per cent on personal (but not corporate) income, followed by Serbia's introduction of a 14 per cent rate on salaries in 2003. In 2004 Ukraine adopted a flat tax of 13 per cent, and 2004 also saw Slovakia launch a comprehensive flat-tax system with Income Tax, Corporate Tax and Value Added Tax all levied at 19 per cent. Georgia's parliament voted to introduce a flat tax in December 2004 and a 12 per cent rate was implemented in January 2005. Similarly Romania unveiled a flat tax of 16 per cent in January 2005, following the election victory of the National Liberal Party/Democratic Party alliance in late 2004. The most recent countries to adopt a flat tax have been Macedonia in 2007 (at 12 per cent and falling to 10 per cent in 2008), and Bulgaria in January 2008 (at 10 per cent). At the beginning of 2008 11 separate countries have adopted a flat tax.

A chief advantage of a flat tax is the administrative simplicity that results from a uniform rate. This factor is especially evident if tax evasion is high, since an increase in compliance will reduce the dead weight loss of collection. The same logic applies to tax avoidance and although it's hard to project hard numbers, the incentives clearly favor economic activity and increased participation rates. The effect of flatter taxes on tax revenue is controversial and depends on the exact position on the infamous Laffer curve, however the rule of thumb 'what you lose by lowering rates, you gain by broadening the base' (Whitmore, 2005) seems typical. Public revenues rose in Estonia by 0.2 per cent of GDP, by over 20 per cent in each of the first two years following Russia's adoption (Lynn, 2004), rose in the Slovak Republic (Fund, 2005), and rose in Romania (Ionita, 2006). Although these boosts to government coffers may stem from alternative but simultaneous economic reforms (or other factors entirely such as surging oil prices), it's clear that many pessimistic predictions have not borne fruit (see Aligica and Terpe, 2005). Legitimate debates will discuss whether capital follows lower wages rather than lower taxes; whether higher Value Added Tax offsets a low flat tax;[4] and what if the current 'sprawling' complexity is simply an emergent and efficient response to the complexity of income? (Kay, 2005; Kay and King, 1986; Hettich and Winer, 1999). However these results ignore the deeper properties of the flat tax – the theological element (Evans,

2006a). Opponents point to a decreasing marginal utility of wealth as justification for progressive taxation whereas advocates focus on the efficiency (allowing resources to flow to their highest return), equity (an even distribution of the tax burden), simplicity, and incentives for political responsibility. These normative dimensions allude to the certainty, convenience and fairness criteria set forth by Smith (1991 [1776]), which form the cornerstones of the classical liberal tradition. Indeed the twin champions of economic liberalism in the twentieth – century Friedrich Hayek and Milton Friedman – both advocated a flat tax (see Hayek, 1956, p. 265–284; Hayek, 1960, p. 315; Friedman, 1962, p. 175). These statements formed the basis of the flat tax epistemic community that created and supports the policy idea, embodied by Robert Hall and Alvin Rabushka's classic proposal (Hall and Rabushka, 1995).

The flat tax has received academic attention but mainly in the form of impact assessment or projections based on wider tax reform. Ventura (1999) found that a Hall–Rabushka flat tax has a positive effect on capital accumulation, aggregate labour in efficiency units' increase, and the distribution of wealth becomes more concentrated; and Stokey and Rebelo (1995) claim that tax reform will have little effect on the US economy. However Heath (2006) provides a long list of academic literature that predicts various beneficial effects. Due to the freshness of the flat tax as a viable policy, most information about its dissemination and adoption is in popular press and takes the form of opinion editorials or other country-specific advocacy.[5] Deeper analysis will take the form of an overview (Grecu, 2005; Forbes, 2006), a specific proposal (Foreman, 1996; Armey, 1996; Scott, unpublished; Teather, 2005), or both (Heath, 2006). Murphy (2006) offers a general critique of flat taxes, focusing on suggested implementations for the UK. However the literature that specifically looks at *how* the flat tax has been spread, incorporating the rise of the flat tax into a theoretical framework, is still in an incipient stage. To do this requires a systematic application of a comparative method.

THE COMPARATIVE METHOD

It might be tempting to believe that a flat tax is contagious, and in 2001 it spread from Estonia, Latvia and Lithuania in two directions simultaneously – to the north-east (i.e. Russia), and to the south-west (i.e. Kaliningrad). However it'd be inappropriate to treat Kaliningrad and Russia as equivalent instances. Kaliningrad is a small port on the Baltic Sea, encircled by Lithuania to the north and Poland to the south. When the USSR collapsed and the so-called 'Baltic Nations' of Lithuania, Estonia and Latvia became independent countries, Russia strategically retained reign over Kaliningrad to keep a border with Poland (and, therefore, Central Europe). Consequently it's somewhat inaccurate to say that the flat tax had been adopted by *all* Baltic nations by 1995, since Kaliningrad, like Russia, introduced a flat tax in 2001.

This example demonstrates the inherent difficulty in understanding the diffusion of economic ideas between political entities, because conventions and assumptions that we take for granted, analogical thinking and broad empirical generalizations can mask, confuse (and sometimes contradict) the processes at work. There is therefore a danger that the obvious becomes lost.

The standard methodological approaches have serious limits in dealing with topics that combine issues related to the spread of ideas and issues of comparative political economy. To analyze the spread of economic policy ideas requires multiple cases, and at the same time the retention of the holistic properties that put us in the position to capture precisely the multicausal paths toward the adoption of the idea. Qualitative methods get bogged down in details when comparing multiple cases involving intricate configurations of factors, while quantitative methods oversimplify – sometimes up to the point of irrelevance – complex and conjunctural causal relationships. Consequently a synthetic 'comparative method' is needed. An adequate study of the spread of economic policy ideas requires a combination of the two approaches, so that we can retain the holistic value of each individual case, but also make comparisons across multiple cases – to appreciate that the process of adoption in Estonia was different from that in Serbia, but that they must be combined somehow, in order to understand the implications for Hungary. One methodological technique that provides such a combination is 'the comparative method', which is 'a technique that uses Boolean algebra to simplify complex data structures in a logical and holistic manner' (Ragin, 1987, p. 14). Since this approach provides a frame into which multiple case studies are analyzed, it has the potential to better uncover process rather than essence, and adjudicate between alternative theories. Before the comparative method is performed, however, we must define the degrees of analysis (the number of cases and the number of conditions); define the binary conditions; and state the theories being examined.

Degrees of Analysis: Number of Cases

The comparative method takes a number of cases, and ascertains the presence (or absence) of various conditions for each case. The intention is to uncover which conditions, and which *combinations* of conditions lead to a pre-defined outcome – in our case that outcome is whether the country has adopted a flat tax on personal income. As of January 2008 there are 11 countries that have adopted a flat tax, and although there's no objectively correct way to decide which cases are of interest, it makes sense to keep the analysis close to the environs of the adopters. In other words, since the adoption of the flat tax thus far is a European phenomenon, this study will focus on Europe.

To be more precise the flat tax is synonymous with post-Soviet economic reforms, and therefore the initial cases of interest are those European countries that were formerly communist. Consequently this study will go beyond the nine cases used in section one and will focus on 20 case studies: Albania; Belarus, Bosnia and Herzegovina; Bulgaria; Croatia; the Czech Republic; Estonia; Georgia; Hungary; Latvia; Lithuania; Macedonia; Moldova; Poland; Romania; Russia; Serbia and Montenegro; Slovakia; Slovenia; and the Ukraine.

Degrees of Analysis: Number of Conditions

Having decided upon the number of cases, the second degree of analysis that needs to be established is the number of conditions. There are many factors that have legitimate claim to being relevant, but since this is an exploratory study it makes sense to begin with a relatively few conditions that seem especially pertinent given preliminary analysis. A strength of the comparative method approach is that conditions can be expanded or neglected as appropriate, in an iterative process. The first condition (A) focuses on the internal fiscal situation, and whether the country has a monetary incentive to alter its taxation revenue – either to bring more people into the tax system (and reduce tax evasion), or to correct shortfalls in revenues (due to budgetary pressures). The second condition (B) is the external fiscal situation, and looks at the threat of capital flight that a country faces. Levels of foreign direct investment (FDI) and the ratio of imports and exports to GDP help ascertain the degree to which an economy is interrelated with its neighbors. These two conditions show how fiscal pressure for its own sake, or fiscal pressure as a consequence of the action of others, might make a flat tax a policy priority. The third condition (C) looks at how much a country belongs to an international community. This is similar to the second condition since it measures the external relationships of a country, but focuses on social rather than economic grounds. The fourth condition (D) looks at civic culture; to see what role public debate might have during the policy adoption process. It is important to know whether having a literate, educated and public debate alters the propensity for the flat tax to spread. The fifth condition (E) asks whether a policy champion promoted the flat tax, and if so whether that person was a political opinion leader. In other words to what extent is policy implementation dependent on it having an individual espouser? And the sixth condition (F) is a crude measure of contagion, by looking at whether there'd been a precedent.

This list is by no means exhaustive, and a number of additional conditions come to mind, such as: Did the flat tax possess media support? Was it part of an electoral policy? What was it's timing? Was the proposed flat tax revenue neutral? Had there been rigorous impact assessment performed? However all of these issues are somewhat represented in the six chosen conditions, and at this stage of analysis a broad understanding is more important than a crude list of preconditions since we are in the midst of flat-tax expansion. If we focus too much on the specific details of conditions in the adopted countries, then there's no scope for it to spread further and we have created a closed system. Rather, we must look at fundamental conditions, which can then be translated into the climates of countries that are yet to adopt a flat tax. This is the only way to straddle the middle ground and say that the flat tax can spread farther, and there are common preconditions that can be used to predict where. Broad conditions are required to prevent analysis from being merely descriptive.

Binary Conditions

The comparative method is based on Boolean algebra, 'the algebra of logic and sets' (Ragin, 1987, p. 85), a key feature of which is the use of binary data. If a condition is present, we denote it with a '1', if it is absent, it receives a '0'. Therefore we must tighten the definition of each condition, and define our assessment criteria. We have already defined the outcome (X) as: 'whether the country has a flat tax on personal income', and so for countries that have adopted a flat tax $X=1$, and for those who haven't $X=0$. The conditions are somewhat more complicated for two reasons: timescale, and the trade-off between accuracy and objectivity. Acknowledgement of such problems is the first step to solving them, and we offset the issue of with which time period we're concerned with the following rule: for an adoptee it's 'prior to adopting', for a non-adoptee it's 'currently'. Since we're performing process-driven analysis rather than taking a snapshot of an arbitrarily defined moment, the timescale depends on whether adoption has taken place. If it has, we're concerned about the conditions prior to the adoption. If it hasn't, we're interested in the present situation. The second issue is whether we wish to be vaguely right or precisely wrong, and we choose the former due to the intent to stimulate further research, which enables us to refine the judgement. Therefore rather than use a narrow question (with an objective answer), we shall use the most accurate indicator and utilize a rigorous case study method to answer it as crisply as possible. It might be less subjective to decide condition A with 'Was the government budget balanced?', but this fails to fully reflect the fiscal situation in the country. Therefore we will use the looser question of 'Did/does the country have a problem raising tax revenue' and use levels of tax evasion and the budget deficit as evidence to answer it. If the country did/does have an internal pressure to reform tax revenue A=1, if it didn't/doesn't then A=0. Again, there are a number of objective statistics relevant for condition B, but the binary condition will be the broader issue of 'Did/does the country fear capital flight?', when B=1 is the answer if yes, and B=0 if not. C=1 if the country was/is an integrated part of the international community, and C=0 if not. If the population was/is engaged with political debate D=1, and D=0 if not. Condition E depends on whether an opinion leader led/leads the flat-tax campaign, with E=1 if they did/do, and E=0 if not. Finally, condition F=1 if a neighboring country had/has previously adopted a flat tax, and F=0 if they hadn't/haven't.

Theories Being Examined

Prior to collecting and evaluating the evidence, it is worth introducing several theoretical frameworks, so that the results can be seen in conceptual context. The reason for such an analysis is not simply to document what happened and when, but to tease out potential 'I' relationships that enlighten us as to why they happened then, and how they might happen again. Discussion of alternate theoretical frames also reinforces the choice of conditions, since they each possess attributes of broader themes. For example, conditions A and B (the role of budgetary pressure and the threat of capital flight) are part of an interest-explanation that explains policy change by the pecuniary incentives faced by actors.[6] A looks at whether it's in a country's own domestic interests to adopt a flat tax, regardless of the activity of neighbours. B asks whether the policy in other countries affects the domestic interests, demonstrating that policy reform can be strategic. Together they answer both facets of interest-driven policy: whether is it domestically rational, and whether it is strategically rational. Ideas-explanations focus more on the role of institutions and individuals,[7] and in this respect three conditions are relevant. Condition C looks at international influence, to gauge whether ideas are transmitted through shared institutions. Condition D looks at domestic institutions, and whether the media and public debate/public opinion lead policymakers. And condition E captures the individual element, and whether key individuals and outstanding leaders ultimately dictate policy (Harberger, 1993). Condition F is a crude measure of contagion, and confirms whether it's fruitful to study the adoption of the flat tax in the first place. After all, if the spread is an automatic process with a clearly predictable pattern, it might suggest that economic explanations are irrelevant. If, however, condition F *isn't* enough, there must be something else at play.

The conditions reflect thus compelling theories. A theory that emphasizes the interests of the actors predicts the importance of conditions A and B; a theory that emphasizes the ideas and beliefs focuses on C, D and E; a 'non-theory' can be captured by F; while a multi-causal path dependent theory emphasizes the role of E for some countries, and A, B and F for others. In other words, the very fact that conjunctural causation and multi-causal paths are a real issue, legitimizes the efforts to explore unorthodox methods and approaches.

GENERATING THE TRUTH TABLE

A Note on the Data

In order to identify the presence or absence of the six conditions, case studies of all 20 countries of interest must be performed, focusing on the criteria outlined in the previous section. Aside from formal flat-tax proposals; scholarly articles on the effects of flat taxes; official data about relevant variables; and other archival records (such as survey data), these case studies make extensive use of mainstream media reports and interviews. These sources are particularly relevant because between them they manage the difficulties created by the subjective nature of the analysis. For example, it is possible to ascertain the official statistics on the size of imports and exports relative to GDP, and it's even possible to utilize projections and formal estimations of the size of the informal economy (and hence the level of tax evasion). However these objective facts are irrelevant for condition A if the domestic policy makers are either unaware of them, or do not see them as a problem. In short, we need to go beyond establishing the retrospective evidence, and uncover whether it's an issue for the public and the policy makers. Mainstream media is a crucial way to judge whether the conditions were relevant. But the press is an imperfect measure of the local environment, and this is explicitly recognized by condition D – in some countries civil society isn't developed so that policy debate mirrors public debate. Therefore interviews were required to acquire information first-hand. There were two types of information of interest. Firstly, information to compensate for imperfect secondary sources (and fill in the missing gaps needed to judge whether the conditions are present or absent.) Secondly, interviews of key players were required to go beyond the public debate, and shed light on the decision-making of the policy makers who actually implemented a flat tax.[8] The range of interviews was large, from international experts such as Alvin Rabushka (Hall and Rabushka, 1995), Allister Heath (Heath, 2006), David Storobin, Daniel Mitchell, Howard Scott and Corin Taylor to key players including Mart Laar (former Prime Minister of Estonia), Martin Bruncko (former Economic Adviser to the Slovakian Finance Minister); Dusko Stojkov (Adviser to the Serbian Finance Ministry), and other national experts and decision-makers who wished to remain anonymous.

Applying the Conditions to the Cases

Condition A: Tax evasion and budget pressure

Since all 20 cases are transition countries, we might expect condition A – internal pressure to generate revenues from taxation – to be prevalent throughout. However these transitions occurred at different times, meaning that we can legitimately expect deviations. Although to Western eyes the structural similarities are blinding, this belies the differences that are of special interest in trying to uncover why economic ideas spread to some countries and not others. Rather than seek absolute values that reinforce the original decision to group the cases under scrutiny, we are more concerned with relative indicators that separate the countries (taking their broader similarities as given). For example all 20 countries possess large informal sectors, but our concern is which countries have an *especially* large shadow economy. While by definition this issue is impossible to calculate, using figures provided by Schneider (2003), we can estimate that the average shadow economy labour force (for selected former Soviet Union and CEE countries) is 29.7 per cent of the working age population.[9] The only countries that have levels more than one standard deviation higher than this average are Belarus, Georgia, Russia and the Ukraine. We can also add Serbia to this list since budgetary issues were important in the build up to the flat tax – although reforms of VAT contributed more to the budget surplus, there are estimates of 30–40 per cent of national output avoiding consumption tax. It is also important to add the Czech Republic, Hungary and Poland since their budget deficits were forecast to remain into 2007.[10]

Condition B: Capital flight

With regard to tax regimes, a discrepancy between two neighboring countries provides an incentive for individuals or firms to choose the more liberal rates, thereby causing capital flight away from higher tax nations. According to Kevin Wadell 'pressure comes from competing economies' (Tzortzis, 2005). The two simplest proxies to assess the degree of competitiveness between countries are the ratio of exports to gross domestic product (GDP), and amounts of foreign direct investment (FDI). The former reflects how open the economy is, and the latter measures its intake of foreign capital. The level of exports of goods and services (as a percentage of GDP) differs dramatically between the countries concerned (ranging from 23.7 per cent in Serbia to 79.9 per cent in Estonia), but the following have exports above 50 per cent of GDP: Belarus; Bulgaria; the Czech Republic; Estonia; Hungary; Lithuania; Moldova; Slovakia; Slovenia; Ukraine.[11]

While exports can be positive-sum between competing nations (for example countries benefit from reductions in trade barriers with neighbors), FDI is a better measure of competitiveness since funds are scarce and therefore one country's ability to entice new investment is more likely to reduce that which is available to its neighbours. CEE nations who received more than $0.5 billion in 2000 and 2001 are Bulgaria; Croatia; the Czech Republic; Hungary; Poland; Romania; Russia; Slovakia; Ukraine (UNCTAD, 2002).

Combining these two proxies (to see which countries feature in both) suggests that condition B is present in Bulgaria; the Czech Republic; Hungary; Slovakia; and Ukraine; but this fails to tell the whole story. As discussed previously these objective statistics are irrelevant unless they are present in the minds of the decision-makers, and therefore further sources are required to validate the initial picture, and alter the list above. The case of the Czech Republic is confirmed with the words of the shadow finance minister – Vlastimil Tlusty – who believes that 'if a neighbouring country [adopts a flat tax] it's necessary to follow suit' (Reynolds, 2004). And similarly in Hungary, where former President (and leader of the opposition party FIDESZ-MPP) Viktor Orban says 'Budapest will have "no choice" but to jump on the "flat tax bandwagon" to retain the country's share of foreign investments that will otherwise flow to flat tax nations' (Storobin, 2006). However, Latvia *should* be on the list; Heath claims that 'At 25%, the rate was chosen to undercut Estonia's; the fact that Latvia felt forced to follow Estonia's lead confirms the power of tax competition and the need for countries to attract capital' (Heath, 2006, p. 82). Georgia's rate of 12 per cent was no coincidence if it was deliberately chosen to undercut Russia's; and Serbia also feared capital flight. Interestingly, although Slovakian politicians knew that a flat tax would provide a competitive edge, it was not a key consideration and therefore not a precondition of flat-tax adoption.

Condition C: Membership of international community
The countries that joined the World Trade Organization in 1995/96 were: Bulgaria; the Czech Republic; Hungary; Poland; Romania; Slovakia; and

Slovenia. Those who joined from 1999–2003 were: Albania; Croatia; Estonia; Georgia; Latvia; Lithuania; Macedonia; and Moldova. Those who aren't members are: Belarus; Bosnia; Russia; Serbia; and Ukraine. The Czech Republic, Estonia, Hungary, Latvia, Lithuania, Poland, Slovakia and Slovenia are members of the EU, and although Bulgaria and Romania joined them in 2007 it is too early to count this as having an institutional effect.[12] If we take early membership of the WTO and membership of the EU (of at least a year) we are left with the Czech Republic, Hungary, Poland, Slovakia and Slovenia.

Condition D: Civil society
There are various means to judge whether the population of a country is engaged in political debate, none of which are perfect. It is possible to use indicators that determine the capacity for civil society – such as literacy rates or tertiary education, but these are crudely elitist. Constitutional factors can be used such as the existence of a free press, and whether that generates independent media. Institutions that might indicate civil society – such as the Catholic Church – help as well. Opinion polls help establish whether political issues are known to the public, but not whether they're understood, therefore voter turnout (and other measures of voter apathy) are required to offset a reliance on instrumental factors. And as before, expert judgement provides the narrative that binds the story together – for example Garton-Ash contrasts two of the cases under scrutiny: 'Slovakia had a vibrant civil society – or what Slovaks call "the third sector". There was the Catholic Church. There were independent radio stations, magazines and the private television channel Markiza. And there were numerous nongovernmental organizations [NGOs]. . . When I described this civic campaign to opposition friends in Serbia a week later, they threw up their hands in envious despair' (Garton-Ash, 1999, p. 358).

It's important to distinguish between the presence of external networks that disseminate ideas (i.e. epistemic communities), external NGOs that influence domestic policy (such as the Soros Fund), and genuine domestic organizations that stimulate and facilitate debate. While all three contribute to civil society more generally, we are only interested in the last type. These are apparent in larger countries with an established dissident culture (such as the Czech Republic, Hungary and Poland), but not in those most tightly controlled during communism (e.g. Albania, Russia, Romania), or those governed by more authoritarian means (Belarus). Since civil society is reliant on an established middle class and stable governance, the Balkan nations afflicted by war (Bosnia, Croatia, Macedonia and Serbia) lack the requisite domestic institutions. Of those remaining the relatively recent revolutions (Georgia and Ukraine) are too fresh to have created a genuine civil society and too small (as is Moldova).

Condition E: Policy champion

Establishing the presence of a policy champion runs the risk of appealing to hindsight, since it would be easy to identify a key proponent of a flat tax in countries where it's been adopted. Therefore the criteria must be strict, and reveal someone who believes in the flat tax's 'theological' properties (Evans, 2006a), as well as being in a position of political influence – either as president, prime minister, minister of finance, or a chief adviser to either position. Despite the degree of influence people such as Alvin Rabushka have regarding the flat tax, he wouldn't qualify as a policy champion on the grounds that he doesn't occupy a position of domestic influence. Such international advocates are the fuel that spreads the ideas, but not the ones who implement them. The advantage of defining the policy champion relatively precisely is that the burden of proof shifts from the motivations of the many actors involved in the adoption process, to assessing the merits of those claiming to steer events. Rather than trawl through the evidence searching for a policy champion, we assume that if that person exists, they'd make themselves known. Therefore each country is assigned a '0', unless they can prove otherwise. Policy champions are Laar (Estonia); Illarionov (Russia); Niklos (Slovakia); Stolojan (Romania). An interesting case is Hungary where Vickor Orban – currently in opposition – is a known advocate. In this country a new election – or new coalition government – would be the constitutional moment required to thrust Mr Orban into becoming a policy champion. Indeed this event occurred in Macedonia when the center-right VMRO-DPMNE party won the 2006 election. The incoming Prime Minster Nikola Gruevska made the economy his main priority and a proposed flat tax was a central part of these reforms.

Condition F: Precedent

Since this is a crude measure, it is easy to determine: for flat-tax countries, has a neighboring country (i.e. shares a border) already adopted a flat tax; for non-flat tax countries, has a neighboring country already adopted a flat tax? Estonia, Russia and Serbia are the only countries that fail to satisfy the first condition, and only Slovenia fails to satisfy the second. This condition highlights the few instances where geographical proximity *isn't* a precondition of flat-tax adoption, and is of interest for two reasons. First, it indicates cases where ideas *might* dominate interests, since adoption cannot be explained by a domino effect. Second, it helps us identify 'isolated' countries where ideas channels (such as epistemic communities) might be

Table 8.1   Truth Table for Flat Tax Adoption in Central & Eastern Europe (1994–2008)

Country	Conditions						Outcome
	A	B	C	D	E	F	X
Albania	0	0	0	0	0	1	0
Belarus	1	0	0	0	0	1	0
Bosnia&H	0	0	0	0	0	1	0
Bulgaria	**0**	**1**	**0**	**0**	**0**	**1**	**1**
Croatia	0	0	0	0	0	1	0
Czech Rep.	1	1	1	1	0	1	0
Estonia	**0**	**0**	**0**	**0**	**1**	**0**	**1**
Georgia	**1**	**1**	**0**	**0**	**0**	**1**	**1**
Hungary	1	1	1	1	0	1	0
Latvia	**0**	**1**	**0**	**0**	**0**	**1**	**1**
Lithuania	**0**	**1**	**0**	**0**	**0**	**1**	**1**
Macedonia	**0**	**0**	**0**	**0**	**1**	**1**	**1**
Moldova	0	0	0	0	0	1	0
Poland	1	0	1	1	0	1	0
Romania	**0**	**0**	**0**	**0**	**1**	**1**	**1**
Russia	**1**	**0**	**0**	**0**	**1**	**0**	**1**
Serbia&M	**1**	**1**	**0**	**0**	**0**	**0**	**1**
Slovakia	**0**	**0**	**1**	**1**	**1**	**1**	**1**
Slovenia	0	0	1	0	0	0	0
Ukraine	**1**	**1**	**0**	**0**	**0**	**1**	**1**
N=20(11)							

required to offset the lack of interest channels (such as structural similarities with neighboring states).

REDUCTION AND BOOLEAN ANALYSIS

Table 8.1 shows the truth table constructed from the analysis in section four, following the technique laid out by Ragin (1987). To maintain close dialogue with the cases the name of each country is retained, and equivalent cases (such as Albania and Bosnia) have not been combined. Although six conditions imply a far greater number of logically possible combinations of conditions (i.e. $2^6 = 64$ rows), for simplicity only observed cases are reported. Note that this doesn't affect the final analysis since only cases that lead to a flat tax (indicated in bold face) are used in the data reduction stage of the analysis.

Prior to reducing the truth table into a set of results, it is worth reiterating the tentative nature of the comparative method. There are two separate matters of judgement that are open to debate; the first is the choice of conditions (A, B, C, D and E); and the second is the establishment of presence or absence (for each of the cases). The plausibility of the results can be used to re-assess *both* matters of judgement, but we should not confuse validity ('0' or '1' *given* A) and soundness (the *choice* of A). Since this is an exploratory study the results are intended to lead toward a refined version of the initial conditions, and insights into which ones require elaboration and further enquiry.

Results

Using uppercase letters to denote presence, and lowercase to denote absence of each condition, the 'primitive' form of the data is as follows:

$$X = aBcdeF + abcdEf + ABcdeF + aBcdeF + aBcdeF + abcdEF + abcdEF + AbcdEf + ABcdef + abCDEF + ABcdeF$$

Notice that there are repetitions and therefore the 11 results can be condensed into seven unique products:

$$X = abcdEf + ABcdeF + aBcdeF + abcdEF + AbcdEf + ABcdef + abCDEF$$

At this point we can utilize 'Boolean minimization', 'If two Boolean expressions differ in only one causal condition yet produce the same outcome, then the causal condition that distinguishes the two expressions can be considered irrelevant and can be removed to create a simpler, combined expression' (Ragin, 1987, p. 93).
    Hence:

(i)   abcdEf combines with abcdEF to produce abcdE
(ii)   ABcdeF combines with ABcdef to produce ABcde
(iii)   ABcdeF combines with aBcdeF to produce BcdeF
(iv)   abcdEf combines with AbcdEf to produce bcdEf
(v)   abCDEF remains.

These leaves the following five combinations of conditions that have led to a flat tax:

$$X = abcdE + ABcde + BcdeF + bcdEf + abCDEF$$

The first minimization shows that *geographical* proximity is an irrelevant condition if a policy champion exists, and there are no budgetary or trade pressures, nor influence in international institutions or a developed civil society. The second shows that precedent is also immaterial if both measures of financial pressure exist, and there is no civil society, institutional influence, or policy champion. The third says that budgetary pressures make no difference if there are external financial pressures, a precedent, and the absence of the remaining conditions. The fourth shows another situation in which condition A is irrelevant, this time when a policy champion is the only present condition. Finally, it's important to retain the only primitive form that cannot be reduced, namely the lack of internal and external financial pressure, but the presence of civil society, international influence, a policy champion and precedent.

This process sharpens the thinking on flat-tax adoption, and applying the results back to the original cases yields several insights. A number of cases validate the interest-explanation that predicts that internal budget pressures, external capital flight pressures, and precedent will lead to the adoption of the flat tax. This holds for Ukraine and Georgia – neither of which had institutional influences, civil society or a real policy champion. The idea-explanation is relevant for two reasons: firstly, the absence of a policy champion is offset by precedent; and secondly, both countries had recent revolutions. These genuine 'constitutional moments' (Ackerman, 1992) are an occurrence of circumstance, and are represented by the lack of a developed civil society. To understand the relationship between the two interest-explanations (A and B) compare Latvia and Lithuania with Belarus. All three have low institutional influence, low civil society, no policy champion but they all have precedent. Also while Belarus has internal pressure to raise tax revenue, Latvia and Lithuania have external pressures over capital flight. Again this supports the interest-explanation, but also shows that external factors are more telling than the internal factor. Were Belarus to feel pressure from competing countries it would take the same expression as Latvia and Lithuania, and therefore be expected to adopt a flat tax – since just one condition is missing me might call Belarus 'ripe'. Note also that there are no cases with AbcdEF, which is also one condition away from Belarus. Although this case lies in counterfactual space we'd expect the addition of a policy champion to make flat tax adoption in Belarus more likely, showing another possible avenue that would lead to a flat tax: the former being an interest-channel, the latter an ideas-channel.

Intuitively we might expect all conditions to independently increase the likelihood of flat-tax adoption, and the only way to test this is to find a case with all conditions present. Such a case doesn't exist, however, suggesting two things. First, the two cases that come closest to a 'full house' are the

Czech Republic and Hungary: both lack a policy champion (E). Since we know that the Hungarian opposition party advocate a flat tax, this is another 'ripe' country, should they come to power. But secondly, the fact that no current adoptee has all conditions present suggests that they might offset each other, and we have the evidence to speculate how. Slovakia is the only flat-tax country that we've judged to have international influence and a developed civil society. One option is to reappraise the initial judgement, and question whether Slovakia warrants a '1' for each condition. The alternative is to expand those two conditions, to see what they're really representing. Condition C might merely be a proxy for 'bigness' or 'development', and demonstrate why the flat tax is associated with small, poorer countries (and therefore explain why it has thus far failed to spread to Western Europe). But if this is the case, Russia should be adapted to have this condition present. What this implies is that the condition as we've defined it is inadequate (either being too imprecise to succinctly capture the current situation, or too tight and therefore letting Russia through the net), but the reason for the original definition was to establish the legitimacy of the traditional ideas-explanation: that ideas transmit by becoming embedded within institutions. This analysis contradicts that assertion, since the flat tax is more consistent with separate, isolated countries rather than members of the same club, sharing institutional structures. Therefore our understanding isn't satisfied, but we've adequately dealt with one of the competing theories: if ideas *do* matter we need a more refined concept than as captured by condition C.

So countries that appear to be only lacking a policy champion (such as the Czech Republic, Hungary, Poland), might be an illusion: we have no cases with either of their condition *but with* a policy champion, therefore we do not know if that would make the difference. On the contrary, as discussed above, the presence of some conditions may offset an ideologically committed opinion leader. Whereas condition C might be a reflection of general size and influence, condition D might represent the lack of something else: a constitutional moment. Since constitutional moments are characterized by 'procedural irregularities' (Ackerman, 1992) these are harder to achieve under the watchful eye of the public. While it's true that constitutional moments possess an 'energized, proactive public taking an active and maybe even directive part in the extended deliberations of a constitutional moment' (Burnham, 1999, p. 2249) it's not clear that mass media is a necessary condition. On the contrary, we might see the people shouting on the streets, politicians seizing the moment and a silent press. For this reason we might expect D and E to offset each other: if there's no real civil society and a constitutional moment appears, radical reforms can be made without a policy champion (e.g. Georgia, Ukraine and to a lesser extent

Latvia, Lithuania and Serbia); however if the policy is going to come up against the gatekeepers of debate it takes a strong politician, with convictions, to pass it through (Slovakia).

Finally, one case appears to contradict the theory that *either* interest-explanations (captured within conditions A and B), combined with precedent (F) matters; *or* an ideas-driver/policy champion (E) has to lead and define the reforms. This is the case of Serbia (ABcdef) but two important caveats must be applied. First the measure of precedent is crude and only looks at geographical proximity. When Serbia adopted a flat tax, Estonia, Latvia, Lithuania and Russia had all already done so, and although this represents the crossing from Eastern Europe to Central Europe, the Serbian debate was influenced by the knowledge that it had already been done. Second, it's debateable whether Serbia's flat tax should count as being analytically equivalent to the others. As already mentioned, Alvin Rabushka contests whether Lithuania's flat tax truly qualifies, and in the case of Serbia *only* salaries are taxed at a flat rate – other forms of personal income are taxed at different rates. Also when Serbia adopted the flat tax it was part of broader reforms where the centerpiece was the introduction of VAT. It was VAT that was seen as the weapon to solve the fiscal imbalances, and the flat tax involved significantly less political capital than in other adopting countries. Finally, other reports fail to include Serbia as a flat-tax adoptee.[13]

Factoring: How and When do Interests-Explanations Matter?

Since the prevailing theory of concern is the interest-explanation, it would be useful to perform a technique called 'factoring' to focus in more detail on the interest conditions. We have already established that condition B rather than A is the most important factor and indeed it is an appeal to competitiveness over FDI that is most evident in reports. Therefore we can separate the minimized expressions into two sets: those consistent with the presence of B, and those consistent with the absence (b). Thus:

$$X = b(aCDEF + acdE + cdEf) + B(Acde + cdeF)$$

The striking result is that in each case where there was no real consideration over the threat of capital flight, condition E is present. And in each case where there *was* financial pressure from external sources, condition E is absent. In other words a policy champion was not necessary in countries that had an interest to adopt a flat tax anyway, but if that interest is nonexistent, ideas-drivers can still get the policy implemented. Therefore *both* are necessary conditions to explain the spread of the flat tax.

CONCLUSION

This chapter used the case of the flat tax in Eastern Europe to illustrate the complex dynamics of economic ideas in the post-communist world to challenge the claim that Eastern Europeans had a purely passive role in the 'neoliberal revolution' taking place in their part of the world, and at the same time to show how one could get more disciplined insights into the ways in which 'ideas' and 'interests' affect the spread of a specific economic policy. With the mono-causal deterministic assumption discarded, one could explore multi-causal paths and patterns through the comparative method illustrated by the chapter. Although theories based on the driving force of interests could explain some cases, they cannot explain all. Therefore even with six simple conditions, an epistemic element *has* to be integrated. In conformity with the more theoretical discussion of section two, we have thus seen that ideas, interests and consequences are all requisites for a convincing explanation. Yet, we have also seen that, for some cases, the ideas-based approach is sufficient to explain adoption – and it is these cases which act as precedent for others to follow.

The importance of these cases is a reminder of the volatile but far-reaching modus operandi ideas have in driving and shaping the social and economic change process. At the same time, this imperfect but illuminating exercise in comparative analysis demonstrates that in the 'neoliberal revolution' the principles and directions of motion, far from being a pure function and expression of 'the West' and its pro-market economics epistemic communities, could be in fact inspired by far more diverse places and contexts.

NOTES

1. This personal allowance creates a degree of progressiveness into the flat tax but a debate as to whether this makes it truly flat is largely semantic. If the allowance is defined as a percentage of income earned below a particular threshold, then we have a progressive system with two rates (one of which is zero). If instead the allowance is defined as a non-taxable exemption it's a single flat-rate system. The distinction is largely irrelevant since it doesn't alter the substance of the policy or the novelty of its implementation. Our view is that the 'flat taxes' under scrutiny are genuine because all taxable income is taxed at a flat rate.
2. For clarity, and to fit into existing studies, the year of adoption refers to when the flat tax hits the people.
3. Some commentators don't consider that Lithuania's 33 per cent rate is equivalent to its neighbors, since it is too high to be competitive, and fails to account for other forms of income (see Rabushka, 2005). Like Lithuania, Serbia levies different flat rates on alternative sources of income.
4. *The Economist* 2005a and b.
5. For examples see Epstein (2005); Pirie (2005); Bartlett (2005); Gurdgiev (2005); and *The Economist* (2005b).

6. The predominant method of rational-choice political science, which stems from the interest groups theories of Olson (1965) and Becker (1983).
7. See Hall (1989); Goldstein (1993); Goldstein and Keohane (1993), Braun and Busch (1999), Legro (2000) and Campbell (2001).
8. We deliberately chose broad conditions, and therefore cannot fulfil the binary conditions by simple recourse to objective facts. Interviews are used to show that subjective criteria do not mean arbitrary criteria; it simply acknowledges that the analysis is tied to personal judgement. Subjectivism can be both a help and a hindrance, but the crucial point is that it exists, and therefore must be countered. And the potential pitfalls caused by a reliance on judgement have been checked by ethnographic fieldwork in a key case (Romania) and formal interviews.
9. See Table 2 (Schneider, 2003), figures for 1998/99, not including Albania, Bosnia, Serbia.
10. See Table 4 of Institute of International Finance (2006).
11. Eurostat (figures are an average of 2000–2004).
12. To some extent the process of accession might be seen to indicate an institutional convergence. We leave this issue open and suggest refining the issue of international community membership to incorporate more detail.
13. See Table 1 of Keen et al. (2006).

9. Neoclassical economics, new institutionalism and the Eastern European economic reform experience

The image of an Eastern European landscape of economic ideas homogenized, stalled and held up under the spell of Western economics has a twin: the image of a rigid and unchanged Western dominant paradigm – the notion of an unmovable, Olympian neoclassical economics, that has reached a stage of mature invulnerability and scientific rectitude. Yet, a closer look at the conceptual and theoretical dynamics set into motion by the encounter between the neoclassical paradigm and the Eastern Europe reform experience after 1989 tells a different story. The limits of policies and approaches inspired by neoclassical economics seem to have invited a challenge from new perspectives. The most influential of them was the so-called 'new institutionalism'. And it may be the case that the rise to preeminence of the new institutionalism as a potential challenger to the supremacy of the neoclassical paradigm both in East and West could be in the end the most significant epistemic outcome of the reform experience. A very notable episode in the history of economic thought may thus be taking shape: After replacing Marxism in Eastern Europe, neoclassical economics comes to face a paradigm challenge mounted from a perspective that was reinforced and inspired by the accumulated lessons drawn from the encounter between the neoclassical views and the realities of transition. This chapter explores this neglected but intriguing facet of the Eastern European social and intellectual experience.

The fact that Western neoclassical economics ideas were able to take over rapidly in Eastern Europe, and to establish their dominance over the void left by the demise of Marxism, should not distract from the fact that the European revolution of 1989 took the mainstream economics unawares about how to offer guidance for rapid transition to markets and democracy. Probably the most concise and clear expression of the first reactions of the social scientists involved in the study of social transformation at the beginnings of the 1990s was articulated by Douglass C. North in the opening remarks of a conference dedicated to the problem of economic change in

Eastern Europe: 'We live in an era of unprecedented societal change but the tool box of the social sciences for modeling the process of this change – economic, politic and social – is almost empty' (North, 1996). Mainstream economics lacked a general theory of economic systems and structural change but, as North noted, the box was not totally empty. The projects of political and economic reform in Eastern Europe at the turn of the decade were predominantly influenced by a series of models of political and social order. The models' key elements were built around neoclassical economics and the standard state-centered political theory, and their expression at the public discourse level where an endless set of variations on such broad themes such as 'Democracy', 'Market Economy', 'State', and 'Civil Society' (Johnson, 1989; Jonas, 1990; Ostrom, 1993; Blejer and Coricelli, 1995; Wagener, 1998).

The initial applications of the 'model' assume that a functional, contradiction-free relationship between those elements existed, and they expected that individual behavior and informal structures would rapidly adjust to the newly established formal institutions. Furthermore, due to their selective stress on the most formal and general aspects of the institutions and in spite of some limited discussions about 'Civil Society', they tended to disregard the social and cultural context in which the new institutions of democracy and market economy were supposed to function. Most importantly, the 'model' lacked the historical dimension. The references to historical processes, the time dimension and the long-term perspective were rare and mostly rhetorical (Murrell, 1992; Kovács, 1994).

Actual developments in the transitioning countries have shown that the relationship postulated between the key elements of the model was not so harmonious and that the model's projections were not accurate. Moreover, as time went by, it became increasingly clear that the vision of reforms based solely on a variant or another of the mainstream state-centered political theory and market-centered neoclassical theory lacked the force expected from them. There was a real need to rethink and reformulate the conceptual and theoretical structure behind the reform projects and policies (Chang and Rowthorn, 1995; Clague, 1997; Ostrom, 1993). That did not mean a total rejection of the initial models but an acknowledgement of the fact that although they were promising starting points for further theoretical development as well as relevant criteria for the creation of complementary approaches, they were nevertheless only of a limited usefulness. Thus, the very process of rapid transformation and reform set up and inspired by the neoclassical economics came to challenge at a foundational level the way economic policy and potentially even economics were conceptualized.

INSTRUMENTS AND TARGETS: THE NEOCLASSICAL APPROACH TO ECONOMIC POLICY

To be more precise, in the case of economics there was an overconfident reliance on a traditional model of economic policy emerging out of the postwar neoclassical synthesis and development economics. As explained by Eggertsson, (1997, 63–4), the model was not very complicated and it described the relation between 'targets' and 'instruments' within given 'systemic parameters'. A policy had targets (that is goals or desired values of endogenous variables derived from the preferences of policy makers) and the targets were reached by applying instruments (exogenous variables controlled by policy makers). The policy model prescribed what target values were attainable and how they could be attained. Policy targets may have been conceptualized as absolute, or the target variables may have been weighted together in a target preference unction. Policy instruments were employed either to attain absolute targets or to maximize the target preference function. In the case where targets were fixed, (or when target preference functions were subject to unlimited maximization), two maxims ruled the policy: (1) 'the number of instruments should be (at least) equal to the number of targets', and (2) individual instruments should not be assigned to specific targets; instead all instruments should be coordinated and directed toward the set of targets (Hansen, 1963, p. 7; Tinbergen, 1967; Eggertsson, 1997, p. 63). It is very important to note that the model had important implications for policy. The interrelationships among the variables in the model were crucial. If the model could be divided into autonomous departments, then 'all endogenous variables and instruments in the model could be prearranged in a causal ordering from the first order to the highest order. Then the instruments of the lower order could influence targets of the higher order without affecting lower orders of the system. However, the use of first-order instruments had repercussions not only for first-order target variables, but also for endogenous variables at higher levels throughout the system.' (Hansen, 1963, pp. 18–22; Acoccella, 1998; Eggertsson, 1997, p. 63)

Implied in that view of economic policy is the notion that there are two types of economic policies: quantitative policy and qualitative or structural policy. Quantitative policy takes as given the structure of the economic system and manipulates existing economic relationships toward a specific target. Structural policy, on the other hand, seeks to change the structure of the system (and implicitly of the equation defining it). If in the case of quantitative policy, the (immediate) goal is to achieve a new value for a target variable in the quantitative policy model, then in the case of qualitative policy the objective is to add new variables and to create a new relationship between (new) instruments and targets (Eggertsson, 1997, p. 64). Mainstream economic theory was relevant primarily for quantitative policy. In that view, the economic system was exogenous and in most cases reduced to several primitive parameters. The approach seemed to have universal validity as most of its applications were used in the case of the stable Western system (although its relevance had been a matter of debate even in that case). Unlike quantitative policy, structural policy could not be employed effectively without a theory of institutions and institutional change (North, 1997, pp. 14–16; Eggertsson, 1997, p. 63). Structural policy required a different type of approach based on a deeper understanding of the social, cultural and historical context of economic policy decision-making. Moreover, in most cases those cultural, social and institutional elements were not the context but part and parcel of policy-making.

The problem with this dichotomy created by the conceptual separation between structural policy and quantitative policy was that prior to 1989 economists specialized mostly in quantitative policy. Structural policy issues were relegated to what was increasingly seen as the periphery of the field: development economics, economic history and comparative economic systems. But that approach backfired after the collapse of Soviet-style communism when the mainstream found itself unprepared to deal with the profound structural policy issues imposed on the agenda by the transition process. The reform experience profoundly challenged the traditional approach. In policy area after policy area the reform experience exposed the inability of the field to identify or anticipate crucial problems and to articulate credible solutions. Out of that, a series of very important lessons emerged that not only contributed to a better understanding of the nature of structural policy but also to the emergence of a new and enhanced approach.

Those practical and theoretical challenges arose at a time when in the West a series of scholars coming from different disciplines and directions were converging upon an innovative approach to economic and political problems (Olson, 1990; North, 1990, 1994; Ostrom, 1993; Hodgson, 1988). The work of those authors had a number of features in common, such as disregard for traditional disciplinary boundaries; emphasis on institutions and institutional arrangements; an awareness of the limits of orthodox political, social and economic theories; and a deep concern for the direct policy relevance of their theories. The collapse of the communist system had already given a great impetus to their work but the new problems generated by the reform process and the limits of the orthodox approaches to these problems pushed them into the limelight. The label of 'institutionalism' was used to denote this family of theories and models that built on their divergence from the neoclassical approach as a key element in defining their identities. It is important to note that there are sufficient common elements and family resemblances between the members of this federation of theories (besides their skepticism regarding mainstream economics standards) that justify clustering them together. Yet there are also substantial differences. One such key difference in the institutionalist camp is between the 'new institutionalism' (an approach that builds on neoclassical insights by integrating concepts such as transaction costs, nature of the goods, property rights and information asymmetries) and the 'old institutionalism' (an approach that represents a more radical departure from the neoclassical assumptions that is directly rooted in the works of nineteenth century American authors such as T. Veblen and the German Historical School). Both strands are organized around the concept of institution and demonstrated the potential to offer a coherent articulation of the transition experience in a way that seemed to be pertinent to the problems confronting the people and decision-makers in that part of the world. The discussion in this chapter is focused mainly on the new institutionalism. Yet one should keep in mind the many commonalities and the fact that sometimes the boundaries between the two are difficult to draw.

THE REFORM EXPERIENCE AND THE INSTITUTIONALIST PERSPECTIVE

One of the most interesting facets of the intellectual history of the transition process was given by the perceived measure in which the intuitive and practical conclusions derived from the historical experience of transition converged with and supported the theoretical conclusions of the institutionalist approach. One could even say that the new institutionalism was strongly reinforced by the transition experience and that the present interest in it owes a lot to the Eastern European evolutions. That, in fact, when seen from a broader perspective, they reciprocally reinforced each other: the practical experience validated the importance of the new approach and the new approach helped to clearly articulate the conclusions of the experience. An overview of this rich area of convergence will help us to get a better grasp of this process and to understand the direction in which both the logic of the theory and the practice of reform have been pressing – while at the same time offering some key aspects of the contour of the new perspective.

One of the foremost aspects of the Eastern European evolutions was no doubt related to the fact that the high rate of (forced) savings did not prevent the economic collapse of the communist countries in Eastern

Europe, even though those savings were systematically invested in the 'productive sector' (Spulber, 1997). This in conjunction with the postwar experience in the Third World that demonstrated there was no clearly positive link between the transfer of resources (economic aid) and economic growth in the absence of an adequate institutional, ideological and cultural environment, made a very powerful case for the new approach. The history of technological transfers in the Third World and Eastern Europe has also confirmed that technology alone is not the most important motor of economic development. As for human capital, it has been observed that the productivity of Central Eastern European individuals in general increased several times within a Western institutional and organizational setting as compared to their performance in their countries of origin. Therefore, it was proper to conclude with the institutionalists that the transfer of physical capital or an increase in human capital through education does not suffice in cases when the institutional structure hampers the efficient use of such resources (Clague, 1997; Olson, 1990; North, 1990).

From this perspective, and on the basis of the practical conclusions that emerged from the reform process itself, an implicit consensus slowly took ground that it was necessary to overcome the reductionist tendency of discussing reform in terms of two or three key policies and variables (Clague, 1997). In fact, it was said, 'reform' consists of many different types of policies. Each type has its specific features and a strategic dimension that is given by the social and institutional context. For example, some policies require popular participation, some require 'insulation of technocrats from political pressure', some will benefit almost everybody, some will negatively affect important segments of the society, some will have immediate effects, and some will work only in the long run. A monolithic approach to reform and a mechanical implementation of ready-made policies projected around notions like the 'market' and the 'state' failed to reflect the complexity of the problems confronting societies in transition. Instead, a 'political economy' approach was needed that could take into account sectional and regional differences, individual and group interests, the institutional structures needed to coordinate their actions, factors such as the balance of economic or political power among different groups, sectors or regions, as well as the conflict and strategies they generate and the new institutionalism was able to capture them (Dixit, 1996). The strength of institutionalism was, in large measure, the result of its ability to signal its willingness and capacity to incorporate an interdisciplinary perspective:

> It is disturbing for many economists to be forced to acknowledge the length of the process leading from plan to market and also the need to resort to history and political science to understand what is going on. The economics of

transition cannot be reduced to just economics (whether macro or micro), nor can it easily be merged in a single approach. (Lavigne, 2000, p. 17)

It looked like an approach was needed that had the ability to incorporate an interdisciplinary perspective that could take into account factors as varied as individual and group interests and their socio-cultural determinants, the institutional structures needed to coordinate their actions, the balance of economic or political power among different groups, sectors or regions, as well as the conflict and strategies they generate (Dixit, 1996).

As time went by, people started to increasingly believe that a reform program should not become a prisoner of one reform-policy vision or one theory or another. For example, more and more voices argued that a vision exclusively focused on macroeconomic aggregates could not capture adequately the complexity of individual and group behavior or the institutional and organizational dynamics during a period of social change (Boettke, 2001). They pointed out that the reform process offered plenty of examples of how inadequate the aggregate demand management measures were in a context in which the basic institutional structure did not permit proper economic processes of adjustment. Phenomena like monetary overhang demonstrated the importance of the institutions that determine and shape the market process. In many cases, the demand management policy and in general the entire macroeconomic policy was undermined by the very structure of the economy they were supposed to stabilize. The initial emphasis was indeed in conformity with the standard mainstream policy model that was concerned primarily with quantitative micro- and macroeconomic relationships and that postulated a coincidence between, on the one hand, the preferences of policymakers and social actors and, on the other, the standard objectives as defined by theory. However, after less than a couple of years of reform policies it become more and more evident that that perspective neglected the incentives and behavior of political actors or the influence of political processes on 'targets', 'instruments' or the resource allocation. Therefore, it comes as no surprise that under the pressure of transition experience the policy models that tried to incorporate both the private and political actors' strategies and behavior and thus to endogenize the choice of targets and instruments came to challenge the traditional approach.

Thus, the new theoretical vision and the partial conclusions of the reform experience converged on the idea that an exaggerated emphasis has been put on macroeconomic measures and privatization while too little has been said for instance about the legal system and legal reform as key to overall institutional reforms (Eggertsson, 1997). It appeared that the role of the legal system and the way it regulates market behavior, property rights, contracts and social cooperation in relation to different institutional and cultural settings was even more important than initially thought. The gap between the enacted legislation and its enforcement in many post-communist countries was a problem too manifest to be neglected (Clague, 1997). In this respect, the role played by private organizations and informal social methods in complementing the government in law enforcement became evident, too. Thus, as time went by, it became clearer and clearer that the policies available were very imprecise instruments even when a 'correct' understanding of the economy and a 'correct' theory about its operation were assumed. Their limitation came from the fact that they were focused on the formal rules only 'when in fact the performance of an economy is an admixture of the formal rules, the informal norms and their enforcement characteristics'. Changing merely the formal rules will produce the results only 'when the informal norms are complementary to that rule change, and enforcement is either perfect or at least consistent with the expectations of those altering the rules' (North, 1997, p. 16).

Hence, both the new institutionalism and the practice of reform reinforced the idea long established in the old institutionalist literature that it was wrong to think that the nature and the functioning of institutions and organizations in a society depend only on the content of the norms, laws and rules and the effectiveness of the law-enforcement agencies. The degree to which those rules are observed and the way people understand, interpret and value those rules and are at least as important as their content. A minimal observance of rules is a prerequisite for any successful reform. The cultural, conjunctural and historical factors that determine the acceptance and observance of rules and the way the conflict between individual interests and rules is defined and managed are of maximal importance for the reform process (Kovács, 1994; Tismaneanu, 1995; Boettke, 2001). Consequently, the rate and direction of change will be determined not only by the 'strength' of the existing organizations and institutions but also by the nature and adaptability of the belief system. Hence, the reformers had to focus with equal force on two key elements: incentive structures and existing mindsets.

Regarding the incentives, as time went by, both the conceptual and empirical developments threw a high dose of skepticism on the approaches which ignored the social context and individual incentive mechanisms, relied on moral exhortation to citizens to act contrary to what they perceived as their immediate self-interest, and naively expected the people to react only to certain incentives while ignoring other ones. In the early 1990s, the implicit assumption in all post-communist countries was that the future of the reform was assured as long as the popular support and the political will were there. However, the political will and a favorable public opinion were merely the necessary but not sufficient conditions. It became evident that people tended to react to concrete, local and short-term incentives (Boettke, 2001; Dixit, 1992). Citizens were capable of expressing their support for reform in polls and public meetings, while at the same time acting or making decisions that were exactly contrary to the reform at their workplace or in their daily business. Crucial aggregate outcomes may emerge from apparently disjointed and unimportant individual actions.

In a similar vein, Eastern European developments reinforced the notion that the key to a successful reform of government bureaucracy is to try to understand the incentives that individual bureaucrats face, the way they participate in informal networks, the information flows, the nature of their specific tasks and the relationships between them and other organizations and institutions. For instance, a highly regulated economy necessarily generates a strong informal sector, and, by the very nature of their work, bureaucrats are bound to become directly and indirectly involved with the shadow economy. This is not a problem that could be solved by moral exhortations. Instead, a clear understanding of the system of incentives set up by the formal and informal institutional structures is required and institutionalism offered the theoretical structure able to capture this issue (Murrell, 1997). Regarding the mindsets and mental models, it is true that macroeconomics did acknowledge long ago that incomplete data and models can undermine the efforts of policy makers and the various lags of uncertain length can undermine the timing of measures (Hansen, 1963, pp. 31–6). But the reform process suggested that additional elements were needed in order to render the theory relevant. If the social actors in their attempts to advance their private goals rely on private policy models of the physical world and the social system, then 'successful structural policy must allow for interactions between public policy models and private models, and revisions to both in response to new data' (Eggertsson, 1997, p. 71). Consequently, the issue of communication and information becomes crucial as 'an important aspect of public policy is to provide the subjects of policy – actors whose behavior the policymaker seeks to change – with the information needed to revise their private models' and hence to help the coordination of different models at different levels. The conclusion was that the revision of models (learning) was vital for the success of public policy and becomes of great practical interest (Eggertsson, 1997, p. 71).

Another very important convergence area of the new institutionalist views and the conclusions of the reform practice was regarding the state's capability problem. Both revealed that there is no linear and universal relationship between the dispersion of power and economic growth (Chang and Rowthorn, 1995; Olson, 1993). Under special circumstances, the concentration of political power at the governmental level – rather than its diffusion – is a decisive factor of economic growth. Nevertheless, there is a direct relationship between economic performance and the government's position in relation to different groups and centers of power. If the government is too weak and is systematically blackmailed into giving privileges or redistributing resources to special interest groups, the result will be widespread corruption and economic stagnation. From this point of view, it was concluded that the constitutional framework is extremely important but not sufficient in itself to secure an efficient state. Each factor – constitutional or extra-constitutional – that affects the limits and distribution of power or the functioning of the government should be examined.

One of the areas in which the new institutionalism had its most significant and original impact in helping to articulate the reform experience was regarding the issue of the social capital and of the informal networks of cooperation. Irrespective of the problems raised by its definition and conceptualization, highlighting this dimension of the social order has been one of the foremost contributions of the new institutionalism. From the institutionalist standpoint, cooperation is as important as competition for the sound functioning of any economic or political order. Social networks of cooperation and social capital – that is, the personal and communitarian relations between individuals that can serve as a resource that promotes their interests – are the fundamental elements of any economic and political system (Coleman, 1987). Efficient economies and good governments are built on and sustain the development of social capital. Consequently, as the reformers learned rather rapidly, the complementarity between markets, political hierarchies, social networks and other institutional arrangements must be seriously considered by any social transformation project. Social networks operate in a subtle and inconspicuous way and perform many functions that cannot be effectively performed either by the state or by the market. They generate reciprocity, trust and social arrangements that facilitate cooperation and exchange as well as reduce opportunism and improve information flows (Shapiro, 1987).

On the other hand, it was noted, the structure and function of social networks – and the social capital they engender – is directly related to the institutional framework. Social networks that are functional in a specific institutional context could become dysfunctional when this context is changed. For example, networks of cooperation generated within communist institutional structures can be a source of corruption and a constant threat to the institutions created by reform. The reverse could also be true: networks of cooperation that were parasitic and subtly undermined the communist structures could be a hotbed of entrepreneurship in the new reformed environment. Once this perspective is accepted, the entire literature focusing on the formal institutions of the market and state looks like an attempt to study only the tip of the iceberg. There is an entirely unexplored continent of informal relations, arrangements, institutions and processes that in fact dictate the structure and performance of the formal ones and required the readjustment of the balance between the study of the formal and the study of the informal (Raiser, 1996). Methods that were developed and used up to that point only regarding formal institutions started to be applied to the vast continent of the informal.

A very important point that emerged with clarity but was largely overlooked initially by reformers was how much history matters. Coherent theoretical frameworks are not enough to understand today's institutions and to reflect the relevant dimensions of the range of policies faced by the reforming societies. As North (1997) put it, the structure and functioning of an economic or social system is difficult to understand without a clear view of its history and the current interplay:

> Because the experience of every society has been unique, the political structure and the informal constraints of norms, conventions, and internally held beliefs will differ for each economy. They constrain the choice set not only because the organizations of the economy have been built on the foundations of that institutional structure, so that their survival depends on its continuance, but also, and perhaps more fundamentally, because the belief system that is a complementary part of that scaffolding tends to change very slowly. Not only is the scaffolding what makes path dependence so important, but it is equally the explanation for the difficulties involved in reconstruction when much of the scaffold crumbles, as happened in 1989 in Eastern Europe. (North, 1997, p. 15)

Thus time, gradual change and historical accidents emerged as key elements in the understanding of the current situation and the future-oriented policy process. First, the lengthy lags between the moment when a policy was initiated and the moment when the new structures were adjusted came to be considered not as accidents but the norm. Once the fundamental incentives were introduced, public and private actors needed to experiment for some time with the organizations of the market economy. Learning and time came to occupy a crucial position in the theory and practice of reform. Financial firms, manufacturing centers, public administration systems and legal systems could not be organized without an implicit learning process. It was clear that structural change involved substantial lags in learning and adjustment, but the reform experience increasingly revealed the importance of even longer, more remarkable lags and path dependence (Arthur, 1994; North, 1990). In other words, the institutions and social structures affected by reforms should be viewed not only from today's perspective but also as a result and a part of a historical process (Putnam et al., 1993). Each institutional feature that the reformers wanted to develop was a part of a complex set of institutions, organizations, social networks and beliefs. The efficient institutions of the West have evolved over a long period of time, and the evidence to date suggests that their development in post-communist societies will take time as well. Reformers came to acknowledge that they do not know how to create such complex structures within a short period of time. It was concluded that any informed approach to this problem should be aware of the constraints imposed by the 'path dependence' – the constraints that past events and structures impose on the present and future policies (Arthur, 1994).

To sum up, the structural economic policies required by the reform process and the problems encountered by those policies bolstered the legitimacy of the institutionalist approach that was stressing precisely some of the structural and historical parameters simply assumed or neglected by the neoclassical approach. While discussing these areas of convergence between the new institutionalist vision and the conclusions of the reform experience it is important to note that although similar ideas could be found in other bodies of literature, the new institutionalism gave them a fresh vision combined with a robust theoretical framework. A brief overview of that vision is thus important in understanding the nature of the relationship between the new institutionalist thinking and the reform experience.

THE BASIC VISION

The toolbox mentioned by North started to gain new components primarily because a fresh way of framing the social economic and political reality started being used. At the most fundamental level, the new approach has been characterized by a specific vision of social order and the best starting point for any discussion of its relevance and its association with the transition issues is to briefly depict this vision. As some of those directly engaged in this effort liked to put it, a different set of conceptual lenses started to be used to approach the complexity of social change. The distinctive aspect of this vision is derived from the key role played by the concept of institutions in its architecture. Due to this, the most common way to identify it has been as the 'new institutionalism'. For many scholars and practitioners familiar with the Eastern European reform experience, the new institutionalism proved to be more than a broad vision of social order or the mere result of reflection on the historical experience of the years of reforms: its strength and appeal was mostly due to the robustness and applicability of its theoretical foundations. Probably in their eyes the most important feature of its theoretical corpus has been its remarkable combination of not only pluralism and flexibility, but also rigor and unity. By embracing the broader concept of 'institution', the approach produced a conceptual unity while avoiding from the very beginning the trap of being either state- or market-centered. From this perspective, the state and the market are sets of institutions among others with their specific features, structures and performance. They are part and parcel of (and sometimes lost in) the complex webs and layers of rules, norms, decisions and relations that characterize a substantive social system. What was liked most about it was that far from neglecting their importance, the new institutionalism illuminated the fact that this importance was relative: a function of, on the one hand, the specific configuration and state of the system and on the other hand, of the way the problem has been analytically defined, and the research strategy designed.

What many scholars and practitioners liked was the basic institutionalist line that allusions to 'markets' and 'states' or to 'socialism' and 'capitalism' do not take us very far 'in thinking about patterns of order in human societies' (Ostrom, 1993). They resonated with the idea that to indiscriminately use such labels as conceptual pivots to address the multitude of relationships that individuals pursue in human societies is not only an error from a social scientific point of view but also could lead to very serious practical consequences. 'These abstractions somehow achieve a sense of reality in our imagination and depending on our degree of attraction or aversion may become either nirvana models or diabolical machines' (Ostrom, 1993, pp. 390–93).

And thus many hoped that the new institutionalist vision may be able to overcome this theoretical dead-end and policy danger by looking at societies as larger aggregate structures of social relationships in which each set of norms, relationships and each form of association is nested in other configurations of relationships with complex areas of overlapping (Granovetter, 1986; Ostrom, 1993). They argued that conceptually it is possible to slice, aggregate and re-aggregate these relationships in many different ways. For instance, it is easy to conceptualize the nature of order in human societies as being constituted with reference to market and states or to markets and hierarchies. However, using such simplified conceptions fails to realistically capture the nature of social order:

> Markets and states are not isolable autonomous realms that exist as mutually exclusive domains of life . . . We thus might realistically expect to find some combination of market and non market structures in every society . . . The options are much greater than we imagine, when we do not allow our minds to be trapped within narrowly constrained intellectual horizons. (Ostrom, 1993, p. 393).

The new vision was perceived as offering the premises to escape this narrow intellectual horizon.

Taking the concept of institution seriously and accepting a much more pluralistic and flexible conceptual framework has direct consequences for the way the factors determining the economic or political performance of a society are understood. A direct result is that, as has already been mentioned, the economic and political performance of a society has started to be seen as not primarily determined by the availability of resources and related constraints but by institutional successes or failures (Olson, 1993; Ostrom, 1993). In other words, an inadequate institutional framework has increasingly been considered as the main obstacle to development or to a successful transition and the variety, complexity and functionality of the institutional arrangements as decisive for the economic and political accomplishments of a society. In this context, the state, the market and their legislative and regulatory infrastructures are seen as playing an important but only partial role in a process in which other institutions, some of them informal, may be decisive in many circumstances (Ostrom, 1993). This aspect of the problem of economic and political performance has drawn a lot of attention because it opened up an entire area of research focused on these largely inconspicuous, neglected and thus little-known institutional arrangements. Thus the new vision was credited with re-opening a new horizon in which the emphasis shifted on the exploration of the variety, complexity and contextuality of the institutional arrangements that form the essence of any concrete system of social order and on a specific institution-centered conception about the factors determining the economic and political performance.

LESSONS AND THEORETICAL IMPLICATIONS

Looking back it seemed that the transformation in Eastern Europe had been considered initially with an extremely limited conceptual apparatus while post-communist societies faced a complex, multilevel process, in which constitutional, legislative, institutional factors and informal social networks, cultural values and attitudes were all part of the problem. As it was said, that was 'a gigantic natural experiment' that had at its core what was rightly considered the 'awesome challenge' of simultaneously reorganizing the political, economic and legal systems and redefining the national, ethnic and cultural identities. In the absence of a general theory of structural change, the economists' natural response to the 1990s transitions of the former Soviet-type regimes was to try to do their best with the tools they had available. Thus, between 1989 and 1994 standard macroeconomic and microeconomic issues (e.g. stabilization policy and privatization) dominated the literature. As has been explained, the mainstream literature initially had little to say about the complexities of the institutional frame-work of economic organization and public administration (Benham and Merithew, 1995). The rise of institutionalism slowly changed the situation and one can say that by the end of the decade the literature has become more balanced in terms of approaches and issues. Although it may be too early to make an assessment of the practical success of the new institu-tionalist vision, at this point it is clear that the reform experience offered a series of valuable lessons and those lessons have implications on the ideas, paradigms, models and theories used to understand economic and social reality. New institutionalism has incorporated some of them as the policy practice has incorporated others at the same time. The complexity of the process precludes at this point a clear assessment, yet is clear that lessons have been learned and adjustments are made.

It is also important to note that the complexity has been amplified by the competing approaches to reform that emerged in the public debate. Initially, these approaches seemed to differ not on basic paradigmatic grounds but on policy objectives and interpretations of the basic emerging lessons. However, later the cleavage seemed to take an increasingly para-digmatic shape and made even more complicated by the 'shock therapy' vs. 'gradualism' dispute (Aslund, 2002; Kornai, 1990; Lipton and Sachs, 1990; Marangos, 2003; Lo, 1995). As has already been pointed out, usually shock therapy was associated with mainstream neoclassical economics while the gradualist approach was linked to non-orthodox currents like institution-alism and post-Keynesianism. Nevertheless, it was noted that the 'gradual-ism' debate was less a debate about the economic theory or the political economy paradigm but a debate on strategy. Thus, in the end there were two dimensions of the debates generated by the transition experience, related but still different: a strategy debate on the speed and intensity of change and a debate on the theories and models supporting the strategic views. Furthermore the discussion was complicated by the issue of whether or not a specific strategy was really and fully implemented. Each group accused the other of having failed to learn the right lessons. Yet, the list of lessons is not an object of controversy in itself: Countries in transition are quite different from one another because of their historical legacies and their transition policies. In other words, history matters. 'Initial conditions' are important: how long the country was communist and how dogmatic the regime was is crucial for the rhythm and success of reforms. The role of the state in the process is pivotal. Institutions matter. Institution building in transition is more a matter of institutional transformation than of day-to-day economic management.

In spite of the increasing rift, it is important to note that there is a rela-tive consensus on all of the above. The problem is in details, and in the different interpretations. For instance, everybody agrees that structural reform is important. The mainstream school defines structural transformation as the establishing of clearly defined private property rights, restructuring of enterprises, enforcement of hard-budget constraints, a healthy banking system, tax reform, competition on the domestic market and a market-based welfare system. For the unorthodox, institutions have to be built, for they do not emerge spontaneously and the process is longer and more complicated than expected. In a similar way, both schools agree that history and 'initial conditions' matter but are interpreted differently. Mainstream economists basically understand them as macro-economic conditions: macro-economic balances. While for the unorthodox economists, the legacy of the past is partly determined by long run and more complex political and historical processes. The point is that even if we assume that institutionalism is just a fad and will be absorbed by the neoclassical mainstream, the reform lessons changed the perceptions and approach of the dominant paradigm. These debates on the speed and intensity of the reforms, the sequencing, shock therapy vs. gradualism, etc. had deeper implications for the way the policy models and economic ideas were considered. Out of all these emerged, if not a dramatic conceptual shift, at least a deeper understanding of the institutional design tools and frameworks as well as a refined view on the models and approaches of the neoclassical economics. In itself that may be considered an important theoretical result of the reform process and also an illustration of the typical philosophy of science conjecture of what one should expect of a healthy research program.

From the perspective of its proponents, chances are that the new institutionalism will not be simply absorbed by the neoclassical theory. One of the most significant aspects of the new institutionalism, they say, is that due to its intrinsic, hard core 'world view' it does not reject or downplay the particular approaches offered by traditional disciplines such as sociology, history and political science. Rather, by providing a basis for a new conceptual framework, it has given a new relevance to traditional analyses and views and overpasses the standard neoclassical rigidity in this respect. To be more specific, by its very theoretical nature it acts as a link between several disciplines recomposing their segments and conclusions into new configurations and thus augmenting their significance and applicability. This capacity, they insist, is not an accident but the result of its special epistemological and methodological characteristics.

For instance they point out to the multiple levels of analysis approach (Crawford and Ostrom, 1995). The same institutional structure or social process could be described and analyzed in historical, structural or rational choice terms. For instance, the state as an institutional structure could be described in terms of public goods provision functions, as an element in a structure in which the social stratification and its dynamics are topical or using a narrative framework that is focused on the role of conjunctures, personalities, situational logic and their interpretation (Bates et al., 1998). As a consequence, the explanations the new institutionalism generates are mutually enforcing and complementary in spite of the fact that each of them reflects the nature of the specific level they are focused on. The analysis could go even further in this direction. For example, focusing only on the problem of social decisions and taking as a starting point the idea that the decisions of the individuals have a self-referential nature, the notion of levels and meta-levels of decision-making could be introduced as an analytical device. This idea that institutions and rules are nested in another set of rules and institutions that define their parameters of functioning and change is a very powerful research and public policy guide. This power is substantially increased when the structural or historical levels are brought back into picture. The differences between levels, the relationships between them, their mutual enforcement or the possible frictions and tensions emerging from their clash or overlapping constitute an entire research agenda. On the whole, the result is a theoretical set whose elements are capturing different nomological and ontological levels that could be flexibly used in function of the analytical goal and the nature of the problem under research (Dixit, 1996).

This pluralism, argue the institutionalists, doesn't necessarily lead to a lack of coherence. Accepting a pluralist approach and taking into account the whole range of social, cultural and historical factors operating at different nomological levels doesn't mean a compromise from the point of view of intellectual rigor. The very foundation and coherence of the whole system is given by the reference point position bestowed upon a series of models and concepts out of which transaction costs, models of public and common goods, rent-seeking and asymmetric information are crucial (Calvert, 1995; Olson, 1990, 1993; Crawford and Ostrom, 1995; Dixit, 1996; Drobak and Nye, 1997). The key to its consistency is mostly given by the discipline these concepts and models impose at each analytical level. Once cast in decision theory terms, they give the preliminary grammar of the approach. Probably this is the key element of novelty that gives the 'new' institutionalism its specific difference from the old variety of institutional analysis. Various theoretical elements could be and are added to the structure, in function of the nature of the problem and the research objectives but their position in this system is defined in most cases in relation to these core concepts or with a basic model that captures a rational choice process (Olson, 1990, 1993; Drobak and Nye, 1997; Boettke, 2001). It seems that not so much by design but by necessity, the new institutionalism has stumbled upon a combination between on the one side an instrumentalist methodology of modeling, used as a mental tool to impose order on data and to clarify and direct the research path and on the other side a realist–empiricist methodology, used to verify, falsify and keep the theorems derived with the help of formal models in close contact with the social reality (Dixit, 1996). The mixture between them depends on the level and goals of each analysis and the trade-off between realism and instrumentalism is not a-priori determinable but a function of the context and goals of each analysis (Calvert, 1995). This combination between the building blocks and the multi-levels approaches articulated on the background of a series of decision theory models makes, in the eyes of many, the new institutionalism a reliable intellectual tool that has what, in institutionalist terms, could be called 'adaptive efficiency' (Dixit, 1996). The capacity to reconfigure the theoretical structure in a coherent manner gives it special strengths both in terms of analytical power and of capacity to incorporate or harmonize other approaches. Moreover, and extremely important, this intrinsic suppleness rules out the possibility that due to a natural inner tendency towards a closer integration of the different building blocks, the new institutionalism will transform itself into another general, rigid and sterile Grand Theory.

Last but not least, one of the most significant lessons of the transition experience was that time, learning and learning in time matter. From this perspective economic policies are better seen not as blueprints imposed by exogenous policy makers but as part of a broader learning process. Economic policies not only constrain the choices but also alter the economic structure and performance. 'The aggregate of such policies is continually altering the way the economy works. In turn that leads to gradual alterations of the models we devise in a never-ending process of economic change' (North, 1997, p. 15). If learning is crucial, then the correlated problem of 'mental models' becomes crucial too. How people adjust their beliefs, their operational codes, and their values to the new circumstances in conditions of uncertainty becomes a pivotal research issue of both theoretical and practical importance:

> The idea of incomplete and competing models has various implications for policy, although the literature is particularly weak in this area. This outlook weighs against attempts at great experiments or the rapid implementation of structural changes and suggests modesty, incrementalism, and learning by doing. A new category of instruments emerges: measures for changing the information environment and for creating incentives for actors to revise their models and make them more compatible with policy targets. (Eggertsson, 1997, p. 74)

The 'qualitative' or 'structural' policy aimed at structural change is a long way from the classical models with their neatly defined 'targets' and

'instruments'. The dynamics of the environment and of the structural parameters is inherently uncertain and cannot be modeled as a relation between
instruments and targets in the traditional manner. The target of a structural policy would be to increase the learning context of both economic
firms and political units alike. Indeed, a meta-logic of maximization might
apply to this approach too but the difference is in spite of everything visible.
The idea is not to maximize a target neatly defined but create an institutional environment in which cooperation and competition would function
as mechanisms of continuous feedback for organizations in their adjustment process to the environment:

> Various feedback mechanisms are crucial both for coping with incomplete and
> competing models and for directing outcomes in social processes. Makers of
> public policy can advance their aims if they are able to design, or facilitate, feed-
> back mechanisms that inform or punish actors who operate with policy
> models, data, or even goals that are inconsistent with public policy. (Eggertsson,
> 1997, p. 74).

Finally, if one listens carefully to institutionalist authors, probably the
most important lesson of the Central Eastern European reform experience
is regarding our understanding of the limits of what we know. For many
social scientists involved in its study the reform process brought a new sense
of humility that deflated the over-confidence with which the complex
problem of transition was approached at the beginning of the 1990s. The
reform experience reminded the economics epistemic community of the
limits to our understanding and the hubris evident in the writing of orthodox economists received a tough lesson. The transition showed how important it was to 'understand that even if we do have it right for one economy,
it will not necessarily be right for another, and that even if we have it right
today, it will not necessarily be right tomorrow' (North, 1997, p. 15). The
reform experience offered economists the possibility to learn a lot about the
structure and functioning of the economic system and about economic performance. But the reform also taught that in our learning process and in the
policies enacted, there 'are innumerable occasions where we can and do get
it wrong' (North, 1997, p. 15). That happened in the past and there is no
reason that that will not happen in the future:

> Throughout history humans have typically gotten it (at least partly) wrong in (1)
> their understanding of the way the economy works, (2) the synthetic frameworks
> they construct, or (3) the policies they enact (at best blunt instruments to serve
> their purposes), producing unanticipated consequences. We may write economic
> history as a great success story of an enormous increase in material well being
> which has reflected the secular growth in the stock of knowledge. But it is also a
> vast panorama of decisions that have produced death, famine, starvation, defeat

in warfare, economic decline and stagnation, and indeed the total disappearance of civilizations. And even the decisions made in the success stories have typically been an admixture of luck plus shrewd judgments and unanticipated outcomes. (North, 1997, p. 15).

The process of social and economic change is constant and the institutions embody and reflect learning from past experience. Past changes teach lessons embodied in present institutions. Thus, there is a structural inability of the present institutions to solve the new problems created by the ongoing change. For that reason, the belief systems and the mental models reflecting the lessons learned and the accumulated knowledge are crucial. The shifting from a traditional political economy to the modern one based on impersonal markets was a difficult process in which the dynamics of institutional change and belief systems adjustment and learning was crucial (North, 1997, p. 15). Some of the lessons learned in that transition and after were useful for the transition from a 'command' economy to a market economy. But other realities created by the transition or the legacies of the 'command' system required a new learning cycle, a new learning experience. There is nothing shameful in acknowledging the fact that the belief system which has evolved as a result of the cumulative past experiences of both the Western and Eastern European epistemic communities and implicitly, societies has not equipped its members to confront and solve the problems (North, 1997, p. 15). The real problem would be if we shield away the invaluable lessons offered by this gigantic social experiment and refuse to accept the challenge it poses to the current orthodoxies. The irony of this possible situation would be evident as one of the major lessons of the transition experience is that belief systems, their dynamics, the way they are altered, replaced or improved – in a word, learning and knowledge – are the crucial factor in institutional and social change.

CONCLUSIONS

The process of rapid transformation in Eastern Europe challenged the theoretical approaches whose historical basis and source of inspiration were the established Western political and economic systems. The new institutionalism emerged as an approach claiming to be able to capture with rigor and clarity the complexity and dynamics of that process. Very soon, not only had reform-related evolutions pushed the new theoretical framework into the limelight but also seemed to validate it in an unprecedented measure. One of the most challenging implications deriving from this resulting combination of theoretical conclusions and conclusions based on the experience and realities of the Central Eastern European evolutions was that many of the problems raised by the rapid process of social transformation were primarily problems of vision and conceptualization and only then theoretical and technical problems. Thus, the problem of paradigm was raised again in a new and challenging way. It was suggested that the most important intellectual barrier to a better understanding of the reform process has been a rigid and poor conceptualization and the compartmentalization of approaches. Not only does that lead to a fragmented explanation but also to the neglect of otherwise more than relevant dimensions of social reality. The new institutionalism offered what looked to be a viable solution to these problems, by on the one hand basing its theoretical structure on a broader vision of social reality whose focus is less liable to be blurred by traditional notions used to conceptualize this reality and, on the other hand, by undermining the rigid consequences of the intellectual division of labor and overspecialization in social sciences.

Out of this approach some challenging lessons and themes emerged: the profound complexity of social change and an increased awareness of the limits to our understanding and control of it, the importance of time and history, the role of learning, belief systems and mental models, learning in time as a pivotal process and the ever-present possibility of error even in the best epistemic circumstances. These are some of the most important lessons emerging from the reform experience and their significance is not at all minor. One could see how the image of an unmovable, Olympian neoclassical paradigm that has reached a stage of mature invulnerability and stability is being challenged. The question is: will these lessons be enough to profoundly transform the neoclassical paradigm? Will this radical social change experience that has taken place on the eastern fringe of the European world, and which the Western society overlooked and misunderstood more often than not, be sufficient to alter the way economics is understood and applied currently? That remains an open question.

Conclusions

This book was an attempt to explore the ways the economics epistemic communities in Eastern Europe embraced the pro-market neoliberal ideas inspiring the massive transformation in institutions and policies in that part of the world in the 1990s. While engaging in this task, it reviewed a significant part of the relevant literature, brought to the fore fresh facts and perspectives, challenged some old assumptions shaping the perception of the issue, and suggested new interpretations. As such, besides being an attempt to better understand the Eastern European case, the project was also an attempt to use the case as a vehicle to shore up our grasp of the processes associated with the spread and change of economic ideas. With these ends in view the book had to walk a fine line between empirical observations and abstract theoretical frameworks, between the macro-level and the micro-level, between economics and sociology, between epistemology and intellectual history, and indeed, between competing interpretations of existing and new data. The result is a modest but, we hope, constructive step advancing an important research agenda. Probably the best way to mark the progress made in this respect is to simply restate some of the most significant observations emerging from the study.

First of all, the book challenged the widespread practice to approach the case of the rise of pro-market ideas in Eastern Europe as if it was possible to have one single, simple way of framing, explaining and understanding it. How ideas, interests and institutions interact and how beliefs spread and change, the great role played by the contextual and historical factors as well as the intrinsic volatility of the ideas-related social processes, are not at all easy to be captured in a single straightforward conceptual framework. Hence the need of 'pluralism' and a recognition of the limits of any attempt to reduce the East European case to a narrative illustrating the power of one master-theory or another. This successive application of a range of theoretical frameworks – sometimes complementing each other, sometimes challenging each other – was far from able to bring the ultimate explanation of the transformation of economic ideas in post-communist Europe but it was definitely able to lead to a deeper and more nuanced understanding of this transformation. Taken as a whole, the study has demonstrated not only the need for, but also the potential of, a pluralistic approach, an approach that is required by the very nature of the complex phenomenon in question. Yet, among this complexity and variety, one thing remains a constant. One is bound to return again and again to the very substance of the ideas that intrinsically define the phenomenon, to their content: to what those ideas say about the world and what they suggest should be done. That may seem a trivial observation but it is worth restating it because its methodological and analytical implications are so momentous. One cannot separate the meaning or content of ideas from their social life and its context. A study of belief systems and epistemic communities is a study built around the very content of ideas and the ways that content affects human decisions and actions.

This theoretical or analytical remark leads to another, more concrete and applied observation. Our study noted that too often the discussions about the 'neoliberal revolution' in Eastern Europe have been dominated by perspectives that forget to mention what kind of ideas were embraced before the coming of the 'neoliberal hegemony' and with what results. And thus, they create the impression that neoliberalism was a usurper and that better ideas were somehow sidestepped by the march of 'market fundamentalism'. The study warns that if that perspective is adopted, the dialectics between the dominant paradigm before the 1989 transformations and what came after it is entirely overlooked. And that is a real problem as it is precisely this dialectics that may explain better the success of pro-market ideas in Eastern Europe than the arguments that make tabula rasa of 50 years of experimentation with socialist ideas in that part of the world. The way to avoid this error, suggests our study, is simple: one has to look at both the winners and the losers. Never lose sight of the old ideas while tracking the march of the new.

Seen in the light of existing evidence, the neoliberal revolution in Eastern European ideas looks far from being an 'extremist' outburst promoted by 'market fundamentalists' as has been suggested by some authors. In fact, the protagonist was none other than the mainstream 'neoclassical synthesis'. The de facto intellectual standard among Western academic, professional and government economists has also become the standard among Eastern European economists. In other words, the ideas embraced in the post-Soviet countries were the usual combination of Keynesian and neoclassical theories. Before any 'supply side', 'monetarist', 'Austrian', 'public choice' or any other 'market fundamentalism' principles are to be understood and embraced in Eastern Europe, the very basic notion of modern economics had to be absorbed and embraced. Our study has shown that the 'neoliberal revolution' in Eastern Europe was not so much a process of uncritically embracing Hayek's social theory or Friedman's monetarism but one of familiarization with Samuelson's 'neoclassical synthesis'. That is to say that the 'neoliberal revolution' in Eastern European ideas was based, for better or for worse, on what was considered the most scientific and advanced social science paradigm of the moment.

Therefore, one of the first outcomes of an empirically informed view of Eastern European developments is the dispelling of the myth of an Eastern European rush to embrace the theories and ideas that may be considered the mark of 'market fundamentalism'. The same is true about the notion that a harsh 'neoliberal dogmatism' was somehow imposed on the region from outside. If 'neoliberal dogmatism' meant embracing aggregate demand notions of Keynesian inspiration and sound business environment standards, under the guidance of the World Bank, the European Union, IMF, USAID and UNDP, then that claim may be correct. But, one should acknowledge the semantic ambivalence involved and the fact that all this is, in the end, something different from the 'supply side', 'public choice' takeover claimed by some. As our study has shown, the most radical pro-market economists, such as the Austrians, are in fact, more often than not, pretty marginal to their nations' economics epistemic communities. Although the spread of radical pro-market theories is real, any empirically informed assessment has to conclude that these theories are far from being dominant. In fact, the spread of the Austrian views behind the Iron Curtain significantly lagged behind the spread of mainstream economics, and despite some highly visible political rhetoric, the evidence contradicts the claim of a market fundamentalist hegemony. To put it briefly, in that part of the world the 'neoliberal revolution' was at its core a realignment with the modern way of seeing and managing the economy. First and foremost it was an effort to get on the same page with the Western mainstream thinking in terms of markets and their management. In a sense, there was nothing 'radical' or 'fundamentalist' in that. To sum up, the raise of neoliberal ideas was a tamer and more commonsensical process than many authors would want us to believe it was.

A similar recalibration and adjustment to reality is necessary regarding the perception of the salience of the 'shock therapy' vs. 'gradualism' debate as the defining feature of the post-communist transition. The discussions during the transition period were marked by an interesting shift of attention to that debate with an ensuing neglect of the most basic cleavage of real historical significance: the rift between on the one hand, Marxist and etatist-socialist ideas, and on the other, Western, market-friendly ideas. The debates on economic strategy, although indicative of the dynamics of the 'neoliberal revolution in ideas' in Eastern Europe, are not the best and most profound indicator of the magnitude and nature of the changes. The nature of changes was without a doubt more profound and historically significant than the focus on the distinction 'gradualism vs. big bang' entails. One should not confuse a debate on strategy and policy with the foundational change of perspectives predetermining it. Those inclined to consider the policy and strategy position advocated by one side in such a debate as the epitome of neoliberalism in Eastern Europe and as the defining feature of transition are obviously free to label things as they please. Yet, this kind of labeling is misleading as it misses the essence of those historical developments. With that comes an inclination to stop thinking about the real cleavage (socialism vs. market economy) and a temptation to use the focus on the strategy debate as a pretext to reintroduce into the picture through the back door some old socialist ideas and principles. That is the reason why it is necessary to reassert that, as our study has documented, the neoliberal revolution in Eastern Europe was an ampler and more profound phenomenon than the 'gradualism vs. shock therapy' tagging implies. The mark of the transition was a paradigm change and not a debate about economic policy or strategy. And the collapse of socialism, as a system and an ideology, as well as the failure of statism as a political and economic principle, was its premise.

Finally, the book challenges a series of notions that have been increasingly influential in shaping the general perception of the nature and meaning of the Eastern European transition. Chief among them is the concern that the standardization and regimentation of economic thinking as a result of the spread of the Western way of doing economics, and the belief that the Eastern Europeans have been passively embracing this uniformity and standardization resulting from the pressure put by the Westerners. Without denying that the regimentation trend and even the pressure placed by mainstream economics on economic thinking have been real and in many ways stultifying, a closer look at the reality shows that the truth is more nuanced. Criticism, creativity and intelligent adoption and adaptation were always present. Neither did the substance of the Western ideas go unchallenged nor did the realignment of the epistemic communities lead to an absolute regimentation. The more Western ideas permeated the East, the more one could see not only uniformity and regimentation but reactions, criticisms, interpretations, re-evaluations and even new and sometimes surprising developments. For instance, one could see how the bold policy idea of a 'flat tax' took off and gained a new life in Eastern Europe. The case of the flat tax becomes thus a living challenge for those that claim that Eastern Europe had a passive (and even victim) role in the face of the Western, neoliberal invasion. It looks like Eastern Europe, after absorbing the neoliberal worldview, has suddenly become able to experiment by itself, moving on independently of the advice and concerns of the Western countries. One could also see how, for instance, Austrian theory ideas were given a new and very intriguing twist in a direction unrelated to the typical ways of employing and interpreting them. Far from being paralyzed and lost in the rapid developments as has been suggested by some, Eastern Europeans seem to have been fast and resourceful learners, ready to adapt, develop or circumvent the Western imports in interesting ways.

Last but not least, our study revealed how Western ideas themselves had to cope with the challenges of transition. Neoclassical economics did not survive the reform experience unscathed. The move from the academic blackboard to the harsh realities of the post-communist world was not without consequences. In the aftermath of the trials and failures of the neo-classical ideas put to work for the cause of economic reform, the 'new insti-tutionalism' theses received a significant boost. And thus the reform experience came to engender a potential challenge to mainstream domi-nance. The neoclassical paradigm itself was forced to listen to calls for its reform. In summary, one could see emerging the image of a very dynamic field in terms not only of replacing the old with the new, not only of spread-ing the Western economics, but also in challenging and changing it. The diffusion of Western ideas to Eastern Europe meant not only standardiza-tion and uniformity but also diversity, refinement and reassessment. Seen from this perspective, the investigations reflected in this book open up a more nuanced and realistic perspective on the neoliberal revolution in eco-nomic thinking in Eastern Europe, revealing new dimensions that make it an even more fascinating and momentous historical event.

Thus, in the end, one could conclude that our study managed to enhance in more than one way our views on the post-communist dynamics of eco-nomic ideas: We have gained a somewhat better grasp of the facts defining the process, we are more aware of the potential and the limits of the theo-retical equipment we use to study it and we have removed or at least ques-tioned some of the myths plaguing the public discourse about the nature of neoliberalism in Eastern Europe. But the measure of this relative progress is at the same time an indication of how far we still are from a satisfactory account of the spread and transformation of economic ideas. The limits of our theories and the need for new and innovative conceptual frameworks are obvious. Similarly, the gaps in our grasp of the facts are apparent. The symptom of our precarious state of knowledge is ultimately given by the numerous prejudices that continue to plague the discussion regarding the nature, origin and transmission of pro-market ideas. For each confusion clarified and each myth dispelled there are countless other half-truths and misunderstandings that tenaciously keep their hold on minds that, for some reason, seem too eager to believe them. That propensity is a very intriguing phenomenon in itself. As such it deserves a special and separate attention. But independent of the intriguing and enticing research agenda emerging in the wake of their mere existence, the resilience of the myths, half-truths and misunderstandings surrounding 'neoliberalism' should be troubling not only for the adepts of market economy but also for those that strive for accuracy and some objectivity in history, social sciences and public discourse.

And that is precisely the reason why the remarkable Eastern European revolution in economic ideas is so important: the post-communist transition represents a huge and unique natural experiment. Communist and post-communist Eastern Europe may undoubtedly be considered a gigantic and historically unique social laboratory and the transformative role ideas played through their own transformation in this unprecedented historical experiment is hard to exaggerate. We are confronted with an exemplary instance of large-scale social change, driven by a battle of two types of ideas: ideas regarding the capitalist economy and ideas advancing alternatives to it. This is indeed a fertile ground for the study of economic beliefs; a combination of almost ideal conditions for investigating their nature, role, diffusion and change. There are theoretical insights awaiting and there are practical lessons to be learned. And in the end, our better understanding of the Eastern European story means at the same time a better understanding of how and why people embrace, reject and transmit economic ideas that at the end of the day will come to affect their lives in profound ways they have never anticipated.

Bibliography

Acocella, N. (1998) *The Foundations of Economic Policy*, Cambridge: Cambridge University Press.

Ackerman, B. (1992) *The Future of Liberal Revolution*, New Haven: Yale University Press.

Adams, I. (1989) *The Logic of Political Beliefs: A Philosophical Analysis of Ideology*, Savage, MD: Barnes & Noble.

Albert, M. (1993) *Capitalism against Capitalism*, London: Whurr Publishers.

Aligica, P.D. (1999) 'Institutions, culture and the transition process', *Anthropology of East Europe Review*, Vol. 17, No. 2.

Aligica, P.D. (2002) 'Romania' in *The State of Three Social Sciences in Eastern Europe*, Budapest: Collegium Budapest; also in *Three Social Science Disciplines in Central and Eastern Europe. A Handbook on Economics, Political Science and Sociology*, (2002) Kaase, M., V. Sparschuh (eds) and A. Wenninger (co-ed.), Social Science Information Centre (IZ), Berlin and Collegium Budapest.

Aligica, P.D. and H. Terpe (2005) 'The Flat Tax Experiment: The Romanian Case'. Working paper.

Arestis P. and M.C. Sawyer (eds) (2004) *The Rise of the Market: Critical Essays on the Political Economy of Neo-Liberalism*, Cheltenham, UK and Northampton, MA, USA: Edward Elgar.

Armey, R. (1996) *Flat Tax*, New York, NY: Ballantine Books.

Arthur, B.W. (1994) *Increasing Returns and Path Dependence in the Economy*, Ann Arbor: University of Michigan Press.

Aslund, Anders (2002) *Building Capitalism: The Transformation of the Former Soviet Bloc*, Cambridge: Cambridge University Press.

Avramov, R. and V. Antonov (eds) (1994) *Economic Transition in Bulgaria*, Sofia: Agency for Economic Coordination and Development.

Avramov, R. and K. Guenov (1994) 'The Rebirth of Capitalism in Bulgaria', *Bank Review*, (Journal of the Bulgarian National Bank) Vol. 4, 3–24.

Avramov, R. (2007) *Communal Capitalism. Reflections on Bulgarian Economic Past*, Centre for Liberal Strategies [Available only in Bulgarian].

Barry, N. (1989) 'Ideas and Interests: the Problem Reconsidered' in *Ideas, Interests, and Consequences*, London: The Institute of Economic Affairs.

Bartlett, B. (2005) 'The Beauty of the Flat Tax', *National Review* (2 March).

Bastiat, F. (1998) *What is Seen and What is Not Seen*, Prague: Liberalni Institute.

Bates, R.H., R.J.P. de Figueiredo, Jr. and B.R. Weingast (1998) 'The politics of interpretation: rationality, culture, and transition', *Politics and Society*, Vol. 26, No. 4, 603–42.

Becker, G.S. (1983) 'A Theory of Competition among Pressure Groups for Political Influence', *The Quarterly Journal of Economics* Vol. 98, 371–400.

Beeson, M. and A. Firth (1998) 'Neoliberalism as a political rationality: Australian public policy since the 1980s', *Journal of Sociology*, Vol. 34, No. 3, 215–31.

Bell, D. (1960) *The End of Ideology – On the Exhaustion of Political Ideas in the Fifties*, New York: Free Press of Glencoe.

Benham, A.L. and M. Merithew (1995) *Institutional Reforms in Central and Eastern Europe: Altering Paths with Incentives and Information*, San Francisco: International Center for Economic Growth.

Biersteker, T. (1995) 'The Triumph of Liberal Economies in the Developing World', in B. Stallings (ed.), *Global Change, Regional Response: The New International Context of Development*, Cambridge: Cambridge University Press.

Blanchard, O. (1987) 'Neoclassical Synthesis', *The Palgrave Dictionary of Economics*, London: Macmillan Press.

Blackhouse, Roger (1985) *A History of Modern Economic Analysis*, Oxford: Blackwell.

Blaug, M. (1997) *Economic Theory in Retrospect*, Cambridge, New York: Cambridge University Press.

Blejer, M. and F. Coricelli (1995) *The Making of Economic Reform in Eastern Europe: Conversations with Leading Reformers in Poland, Hungary, and the Czech Republic*, Aldershot, UK and Brookfield, US: Edward Elgar.

Blyth, M.M. (1997) 'Any more bright ideas? The ideational turn of comparative political economy', *Comparative Politics*, Vol. 29, No. 2, 229–50.

Blyth, M. (2001) 'The transformation of the Swedish model: economic ideas, distributional conflict, and institutional change', *World Politics*, Vol. 54, No. 1, 1–26.

Blyth, M.M. (2002a) *Great Transformations: The Rise and Decline of Embedded Liberalism*, New York: Cambridge University Press.

Blyth, M.M. (2002b) *Great Transformations: Economic Ideas and Institutional Change in the Twentieth Century*, New York: Cambridge University Press.

Boettke, P.J. (1990) 'Soviet Admissions: Communism: Doesn't Work', *The Freeman: Ideas on Liberty*, Vol. 40, No. 2.

Boettke, P.J. (1993) *Why Perestroika Failed: The Politics and Economics of Socialist Transformation*, London and New York: Routledge.

Boettke, P.J. (1994a), *The Collapse of Development Planning*, New York: New York University Press.

Boettke P.J. (ed.) (1994b) *The Elgar Companion to Austrian Economics*, Aldershot, UK and Brookfield, US: Edward Elgar.

Boettke P.J. (1995) 'Why Are There No Austrian Socialists? Ideology, Science and the Austrian School', *Journal of the History of Economic Thought*, Vol. 17, 35–56.

Boettke, P.J. (2001) *Calculation and Coordination: Essays on Socialism and Transitional Political Economy*, London and New York: Routledge.

Boettke P.J. and P.T. Leeson (2005) 'Socialism: Still Impossible After All these Years', *Critical Review*, Vol. 17, No. 1–2, 177–92.

Bohm-Bawerk E. (1891) 'The Austrian Economists', *Annals of the American Academy of Political and Social Science*, Vol. 1.

Borhek, J.T. and R.F. Curtis (1975) *A Sociology of Belief*, New York: Wiley.

Boudon, R. (1989) *The Analysis of Ideology*, translated by M. Slater, Chicago: University of Chicago Press.

Boyer, R. and D. Drache (1996) *States Against Markets*, London: Routledge.

Braun, D. and A. Busch (eds) (1999) *Public Policy and Political Ideas*, Cheltenham, UK and Northampton, MA, USA: Edward Elgar.

Brown, A. (2007) *Seven Years that Changed the World, Perestroika in Perspective*, Oxford: Oxford University Press.

Brus, W. (1961) *General Problems of Functioning of Socialist Economy*, 2nd edn, Warsaw: State Scientific Pubications.

Brus, W. (1972) *The Market in a Socialist Economy*, London: Routledge & Kegan Paul.

Brus, W. and L. Kazimierz (1990) *From Marx to the Market: Socialism in Search of an Economic System*, New York: Oxford University Press.

Buchanan, J.M. and G. Tullock (1974) [1962] *The Calculus of Consent*, Ann Arbor: University of Michigan Press.

Bukharin, N. (1919/1970) *The Economic Theory of the Leisure Class*, New York: Augustus M. Kelly.

Burnham, W.D. (1999) 'Constitutional Moments and Punctuated Equilibria: A Political Scientist Confronts Bruce Ackerman's We The People', *The Yale Law Journal*, Vol. 108, No. 8, 2237–77.

Calvert, R. (1995) 'The Rational Choice Theory of Social Institutions: Cooperation, Coordination, Communication', in J.S. Banks and E.A. Hanushek (eds), *Modern Political Economy: Old Topics, New Directions*, Cambridge, Mass.: Cambridge University Press.

Campbell, J.L. (2001) 'Institutional Analysis and the Role of Ideas in Political Economy', in J.L. Campbell and O.K. Pedersen (eds) *The Rise of Neoliberalism and Institutional Analysis*, Princeton, NJ: Princeton University Press.

Campbell, J.L. and O.K Pedersen (2001a) 'The Second Movement in Institutional Analysis', in J.L. Campbell and O.K. Pedersen (eds), *The Rise of Neoliberalism and Institutional Analysis*, Princeton, NJ: Princeton University Press, pp. 249–81.

Campbell, J.L. and O.K. Pedersen (eds) (2001b) *The Rise of Neoliberalism and Institutional Analysis*, Princeton, NJ: Princeton University Press.

Caplan, B. (2001) 'What Makes People Think Like Economists? Evidence on Economic Cognition from the Survey of Americans and Economists on the Economy', *Journal of Law and Economics*, Vol. 44, No. 2, 395–426.

Caplan, B. (2007) *The Myth of the Rational Voter: Why Democracies Choose Bad Policies*, Princeton, NJ: Princeton University Press.

Caporaso, J. and D. Levine (1992) *Theories of Political Economy*, Cambridge: Cambridge University Press.

Cassidy, J. (2000) 'The Hayek Century', *Hoover Digest*, No. 3.

Catephores, G. (1989) *An Introduction to Marxist Economics*, New York: New York University Press.

Čekanavičius, L. (2002) *Lithuania: The State of Three Social Sciences in Eastern Europe*, Budapest: Collegium. Also in *Three Social Science Disciplines in Central and Eastern Europe. A Handbook on Economics, Political Science and Sociology*, (2002), in M. Kaase and V. Sparschuh (eds) and A. Wenninger (co-ed), Social Science Information Centre (IZ), Berlin and Collegium Budapest.

Chang, H. and R. Rowthorn (eds) (1995) *The Role of the State in Economic Change*, Oxford: Clarendon Press; New York: Oxford University Press.

Clague, C. (1997) 'The New Institutional Economics and Economic Development', in C. Clague (ed.), *Institutions and Economic Development. Growth and Governance in Less-Developed and Post-Socialist Countries*, Baltimore: John Hopkins University Press.

Coase, R.H. (1960) 'The Problem of Social Cost', *Journal of Law and Economics*, Vol. 3, No. 1, 1–44.

Coase, R.H. (1973) *The Firm, the Market, and the Law*, Chicago: University of Chicago Press.

Coase, R.H. (1995) *Essays on Economics and Economists*, Chicago: University of Chicago Press.

Coats, A.W.B. (1993) *The Sociology and Professionalization of Economics*, London; New York: Routledge.

Coats, A.W.B. (ed.) (1997) *The Post-1945 Internationalization of Economics*, Durham, NC: Duke University Press.

Coats, A.W.B. (ed.) (2000) *The Development of Economics in Western Europe*, London; New York: Routledge.

Coats, A.W.B. and D. Collander (1989) *The Spread of Economic Ideas*, Cambridge: Cambridge University Press.

Cole, K., J. Cameron and C. Edwards (1991) *Why Economists Disagree: The Political Economy of Economics*, London, New York: Longman.

Coleman, J.S. (1987) 'Norms as Social Capital', in G. Radnitzky and P. Bernholz (eds), *Economic Imperialism. The Economic Approach Applied Outside the Field of Economics*, New York: Paragon House.

Conaghan, C. and J. Malloy (1994) *Unsettling Statecraft*, Pittsburgh: University of Pittsburgh Press.

Constantinescu, N. (1973) *Problema contradicţiei în economia socialistă* (The Problem of Contradictions in the Socialist Economy), Bucharest: Editura Politică.

Cowen, T. (1998) *In Praise of Commercial Culture*, Cambridge: Harvard University Press.

Crawford, S. and E. Ostrom (1995) 'A Grammar of Institutions', in S. Haggard and R. Kaufman (eds), *The Political Economy of Democratic Transitions*, Princeton, NJ: Princeton University Press.

Crouch, C. and W. Streeck (1997) 'Institutional Capitalism: Diversity and Performance' in C. Crouch and W. Streeck (eds), *Modern Capitalism versus Modern Capitalisms: The Future of Capitalist Diversity*, Oxford: Oxford University Press.

Csaba, L. (2002/2000) *Hungary: The State of Three Social Sciences in Eastern Europe*, Budapest: Collegium. Also in *Three Social Science Disciplines in Central and Eastern Europe. A Handbook on Economics, Political Science and Sociology* (2002), M. Kaase and V. Sparschuh (eds) and A. Wenninger (co-ed), Social Science Information Centre (IZ), Berlin and Collegium: Budapest.

Cucerai, S. (2003) 'Free Exchange and Ethical Decisions', *Journal of Libertarian Studies*, Vol. 17, No. 2, 1–9.

Cuhel, F. (1994) 'On the Theory of Needs', in I.M. Kirzner (ed.), *Classics in Austrian Economics: A Sampling in the History of a Tradition*, London: William Pickering and Chatto Publishers.

Dăianu, D. (1999) *Transformarea ca proces real* (Transformation as a Real Process), Bucharest: IRLI.

David, P.A. (1994) 'Why are Institutions the Carriers of History? Path Dependence and the Evolution of Conventions, Organizations and Institutions', *Structural Change and Economic Dynamics*, Vol. 5, No. 2, 205–20.

Denzau, A.T. and D.C. North (1994) 'Shared Mental Models: Ideologies and Institutions', *Kyklos*, Vol. 47, 3–31.

Dewatripont, M. and G. Roland (1995) 'The Design of Reform Packages under Uncertainty', *American Economic Review*, Vol. 85, No. 5, 1207–23.

Dic, Lo. (1995) 'Economic Theory and the Transformation of the Soviet-Type System', in H.J. Chang and P. Nolan (eds), *The Transformation of the Communist Economies*, London: St Martin's Press.

Dijmărescu, E., A. Ghibuțiu and N.G. Isărescu (1977) *Datoria externă a țărilor în curs de dezvoltare și lichidarea subdezvoltării* (The External Debt of the Developing Countries and Underdevelopment Elimination), Bucharest: Editura Științifică și Enciclopedică.

Dimitrov, M. (2002) *Bulgaria: The State of Three Social Sciences in Eastern Europe*, Budapest: Collegium. Also in *Three Social Science Disciplines in Central and Eastern Europe. A Handbook on Economics, Political Science and Sociology* (2002), M. Kaase and V. Sparschuh (eds) and A. Wenninger (co-ed), Social Science Information Centre (IZ), Berlin and Collegium Budapest.

Dioscuri-Access Interviews (2003–2006) CEU University Budapest, CADI Bucharest and Institute for Human Sciences, Vienna.

Dixit, A. (1992) 'Theory and policy: reply to Tanzi', *IMF staff papers*, Vol. 39, No. 4 (December), 969–70.

Dixit, A. (1996) *The Making of Economic Policy: A Transaction Costs Politics Perspective*, Cambridge, MA: The MIT Press.

Dobrotă, N. (1986) 'Contradicțiile economiei mondiale contemporane' (The Contradictions of the Contemporary World Economy), in *Tratat de Economie Contemporană* (Treatise on Contemporary Economy), Vol. 1, Bucharest: Editura Politică.

Dobrotă, N. (1993/1995), *Economia politică* (Political Economy), Bucharest: Editura Economică.

Doherty, B. (2007) *Radicals for Capitalism: A Freewheeling History of the Modern American Libertarian Movement*, New York, NY: Public Affairs.

Dolan, E.G. (ed.) (1976) *The Foundations of Modern Austrian Economics*, Kansas City: Sheed and Ward.

Dore, R. and S. Berger (eds) (1996) *National Diversity and Global Capitalism*, Ithaca: Cornell University Press.

Douglas, G.W. and J.C. Miller III (1974) *Economic Regulation of Domestic Air Transport: Theory and Policy*, Washington DC: Brookings Institution.

Downs, A. (1957) *An Economic Theory of Democracy*, New York: Harper and Row.

Drewnowski, J. (ed.) (1982) *Crisis in the Eastern European Economy: The Spread of the Polish Disease*, New York: St Martin's Press.

Drobak, J. and J. Nye (eds) (1997) *Frontiers of the New Institutional Economics*, Washington DC: Academic Press.

Dunn, J. (1989) *The Economic Limits to Modern Politics*, Cambridge, England; New York: Cambridge University Press.

Economist, The (2005a) 'Flat Is Beautiful' (5 March).

Economist, The (2005b) 'The Case for Flat Taxes – Simplifying Tax Systems' (16 April).

Eggertsson, T. (1990) *Economic Behavior and Institutions*, Cambridge, England: Cambridge University Press.

Eggertsson, T. (1996) 'A note on the economics of institutions', in L.J. Alston, T. Eggertsson and D.C. North (eds), *Empirical Studies in Institutional Change. Political Economy of Institutions and Decisions*, Cambridge and New York: Cambridge University Press.

Eggertsson, T. (1997) 'Rethinking the theory of economic policy: some implications of the new institutionalism', in D. North (ed.), *Transforming Post-Communist Political Economies*, Washington DC: National Resource Council, National Academy of Sciences.

Encyclopedia of the World's Religions (1996), *Encyclopedia of the World's Religions*, New York: Barnes and Noble Books.

England, K. and K. Ward (eds) (2007) *Neo-Liberalization: Networks, States, Peoples*, Oxford: Blackwell Publishing.

Englis, K. (1992) *Economics: A Purpose Oriented Approach. East European Monographs*, New York: Columbia University Press [translated by Ivo Moravcik].

Epstein, R. (2005) 'The Case for Flat Taxes', *New Zealand Herald* (31 January).

European Commission (2002) 'Phare Action Programmes Documents', Brussels: European Commission.

Evans, A.J. (2005) 'Ideas and Interests: The Flat Tax', *Open Republic* Vol. 1, No. 1.

Evans, A.J. (2006a) 'The Spread of Economic Theology: The Flat Tax', *Romanian Economic and Business Review* Vol. 1, No. 1.

Evans, A.J. (2006b) 'Libertarianism in Romania', *Revista* Vol. 22, No. 867 20–26 October [translated into Romanian].

Feuer, L.S. (1975) *Ideology and the Ideologists*, New York: Harper and Row.

Foldvary, F. and D. Klein (eds) (2003) *The Half-life of Policy Rationales: How Technology Affects Old Policy Issues*, New York: New York University Press.

Forbes, S. (2006) *Flat Tax Revolution*, Washington, DC: Regnery Publishing.

Foreman, N. (1996) 'Single Rate Tax: The Path to Real Simplicity', Demos.

Friedman, M. (1953) 'The Methodology of Positive Economics', in *Essays in Positive Economics*, Chicago: The University of Chicago Press.

Friedman, M. (1962) *Capitalism and Freedom*, Chicago, IL: University of Chicago Press.

Fukuyama, F. (1992) *The End of History and the Last Man*, New York: Avon Books and The Free Press.

Fund, J. (2005) 'High Taxes Wither Away', *New York Sun* (1 March).

Furet, F. (1999) *The Passing of an Illusion: The Idea of Communism in the Twentieth Century*, translated by D. Furet, Chicago: University of Chicago Press.

Gabrisch, H. (ed.) (1988) *Economic Reforms in Eastern Europe and the Soviet Union*, Boulder, Colo.: Westview Press.

Gamamikow, M. (1968) *Economic Reforms in Eastern Europe*, Detroit: Wayne State University Press.

Gamble, A. (1989) 'Ideas and Interests in British Economic Policy', *Ideas, Interests, and Consequences*, IEA.

Gamble, A. (2006) 'Two Faces of Neoliberalism', in R. Robison (ed.), *The Neoliberal Revolution: Forging the Market State*, London: Palgrave.

Garrison, R. (2004) 'A Roundabout Approach to Macroeconomics: Some Autobiographical Reflections', *The American Economist*, Vol. 48, No. 2, 26–40.

Garton-Ash, T. (1999) *History of the Present*, New York, NY: Random House.

George, A. (1978) *Bridging the Gap: Theory and Practice in Foreign Policy*, Washington, DC: United States Institute of Peace Press.

Gershenkron, A. (1962) *Economic Backwardness in Historical Perspectives, A Book of Essays*, Cambridge, MA: Belknap Press of Harvard University Press.

Glass, J.C. and W. Johnson (1989) *Economics – Progression, Stagnation, or Degeneration? An Introduction to the Methodological Issues Involved in Assessing the Growth of Economic Knowledge*, Ames, Iowa: Iowa State University Press.

Glavan, B. (2004) 'The Failure of OCA Analysis', *The Quarterly Journal of Austrian Economics*, Vol. 7, No. 2, 29–46.

Glavan, B. (2005) 'The Insulation Argument in Neoclassical International Economics: A Critique', *The Quarterly Journal of Austrian Economics*, Vol. 8, No. 3, 3–19.

Gloria-Palermo S. (ed.) (2002) *Modern Austrian Economics: Archaeology of a Revival*, London: Pickering & Chatto.

Goldstein, J. (1988) 'Ideas, Institutions, and Trade Policy', *International Organization*, Vol. 42.

Goldstein, J. (1993) *Ideas, Interests, and American Trade Policy*, Ithaca, NY: Cornell University Press.

Goldstein, J. and R. Keohane (1993a) *Ideas and Foreign Policy: Beliefs*

Institutions and Political Change, Ithaca, NY: Cornell University Press.

Goldstein, J. and R. Keohane (1993b) 'Ideas and Foreign Policy: An Analytical Framework', in *Ideas and Foreign Policy*, J. Goldstein, R. Keohane (eds), Ithaca, NY: Cornell Univ. Press, pp. 3–30.

Gonda, P. and Chalupnicek, P. (2007) *In Defense of the Free Market*, Bratislava: Conservative Institute.

Goodwin, C. (1972) 'Economic Theory and Society: A Plea for Process Analysis', *American Economic Review*, Vol. 62 (May).

Goodwin, C.D.W. and I.B. Holley Jr. (eds) (1968) *The Transfer of Ideas, The South Atlantic Quarterly*, Durham, NC.

Gordon, D. (1995) 'A New Socialism?', *The Mises Review*, www.mises.org/misesreview_detail.aspx?control=62.

Granovetter, M. (1986) 'Economic Action and Social Structure. The Problem of Embeddedness', *American Journal of Sociology*, Vol. 91, No. 3, 481–510.

Grecu, A. (2005) 'Flat Tax – The British Case', Adam Smith Institute.

Gurdgiev, C. (2005) 'Should Ireland Join the Flat Tax Club?', *Business & Finance Magazine* (7 April).

Gyorgy, A. and J.A. Kuhlman (eds) (1978) *Innovation in Communist Systems*, Boulder, Colo.: Westview Press.

Haas, P. (1990) *Saving the Mediterranean*, New York, NY: Columbia University Press.

Haas, P. (1992) 'Introduction: Epistemic Communities and International Policy Coordination', *International Organization*, Vol. 46, No. 1, 1–37.

Hagerstrand, T. (1988) 'Some unexplored problems in the modeling of Culture Transfer and Transformation' in Hugill and Dikinson (eds), *The Transfer and Transformation of Ideas and Material Culture*, Texas: A&M University Press.

Hal, V. (2000) 'Markets for Information Goods' in *Monetary Policy in a World of Knowledge-Based Growth, Quality Change, and Uncertain Measurement*, PLACE: Bank of Japan.

Hall, J.A. (1993) 'Ideas and the social sciences' in J. Goldstein and R. Keohane (eds), *Ideas and Foreign Policy: Beliefs, Institutions and Political Change*, Ithaca: Cornell University Press.

Hall, P.A. (ed.) (1989) *The Political Power of Economic Ideas: Keynesianism Across Nations*, Princeton, NJ: Princeton University Press.

Hall, P.A. (1992) 'The movement from Keynesianism to monetarism: Institutional analysis and British economic policy in the 1970s', in S. Steinmo, K. Thelen and F. Longstreth (eds), *Structuring Politics. Historical Institutionalism in Comparative Analysis*, Cambridge, Mass.: Cambridge University Press.

Hall, P. and A. Rabushka (1995) *The Flat Tax*, 2nd edn, Stanford, CA: Hoover.

Hanley, S. (2006a) 'Blue Velvet: The Rise and Decline of the New Czech Right' in A. Szczerbiak and S. Hanley (eds), *Centre-Right Parties in Post-Communist East-Central Europe*, London: Routledge.

Hanley, S. (2006b) 'Getting the Right Right: Redefining the Centre-Right in Post-Communist Europe' in A. Szczerbiak and S. Hanley (eds), *Centre-Right Parties in Post-Communist East-Central Europe*, London: Routledge.

Hanley, S., A. Szczerbiak, T. Haughton and B. Fowler (2007) 'Explaining the Success of Centre-Right Parties in Post Communist East Central Europe: A Comparative Analysis', Sussex European Institute Working Paper No. 94.

Hansen, A. (1963) *Monetary Theory and Fiscal Policy*, New York: McGraw-Hill.

Harberger, A. (1993) 'Secrets of Success: A Handful of Heroes', *American Economic Review Papers and Proceedings*, Vol. 83, 343–50.

Harvey, D. (2005) *A Brief History of Neoliberalism*, Oxford, UK: Oxford University Press.

Hausner, J., B. Jessop and K. Nielsen (1995) *Strategic Choice and Path-Dependency in Post-Socialism: Institutional Dynamics in the Transformation Process*, Aldershot, UK and Brookfield, US: Edward Elgar.

Havel, J., J. Klacek, J. Kosta and S. Zdislav (1998) 'Economics and systemic changes in Czechoslovakia' in H.J. Wagener (ed.), *Economic Thought in Communist and Post Communist Europe*, London and New York: Routledge.

Hay, C. (2001) 'The 'Crisis' of Keynesianism and the Rise of Neoliberalism in Britain' in J.L. Campbell and O.K. Pedersen (eds), *The Rise of Neoliberalism and Institutional Analysis*, Princeton, NJ: Princeton University Press, pp. 193–218.

Hayek, F.A. (1945) 'The Use of Knowledge in Society', *American Economic Review*, Vol. 35, No. 4, 519–30.

Hayek, F.A. (1956) 'Progressive Taxation Reconsidered' in H. Sennholz (ed.), *On Freedom and Free Enterprise*, Princeton, NJ: Van Nostrand.

Hayek, F.A. (1960) *The Constitution of Liberty*, Chicago, IL: University of Chicago Press.

Hayek, F.A. (1967) *Studies in Philosophy, Politics, and Economics*, Chicago: The University of Chicago Press.

Hayek, F.A. (1973/1974) *Law, Legislation and Liberty*, Chicago: University of Chicago Press.

Hayek, F.A. (1988) *The Fatal Conceit: The Errors of Socialism*, ed. by W.W. Hartley III, Chicago: The University of Chicago Press.

Heath, A. (2006) *The Flat Tax: Towards a British Model*, London: The Tax Payers' Alliance.

Heilbroner, R. and Milberg W. (1995) *The Crisis of Vision in Modern Economic Thought*, New York: Cambridge University Press

Helleiner, E. (2003) 'Economic Liberalism and Its Critics: The Past As Prologue?', *Review of International Political Economy*, Vol. 10, No. 4, 685–96.

Hettich, W. and S.L. Winer (1999) *Democratic Choice and Taxation: A theoretical and Empirical Analysis*, Cambridge, UK: Cambridge University Press.

Heyne, P., P. Boettke and D. Prychitko (2005) *The Economic Way of Thinking*, Saddle River NJ: Prentice Hall (11th edn).

Hirshleifer, J. (1992) *The Analytics of Uncertainty and Information*, Cambridge: Cambridge University Press.

Hirst, P. and G. Thompson (1996) *Globalization in Question*, London and Cambridge: Polity Press.

Hodgson, G. (1988) *Economics and Institutions: A Manifesto for a Modern Institutional Economics*, Cambridge: Polity Press.

Hodgson, G. (1989) 'Institutional Economic Theory: the Old versus the New', *Review of Political Economy*, Vol. 1, No. 3, 249–69.

Horvart, J. (2002) *Slovakia – The State of Three Social Sciences in Eastern Europe*, Budapest: Collegium. Also in *Three Social Science Disciplines in Central and Eastern Europe. A Handbook on Economics, Political Science and Sociology* (2002), M. Kaase and V. Sparschuh (eds) and A. Wenninger (co-ed), Social Science Information Centre (IZ), Berlin and Collegium Budapest.

Hristoforov, A. (1946) 'Central Banks and Modern Banking Theories', *Yearbook of the State Higher School of Financial and Administrative Sciences*, Vol. V, 1–70.

Institute of International Finance (2006) 'Regional Overview: Central and Eastern Europe', EBRD Annual Meeting, Institute of International Finance.

Ionita, S. (2006) 'The Truth about the Flat Tax', SAR Policy Brief No. 18.

Jacobsen, J.K. (1995) 'Much Ado about Ideas: the Cognitive Factor in Economic Policy', *World Politics*, Vol. 47, 283–310.

Johnson, P.M. (1989) *Redesigning the Communist Economy: The Politics of Economic Reform in Eastern Europe*, Boulder, Colo.: Westview Press.

Jonas, P. (1990) *The Structure and Reform of Centrally Planned Economic System*, Boulder, Colo.: East European Monographs.

Junankar, P.N. (1982) *Marx's Economics*, Oxford: Oxford University Press.

Junglich, P., T. Koudela and P. Zantovsky (1998) *Tak pravil Václav Klaus*, Prague: Votobia.

Kaase, M. and V. Sparschuh (eds) and A. Wenninger (co-ed.) (2002) *Three Social Science Disciplines in Central and Eastern Europe. A Handbook on Economics, Political Science and Sociology (1989–2001)*, Social Science Information Centre (IZ), Berlin and Collegium Budapest.

Kahler, M. (1990) 'Orthodoxy and Its Alternatives' in J. Nelson (ed.), *Economic Crisis and Policy Choice*, Princeton: Princeton University Press.

Kalecki, M. (1990) *Collected Works* (J. Osiatynski ed.), Oxford: Oxford University Press.

Karnite, R. (2002) *Latvia – The State of Three Social Sciences in Eastern Europe*, Budapest: Collegium. *Also in Three Social Science Disciplines in Central and Eastern Europe. A Handbook on Economics, Political Science and Sociology* (2002), M. Kaase and V. Sparschuh (eds) and A. Wenninger (co-ed.), Social Science Information Centre (IZ), Berlin and Collegium Budapest.

Kay, J. (2005) 'Why Tax Cannot be Expressed on a Postcard', *The Financial Times* (8 February).

Kay, J.A. and M.A. King (1986) *The British Tax System*, Oxford, UK: Oxford University Press.

Keen, M., Y. Kim and R. Varsano (2006) 'The 'Flat Tax(es)': Principles and Evidence', IMF Working Paper.

Kirshner, J. (1998a) 'Political Economy in Security Studies after the Cold War', *Review of International Political Economy*, Vol. 5, No. 1, 64–91.

Kirshner, J. (1998b), 'Disinflation, Structural Change, and Distribution', *Review of Radical Political Economics*, Vol. 30, No. 1/March, 53–89.

Kirzner, I. (1960) *The Economic Point of View*, Kansas City: Sheed and Ward Inc.

Kirzner, I.M. (2001) *Ludwig Von Mises. The Man and His Economics*, Wilmington, Delaware: ISI Books.

Kirzner, I.M. (2006) 'Calculation, competition and entrepreneurship' in J. High (ed.), *Humane Economics. Essays in Honor of Don Lavoie*, Cheltenham, UK and Northampton, MA, USA: Edward Elgar.

Kitschelt, H., P. Lange, G. Marks and J.D. Stephens (1999) 'Convergence and Divergence in Advanced Capitalist Democracies' in H. Kitschelt, P. Lange, G. Marks, J.D. Stephens (eds), *Continuity and Change in Contemporary Capitalism*, New York: Cambridge University Press, pp. 427–60.

Klamer, A. and D. McCloskey (1990) 'The Economy as Conversation', paper given at AEA meeting in Washington DC, December.

Klaus, V. (1991) *A Road to Market Economy*, Prague: Top Agency.

Klaus, V. (1997) 'The Austrian School: Its Significance in the Transformation Process' in H. Bouillon (ed.), *Libertarians and Liberalism: Essays in Honor of Gerard Radnitzky*, Aldershot, UK: Avesbury.

Klaus, V. (2006) *Ekonomie a Ekonomika*, Prague: Knizni Klub.

Klein, D. and C. Stern (2007) 'Is There a Free-Market Economist in the House? The Policy Views of American Economic Association Members', *American Journal of Economics and Sociology*, Vol. 66, No. 2/April, 309–34.

Knight, J. (1992) *Institutions and Social Conflict*, Cambridge, Mass.: Cambridge University Press.

Knight, J. (2003) 'Explaining the Rise of Neoliberalism' in J.L. Campbell and O.K. Pedersen (eds), *The Rise of Neoliberalism and Institutional Analysis*, Princeton: Princeton University Press.

Knight, J. and D. North (1997) 'Explaining Economic Change: The Interplay Between Cognition and Institutions', *Legal Theory*, Vol. 3, 211–26.

Kornai, J. (1971) *Anti-Equilibrium. On Economic Systems Theory and The Tasks of Research*, Amsterdam: North-Holland.

Kornai, J. (1980) *Economics of Shortage*, Amsterdam: North-Holland.

Kornai, J. (1986) 'The Hungarian Reform Process: Visions, Hopes and Reality', *Journal of Economic Literature*, Vol. 24, No. 4, 1687–1737.

Kornai, J. (1990a) *The Road to a Free Economy. Shifting from a Socialist System: The Example of Hungary*, New York: W.W. Norton and Budapest: HVG Kiadó.

Kornai, J. (1990b) 'The Affinity Between Ownership and Coordination Mechanisms: The Common Experience of Reform in Socialist Countries', World Institute for Development Economics Research of the United Nations University, Helsinki.

Kornai, J. (1992) *The Socialist System. The Political Economy of Communism*, Princeton: Princeton University Press and Oxford: Oxford University Press.

Kornai J. (2000a) 'The System Paradigm', in W. Schekle, W. Krauth, M. Kohli and G. Elwert (eds), *Paradigms of Social Change: Modernization, Development, Transformation, Evolution*, Frankfurt/New York: Campurs Verlag and New York: St Martin's, pp. 111–33.

Kornai, J. (2000b) 'What the Change of System from Socialism to Capitalism Does and Does Not Mean', *Journal of Economic Perspectives*, 14, (1), 27–42.

Kovács, J.M. (ed.) (1994) *Transition to Capitalism? The Communist Legacy in Eastern Europe*, New Brunswick, NJ: Transaction Publishers.

Kovács, J.M. and M. Tardos (1992) *Reform and Transformation in Eastern*

Europe: Soviet-Type Economics on the Threshold of Change, New York: Routledge in association with the Institut für die Wissenschaften vom Menschen, Vienna.

Kowalik, T. (2000/2002) *Poland – The State of Three Social Sciences in Eastern Europe*, Budapest: Collegium. Also in M. Kaase and V. Sparschuh (eds) and A. Wenninger (co-ed.) (2002), *Three Social Science Disciplines in Central and Eastern Europe. A Handbook on Economics, Political Science and Sociology*, Social Science Information Centre (IZ), Berlin and Collegium Budapest.

Kuhn, T. (1962) *The Structure of Scientific Revolutions*, Chicago: University of Chicago Press.

Kuskowski, J. (2007) 'Rockwell on Libertarianism', An interview for the Polish Libertarian Website Liberalis, http://www.lewrockwell.com/rockwell/liberalis-inteview.html.

Kuttner, R. (1997) *Everything for Sale: The Virtues and Limits of Markets*, New York: Knopf.

Lachmann, L.M. (1978) 'An Austrian Stocktaking: Unsettled Questions and Tentative Answers' in L.M. Sporado (ed.), *New Directions in Austrian Economics*, Kansas City: Sheed Andrews and McMeel.

Lakatos, I. (1978) *Philosophical Papers*. Cambridge and New York: Cambridge University Press.

Lakatos, I. and A. Musgrave (1970) *Criticism and the Growth of Knowledge*, Cambridge: Cambridge University Press.

Larner, W. (2000) 'Neo-liberalism: Policy, Ideology, Governmentality', *Studies in Political Economy*, Vol. 63, 5–25.

Larner, W. (2003) 'Neoliberalism?', *Environment and Planning D: Society and Space*, Vol. 21, No. 5, 509–12.

Lavigne, M. (2000) 'The Economics of the Transition Process: What Have We Learned?', *Problems of Post-Communism*, Vol. 47 (Jul/Aug), Issue 4.

Lavoie, D. (1985) *Rivalry and Central Planning: The Socialist Calculation Debate Reconsidered*, New York: Cambridge University Press.

Lawrence, A.Y. (ed.) (1997) *Rational Choice Theory and Religion: Summary and Assessment*, New York: Routledge.

Lee, A., T. Eggertsson and D.C. North (eds) (1996) *Empirical Studies in Institutional Change*, Cambridge and New York: Cambridge University Press.

Legro, J.W. (2000) 'The Transformation of Policy Ideas', *American Journal of Political Science*, Vol. 44, No. 3, 419–32.

Leonidov, A. (1988) *Neoconservatism and Bourgeois Political Economy*, Sofia: Science and Art.

Lipinski, E. (1956) *Studies in the History of Polish Economic Thought*, Warsaw, State Scientific Publishing House.

Lipton, D. and Sachs J. (1990) 'Creating a Market Economy in Eastern Europe', in W. Brainard and G. Peters (eds), *Brookings Papers on Economic Activity*, Washington, DC: Brookings Institution, pp. 75–133.

Lipton, D. and J. Sachs (1999) 'Creating a Market Economy in Eastern Europe: the Case of Poland', *Brookings Papers on Economic Activity*, Vol. 1, 75–147.

Lo, D. (1995) 'Economic Theory and the Transformation of the Soviet-type System', in H.J. Chang and P. Nolan (eds), *The Transformation of the Communist Economies*, London: St Martin's Press.

Love, J. (1996) *Crafting the Third World. Theorizing Underdevelopment in Rumania and Brazil*, Stanford, California: Stanford University Press.

Lovejoy, A. (1948) *Essays in the History of Ideas*, Baltimore: John Hopkins Press.

Lowy, M. (1992) *Redemption and Utopia*, Stanford, CA: Stanford University Press [Published in 1988 by Pressess Universitaires de France as 'Redemption et Utopie'].

Lynn, M. (2004) 'Flat Approach Seems to Generate an Upward Curve', *Liquid Africa*, Comtex (30 November).

Machlup, F. (1962) *The Production and Distribution of Knowledge in the United States*, Princeton, NJ: Princeton University Press.

MacIntyre, A. (1984) *Marxism and Christianity*, Notre Dame, Ind.: University of Notre Dame Press.

Malabra, A.L. (1994) *Lost Prophets: An Insider's History of Modern Economists*, Boston: Harvard Business School Press.

Marangos, J. (2003) 'Was Shock Therapy Really a Shock?', *Journal of Economic Issues*, Vol. 37, No. 4, 943–66.

Marx, K. (1967) *Capital, Vol. I*, New York: International Publishers.

McCloskey, D.N. (1985) *The Rhetoric of Economics*, Madison: University of Wisconsin Press.

McCloskey, D.N. (2006) *The Bourgeois Virtues: Ethics for an Age of Commerce*, Chicago: University of Chicago Press.

McKinnon, R. (1991) *The Order of Economic Liberalization*, Baltimore: Johns Hopkins University Press.

Mecu, C. (1973) *Structuri economice în America Latină*, Bucharest: Editura Politică.

Mehedinţiu, M. (1986) 'Contradicţiile şi legile economice în socialism' (Contradictions and Economic Laws in Socialism), *Tratat de Economie Contemporană* (Treatise of Contemporary Economics), Bucharest: Ed. Politica.

Merton, R.K. (1967) *On Theoretical Sociology: Five Essays, Old and New*, New York: The Free Press.

Michel, D. (1992) *Regulile jocului (Les regles du jeu)*, Bucharest: Editura Humanitas.

Miller, A.H., W.M Reisinger and V.L. Hesli (eds) (1993) *Boulder Public Opinion and Regime Change: the New Politics of Post-Soviet Societies*, Boulder, CO: Westview Press.

Mises, L.v. (1957) *Theory and History. An Interpretation of Social and Economic Evolution*, New Haven, Conn.: Yale University Press.

Mises, L.v. (1981a) [1922] *Socialism*. Indianapolis, IN: Liberty Fund.

Mises, L.v. (1981b) [1947] *Planned Chaos*. Irvington-on-Hudson, NY: Foundation for Economic Education.

Mises, L.v. (1996) [1927] *Liberalism: The Classical Tradition*, Irvington-on-Hudson, NY: Foundation for Economic Education.

Monnerot, J. (1960) *Sociology and Psychology of Communism*, translated by J. Degras and R. Rees, Boston: Beacon Press.

Morales J. and J. Sachs (1989) 'Bolivia's Economic Crisis', in J. Sachs (ed.), *Developing Country Debt and Economic Performance*, Chicago: University of Chicago Press, pp. 57–80.

Munck, R. (2003) 'Neoliberalism, Necessitarianism and Alternatives in Latin America: There is No Alternative (tina)?', *Third World Quarterly*, Vol. 24, No. 3, June, 495–511.

Murphy, R. (2006) 'A Flat Tax for the UK? The Implications of Simplification', ACCA Discussion Paper.

Murrell, P. (1992a) 'Evolutionary and Radical Approaches to Economic Reform', *Economics of Planning*, Vol. 25, 75–95.

Murrell, P. (1992b) 'Evolution in Economics and in the Economic Reform of the Centrally Planned Economies', in C.C. Clague and G. Rausser (eds), *The Emergence of Market Economies in Eastern Europe*. Cambridge, Mass.: Blackwell.

Murrell, P. (1997) 'Missed Policy Opportunities during Mongolian Privatization: Should Aid Target Policy Research Institutions?', in C. Clague (ed.), *Institutions and Economic Development. Growth and Governance in Less-Developed and Post-Socialist Countries*, Baltimore: John Hopkins University Press.

Naim, M. (1993) 'Latin America: Post-Adjustment Blues', *Foreign Policy*, Vol. 92, 133–50.

Nechita, N. (1986) 'Contradicțiile economice și dezvoltarea economico-socială contemporană' ('Economic Contradictions and Contemporary Socio-Economic Development') in *Tratat de Economie Contemporană* (Treatise on Contemporary Economy), Bucharest: Editura Politică.

Nechita, V. (1993) *Mihail Manoilescu – creator de teorie economică* (Mihail Manoilescu – Creator of Economic Theory), Iași: Cugetarea.

Nelson, R.H. (1991) *Reaching for Heaven on Earth: the Theological*

Meaning of Economics, Savage, MD.: Rowman & Littlefield Publishers.

Nelson, R.H. (2001) *Economics as Religion: from Samuelson to Chicago and beyond*, University Park, Pennsylvania: Pennsylvania State University Press.

Nenovsky, N. (1999) 'The Economic Philosophy of Friedrich Hayek (the Centenary of his Birth)', *Bulgarian National Bank Discussion Paper* DP/8/1999.

Nenovsky, N. (2002) 'Improving Monetary Theory in Post Communist Countries – Looking back to Cantillon', *Bulgarian National Bank Discussion Paper* DP/28/2002, November.

Nenovsky, N. (2004) 'Professor Simeon Demostenov (1886–1968) – the Bulgarian Austrian', Unpublished Mimeo.

Nenovsky, N. (2006) *Exchange Rates and Inflation: France and Bulgaria in the Interwar Period and the Contribution of Albert Aftalion* (1874–1956), Sofia: Bulgarian National Bank.

Nenovsky, N., G. Pavanelli and K. Dimitrova (2007) 'Exchange Control in Inter-war Italy and Bulgaria: History and Perspectives', ICER Working Paper.

Nicolae-Văleanu, I. (ed.) (1986) *Subdezvoltarea economică în lumea actuală. Realități și teorii* (Underdevelopment in the Contemporary World. Realities and Theories), Bucharest: Editura Academiei RSR.

North, D.C. (1981) *Structure and Change in Economic History*, New York: Norton.

North, D.C. (1990) *Institutions, Institutional Change, and Economic Performance*, New York: Cambridge University Press.

North, D.C. (1994) 'Institutions and their Consequences for Economic Performance', in K. Cook and M. Levi (eds), *The Limits of Rationality*, Chicago: University of Chicago Press.

North, D.C. (1995) *Understanding the Process of Economic Change*, Princeton: Princeton University Press.

North, D.C. (1996) 'Order, Disorder and Economic Change', paper presented at the Social Capital in Eurasia Kennan Institute Workshop, Washington.

North, D.C. (ed.) (1997) *Transforming Post-Communist Political Economies*, Washington, DC: National Resource Council, National Academy of Sciences.

Ohmae, K. (1995) *The End of The Nation State: The Rise of Regional Economies*, New York: The Free Press.

Olson, M. (1965) *The Logic of Collective Action*, Cambridge, MA: Harvard University Press.

Olson, M. (1982) *The Rise and Decline of Nations: Economic Growth, Stagflation, and Social Rigidities*, New Haven: Yale University Press.

Olson, M. (1989) 'How Ideas Affect Societies: Is Britain the Wave of the Future?', in A. Gamble et al. (eds), *Ideas, Interests & Consequences*, London: Institute of Economic Affairs, pp. 23–50.

Olson, M. (1990) 'The New Institutional Economics: the Collective Choice Approach to Economic Development', in C. Clague (ed.) (1997), *Institutions and Economic Development. Growth and Governance in Less-Developed and Post-Socialist Countries*, Baltimore: Johns Hopkins University Press.

Olson, M. (1992) 'The Hidden Path to a Successful Economy', in C. Clague and C.R. Gordon (eds), *The Emergence of Market Economies in Eastern Europe*, Cambridge, Mass., USA: Blackwell Publishers.

Olson, M. (1993) 'Dictatorship, Democracy, and Development', *American Political Science Review*, September, Vol. 87, 567–76.

Oomes, N. (1998) *Market Failures in the Economy of Science*, Unpublished manuscript.

Ostrom, E. (1986) 'An Agenda for the Study of Institutions', *Public Choice*, Vol. 48, 3–25.

Ostrom, E. (1990) *Governing the Commons. The Evolution of Institutions for Collective Action*, Cambridge: Cambridge University Press.

Ostrom, V. (1993) 'Opportunity, Diversity and Complexity', in V. Ostrom, D. Feeny and H. Picht (eds), *Rethinking Institutional Analysis and Development: Issues, Alternatives, and Choices*, San Francisco: ICS Press, Institute for Contemporary Studies.

Ostrom, E. (1994) 'Economic Performance through Time', *American Economic Review*, Vol. 84, No. 3, 359–68.

Ostrom, V. (1997) *The Meaning of Democracy and the Vulnerability of Democracies: A Response to Tocqueville's Challenge*, Ann Arbor: University of Michigan Press.

Ostrom, E. and S.E.S. Crawford (1995) 'A Grammar of Institutions'. *American Political Science Review*, Vol. 89, No. 3 (September), 582–600.

Ostrom, E., R. Gardner and J. Walker (1993) *Institutional Incentives and Sustainable Development. Infrastructure Policies in Perspective*, Boulder, CO: Westview Press.

Pierson, P. (1994) *Dismantling the Welfare State?*, New York: Cambridge University Press.

Pirie, M. (2005) 'Why the Case for a Flat-Tax System is Irresistible', *Financial Times* (17 February).

Popper, K.R. (1963) *Conjectures and Refutations: The Growth of Scientific Knowledge*, New York: Harper Torchbooks.

Popper, K.R. (1966) *The Open Society and its Enemies*, Princeton, NJ: Princeton University Press.

Popper, K.R. (1979) *Objective Knowledge: An Evolutionary Approach*, Oxford: Oxford University Press.

Porwit, K. (1998) 'Looking Back at Economic Science in Poland, 1945–1996: the Challenge of System Changes' in H.J. Wagener (ed.), *Economic Thought in Communist and Post Communist Europe*, London and New York: Routledge.

Prakash, A. and J.A. Hart (1999) *Globalization and Governance*, London and New York: Routledge.

Przeworski, A. (1991) *Democracy and the Market*, Cambridge: Cambridge University Press.

Püss, T. (2002) *Estonia – The State of Three Social Sciences in Eastern Europe*, Budapest: Collegium. Also in M. Kaase and V. Sparschuh (eds) and A. Wenninger (co-ed.) (2002), *Three Social Science Disciplines in Central and Eastern Europe. A Handbook on Economics, Political Science and Sociology*, Social Science Information Centre (IZ), Berlin and Collegium Budapest.

Putnam, R.D., R. Leonardi and R.Y. Nanetti (1993) *Making Democracy Work: Civic Traditions in Modern Italy*, Princeton, NJ: Princeton University Press.

Rabushka, A. (2005) 'A Competitive Flat Tax May Spread to Lithuania'. *The Russian Economy* (24 March).

Radnitzky, Gerard and Peter Bernholz (eds) (1987) *Economic Imperialism: The Economic Approach Applied Outside the Field of Economics*, New York: Paragon House Publishers.

Ragin, C.C. (1987) *The Comparative Method: Moving Beyond Qualitative and Quantitative Strategies*, Berkeley, CA: University of California Press.

Raico, R. (1994) 'Classical Liberalism and the Austrian School' in P.J. Boettke (ed), *The Elgar Companion to Austrian Economics*, Aldershot, UK and Brookfield, US: Edward Elgar. pp. 320–27; [also published in *Advances in Austrian Economics* vol. 2A, 1995].

Raiser, M. (1996) *Informal Institutions, Social Capital and Economic Transition. Reflections on a Neglected Dimension*, London: European Bank for Reconstruction and Development.

Ray, R.K., A.T. Denzau and T.D. Willett (eds) (2007) *Neoliberalism: National and Regional Experiments with Global Ideas*, London: Routledge.

Rescher, N. (1978) *Scientific Progress: a Philosophical Essay on the Economics of Research in Natural Science*, Pittsburgh: University of Pittsburgh Press.

Reynolds, A. (1999) *The Hong Kong Tax System*, Washington, DC: The Hudson Institute.

Reynolds, M. (2004) 'Look East, Say Flat Tax Advocates', *Prague Post* (9 December).

Richter, M.N. (1972) *Science as a Cultural Process*, London: Frederick Muller.

Risse-Kappen, T. (1994) 'Ideas Do Not Float Freely: Transnational Coalitions, Domestic Structures, and the End of the Cold War', *International Organization* Vol. 48, No. 2, 185–214.

Rizzo M. (1992) 'Austrian Economics for the Twenty-First Century' in B. Caldwell and S. Boehm (eds), *Austrian Economics: Tensions and New Directions*, Boston: Kluwer Academic Publishers, pp. 245–55.

Robison, R. (ed.) (2006) *The Neoliberal Revolution: Forging the Market State*, London: Palgrave.

Roemer, J.E. (1994) *A Future for Socialism*, Cambridge: Harvard University Press.

Rogers, R. (1995) *Diffusion of Innovations*, New York: Simon and Schuster.

Romer, P. (1993) 'Economic Growth', in D.R. Henderson (ed.), *The Fortune Encyclopedia of Economics*, New York: Time Warner Books.

Rothbard, M.N. (1976) 'Praxeology, Value Judgements and Public Policy' in E. Dolan (ed.), *The Foundations of Modern Austrian Economics*, Kansas City: Sheed and Ward.

Rothbard, M.N. (1996) *Making Economic Sense*, Auburn, AL: Ludwig von Mises Institute.

Roy, R.K., A.T. Denzau and T.D. Willett (eds) (2007) *Neoliberalism: Global Experiements with a Shared Mental Model*, London: Routledge.

Ruggie, J.G. (1982) 'International Regimes, Transactions, and Change: Embedded Liberalism in the Postwar Economic Order', *International Organization*, Vol. 36, No. 2, 379–415.

Sabatier, P. and H. Jenkins-Smith (eds) (1993) *Policy Change and Learning: An Advocacy Coalition Approach*, Boulder, CO: Westview.

Salerno, J. (2007) 'A Fairy Tale of the Austrian Movement', available online at www.mises.org/story/2720 (accessed October 2008).

Samuelson, P.A. (1947) *Foundations of Economic Analysis*, Cambridge, MA: Harvard University Press.

Samuelson, P.A. (1951) [1948] *Economics*, McGraw Hill.

Samuelson, P. A. (1955) *Economics*, 3rd edn, New York: Warner Books.

Samuelson, P.A. (1967) 'Marxian Economics as Economics', *American Economic Review*, Papers and Proceedings, Vol. 57.

Schneider, F. (2003) 'The Development of the Shadow Economies and Shadow Labor Force of 22 Transition and 21 OECD Countries', Unpublished manuscript.

Scott, H. 'Could a 10% Flat Rate Tax Work in the UK?', Unpublished manuscript.

Service, R. (2007) *Comrades! A History of World Communism*, Cambridge: Harvard University Press.

Shapiro, S. (1987) 'The Social Control of Impersonal Trust', *American Journal of Sociology*, Vol. 93, No. 3, 623–58.

Sik, O. (1967) *Plan and Market under Socialism*, White Plains, NY: International Arts and Sciences Press.

Sima, J. (2007) 'Notes on Austrian Economics', unpublished.

Sima, J and D. Stastny (2000) 'A Laissez-Faire Fable of the Czech Republic', *Journal of Libertarian Studies*, Vol. 14, No. 2, 155–78.

Simmons, B., F. Dobbin and G. Garrett (eds) (2006) 'Symposium on Global Diffusion of Public Policies', *International Organization*, 60 (Fall).

Skidelsky, R. (1995) *The Road from Serfdom: The Economic and Political Consequences of the End of Communism*, New York: Penguin Books.

Smith, A. (1976) *An Inquiry into the Nature and Causes of the Wealth of Nations*, Oxford: Clarendon Press.

Smith, A. (1991) [1766] *An Enquiry into the Nature and Causes of the Wealth of Nations*, Amherst, NY: Prometheus Books.

Smith, J.A. (1989) 'Think Tanks and the Politics of Ideas', in D. Colander and A.W. Coats (eds), *The Spread of Economic Ideas*, New York: Cambridge University Press, pp. 175– 94.

Smith, J.A. (1991) *The Idea Brokers*, New York: Free Press.

Snowdon, B., H. Vane, and P. Wynarczyk, (1994) *A Modern Guide to Macroeconomics: An Introduction to Competing Schools of Thought*, Aldershot, UK and Northampton, MA, USA: Edward Elgar.

Solo, R. (1991) *The Philosophy of Science and Economics*, Armonk, NY: M.E. Sharpe.

Soros, G. (1998) *The Crisis of Global Capitalism: Open Society Endangered*, New York: Public Affairs.

Spadaro, L.M. (ed.) (1978) *New Directions in Austrian Economics*, Kansas City: Sheed Andrews and McMeel.

Spulber, N. (1979) *Organizational Alternatives in the Soviet System*, Cambridge University Press.

Spulber, N. (1997) *Redefining the State: Privatization and Welfare Reform in Industrial and Transitional Economies*, Cambridge, Mass.: Cambridge University Press.

Stallings, B. (1992) 'International Influence on Economic Policy' in S. Haggard and R. Kaufman (eds), *The Politics of Economic Adjustment*, Princeton: Princeton University Press, pp. 41–88.

Steger, M. (2002) *Globalism: The New Market Ideology*, Lanham, MD: Rowman & Littlefield Publishers.

Stigler, G.J. (1971) 'The Theory of Economic Regulation', *Bell Journal of Economics*, The RAND Corporation, Vol. 2, No. 1, Spring, 3–21.

Stiglitz, J. (2002) *Globalization and Its Discontents*, New York: Norton.

Stokey, N.L. and S. Rebelo (1995) 'Growth Effects of Flat-Rate Taxes', *Journal of Political Economy*, Vol. 103, No. 3, 519–50.

Stone, D. (1996) *Capturing the Political Imagination*, London: Frank Cass.

Storobin, D. (2006) 'The Flat Tax Revolution in Europe', *Global Politician* (8 May).

Strange S. (1996) *The Retreat of the State: The Diffusion of Power in the World Economy*, Cambridge: Cambridge University Press.

Sută-Selejan, S. (1986) 'Confruntări de idei privind actuala criză economică mondială. Originalitatea concepției românești cu privire la această criză' ('Confrontation of Ideas on the Present-Day World Crisis. The Originality of the Romanian Outlook on the Crisis'), *Tratat de Economie Contemporană* (Treatise on Contemporary Economy), Bucharest: Editura Politică.

Szamuely, L. and L. Csaba (1998) 'Economics and Systemic Changes in Hungary', in H.J. Wagener (ed.), *Economic Thought in Communist and Post Communist Europe*, London and New York: Routledge.

Teather, R. (2005) *A Flat Tax for the UK – A Practical Reality*, London, UK: Adam Smith Institute.

Thrower, J. and N. Lewiston (1992) *Marxism–Leninism as the Civil Religion of Soviet Society: God's Commissar*, New York: E. Mellen Press.

Thrower, J. and M. Rodinson (1983), *Marxist–Leninist 'Scientific Atheism' and the Study of Religion and Atheism in the USSR*, New York: Mouton.

Tillich, P. and Carl E. Braceten (eds) (1967) *Perspectives on 19th and 20th Century Protestant Theology*, New York: Harper and Row.

Tinbergen, J. (1956) *Economic Policy: Theory and Design*, Amsterdam, The Netherlands: North Holland Publishing Co.

Tinbergen, J. (1967) *Economic Policy: Principles and Design*, Chicago: Rand Mc Nally.

Tismaneanu, V. (1992) *Reinventing Politics: Eastern Europe from Stalin to Havel*, New York: The Free Press.

Tismaneanu, V. (1995) *Political Culture and Civil Society in Russia and the New States of Eurasia*, Armonk, NY: M.E. Sharpe.

Tismaneanu, V. (1998) *Fantasies of Salvation: Democracy, Nationalism and Myth in Post-Communist Europe*, Princeton, NJ: Princeton University Press.

Tucker J.A. (1990) 'Mises in Moscow! An Interview with an Austrian Economist From the U.S.S.R.', in L. Rockwell (ed.), *The Economics of Liberty*, Auburn: The Ludwig von Mises Institute.

Turnovec, F. (2002) *Czech Republic – The State of Three Social Sciences in Eastern Europe*, Budapest: Collegium. Also in M. Kaase and V. Sparschuh (eds) and A. Wenninger (co-ed.) (2002), *Three Social Science Disciplines in Central and Eastern Europe. A Handbook on Economics,*

Political Science and Sociology, Social Science Information Centre (IZ), Berlin and Collegium Budapest.

Tzortzis, A. (2005) 'Flat-tax Movement Stirs Europe', *Christian Science Monitor* (8 March).

United Nations Conference on Trade and Development (UNCTAD) (2002) World Investment Report, UNCTAD.

Varian, H. (2000) *Internet Publishing and Beyond: the Economics of Digital Information and Intellectual Property*, Cambridge, MA: MIT Press.

Vaughn, K. (1994), *Austrian Economics in America, the Migration of a Tradition*, Cambridge: Cambridge University Press.

Veltmeyer, H., J. Petras and S. Vieux (1997) *Neoliberalism and Class Conflict in Latin America*, New York: St Martin's Press.

Ventura, G. (1999) 'Flat Tax Reform: A Quantitative Exploration', *Journal of Economic Dynamics and Control*, Vol. 23, 1425–58.

Wagener, H.J. (ed.) (1998a) *Economic Thought in Communist and Post Communist Europe*, London and New York: Routledge.

Wagener, H.J. (1998b) 'Between Conformity and Reform: Economics under State Socialism and its Transformation', in H.J. Wagener (ed.), *Economic Thought in Communist and Post Communist Europe*, London and New York: Routledge.

Wagener, H.J. (2002) *Comments – The State of Three Social Sciences in Eastern Europe*, Budapest: Collegium.

Ward, B. (1979) *The Ideal Worlds of Economics: Liberal, Radical, and Conservative Economic World Views*, New York: Basic Books.

Wei, S. (1997) 'Gradualism versus Big Bang: Speed and Sustainability of Reforms', *The Canadian Journal of Economics*, Vol. 30, No. 4b.

Weintraub, R. (1993) 'Neoclassical Synthesis', in D.R. Henderson (ed.), *The Fortune Encyclopedia of Economics*, New York: Warner Books.

Wible, J. (1994) 'The Economic Organization of Science, the Firm, and the Marketplace', *Philosophy of the Social Sciences*, Vol. 2.

Wible, J. (1998) *Economics of Science*, London: Routledge.

White, L.H. (1989) *Competition and Currency: Essays on Free Banking and Money*, Washington DC: Cato Institute.

Whitmore, B. (2005) 'Eastern Europe Embraces Flat Tax: Former Communist Nations See Revenue Rise, Cheating Decline', *The Boston Globe* (22 February).

Wolff, R.D. and S.A. Resnick (1987) *Economics: Marxian versus neoclassical*, Baltimore: Johns Hopkins University Press.

Woodcock, G. (1962) *Anarchism. A History of Libertarian Ideas and Movements*, Harmondsworth: Penguin Books.

Yee, A. S. (1996) 'The Causal Effects of Ideas on Policies', *International Organization*, Vol. 50, No. 1, 69–108.

Index

Abraham-Frois, Gabriel, 55
Academia Istropolitana, 59–60
Academy of Economic Studies,
    Bucharest, 54–5, 66
Academy of Sciences, Czech, 61, 64
Adam Smith Research Center, 63
Alchian, Armen, 63
Anderson, Oscar, 39
Aslund, A., 75, 218
Austrian economics, 20, 24, 104, 137,
    141–59, 173–82
Avramov, Rumen, 56

Balcerowicz, Leszek, 63, 149, 150,
    156
    Balcerowicz Plan, 52
Baltic Economic Management
    Training Project, 56
Bank of International Settlements, 70
Bastiat, Frederic, 146
Berend, Ivan, 63
Blyth, M., 2, 3, 6, 130–33
Boettke, Peter, 148, 159
Bohm-Bawerk, Eugen, 143
Boolean algebra, 188, 190, 197, 198
Boudon, R., 2
Bretton-Woods, 6
Brookings Institute, 156
Brus, Wlodzimierz, 31, 32
Buchanan, James, 63, 147
Budapest University of Economics, 45
Bulgarian Academy of Science, 49, 65
Bulgarian National Bank, 153

Campbell, J.L., 1, 84, 85, 121, 201
Canadian International Development
    Agency, 56
Caplan, Brian, 142–3
Catallaxy Publishing, 157
Catholic Church, 59, 116, 180, 195
Ceaianov, A.V., 39
Ceausescu, Nicolae, 37, 38

Cekanavicius, L., 28–30, 41–3, 49–50,
    53, 57, 62, 67
Center for Economic Policies, 66
Center for Institutional Analysis and
    Development (CADI), 154, 157
center periphery model, 96
Center for Strategic Planning, 156
Central European University, 59
Centre for Social and Economic
    Analysis, 63
Charles Koch Fellowship, 152
Charles University, Prague, 61
Chubais, Anatoly, 155
Civic Education Project, 56
civil society, 192, 195–6, 199, 200, 205
Coats, A.W.B., 2, 15, 81, 86
Colander, D., 2, 15, 81, 86
Collegium Budapest, 10
Comenius University, 60
communism, 1, 5, 36, 39, 69, 75, 81,
    117, 146, 154, 155, 183, 195,
    207
Communist Party, 29, 36–7, 40, 51, 57,
    92, 117
Conservative Economic Quarterly
    Lecture Series (CEQLS),
    Bratislava, 149
Conservative Institute, 149
constitutional moments, 199–200
Cowen, Tyler, 4, 138
critical junctures, 130–32, 134
Csaba, L., 29, 31–2, 44, 45, 52–3, 59,
    62, 63

Denzau, A.T., 1, 14, 130
deteriorating terms of trade, 38
Didier, Michel, 55
Dimitrov, M., 37, 39, 40, 47, 48, 54–5,
    57, 61, 65
Dioscuri-Access, 160–83
Dobbin, F., 84–6
dual economy, 123–5